RELIGIOUS VALUES

By

EDGAR SHEFFIELD BRIGHTMAN

Borden Parker Bowne Professor of Philosophy
in Boston University

THE ABINGDON PRESS

NEW YORK   CINCINNATI

KRAUS REPRINT CO.
New York
1970

Reprinted with the permission of the Licensor
KRAUS REPRINT CO.
A U.S. Division of Kraus-Thomson Organization Limited

Printed in the United States of America

DEDICATED
TO
MY WIFE

CONTENTS

CONTENTS

PREFACE

THE aim of this book is, as the title indicates, to interpret some of the central values in religious experience. Its chief purpose, then, is not to attack or to defend any particular philosophers or philosophic systems, or any particular religious creeds, but, rather, to consider afresh the meaning and value of religion as an actual human experience.

It is impossible, I believe, completely to separate any experience from our thought about it. Hence "pure" religious experience, purged of all admixture of idea and belief, is an abstraction as unreal as is "pure" sensation in psychology. Some mystics and empiricists in religion appear to have forgotten this fact. On the other hand, religious beliefs, apart from the life out of which they grow and by which they are nourished, are abstractions equally unreal. Some contenders for theory in both philosophical and theological circles seem to have forgotten this fact. Neither fact should be overlooked. Our actual experience, whether of religion or of sense objects, is a life of which thought is a necessary and inseparable aspect. Therefore a fruitful study of religious value-experience must face the question of the truth of the fundamental ideas implied by that experience.

In contemporary philosophy of religion, there is a cleavage of opinion between those who find the meaning of religious values in their function of adjusting human social relations, and those who find the unique value of religion in the adjusting of individuals and societies to the ideal purposes of a superhuman being, a personal

9

God. The former opinion may be called positivism or
humanism; the latter, metaphysical theism or personalism. It is not my view that either one of these
two opinions is wholly false and the other wholly true
by itself. Religion has, as positivism believes, a social
origin and a social destiny; it also has a more-than-
humanly-social reference. If the positivist forgets God,
the theist is in danger of forgetting man. Each over-
simplifies the problem; each is in peril of putting a part
for the whole. In this book I hope to do justice by the
humanistic as well as by the metaphysical implications
of religion.

The intent of the book may be made clearer by a brief
preview of its contents. In Chapter I it is shown that,
if religious values are to be recognized, they must be
interpreted reasonably; that is, they must be understood
in relation to our experience and thinking as a whole.
Religious values, Chapter II goes on to say, not only
presuppose reasonable belief but they also presuppose
loyalty to moral obligation; moral values are the basis
of religious values. The next chapter (III) points out
the distinction between apparent and real values; many
experiences that seem convincing and satisfactory in
themselves are seen, when tested by the logical and moral
criteria of Chapters I and II, not to be real values. The
constructive interpretation of religious value-experience
begins with Chapter IV, in which the human values of
religious experience are discussed, irrespective of the
truth of religious belief. In the next chapter (V) it is
shown that many of the most characteristic human
values of religion, as well as other values, are dependent
on faith in a more-than-human God. Chapter VI, "the
watershed of the book," raises the question how the
experiences described in Chapters IV and V may best be
interpreted intellectually. The leading systems of con-

temporary philosophy are examined with a view to considering their relative adequacy as coherent and inclusive accounts of religious value-experience. The study thus far in the book has been a consideration of the more general aspects of the problem. The next three chapters take up the central experience of religion, namely, worship, and undertake to estimate its meaning (VII), weighing doubts about its value (VIII), and studying the fruits which it creates in human experience (IX). Having thus surveyed the meaning of religious values, the book closes with some account of the implications of such a view of religion for the content of religious education.

Isaac Watts was a devoutly religious poet and a connoisseur in religion. In him, as in most great religious natures, there was a union of lofty thought and hóly experience. He was the author not only of hymns which are sung throughout the Christian world but also of a *Logick*. If an *apologia* for writing on the philosophy of religion were needed, Watts would furnish it, for he says, "The great design of this noble science (Logic) is to rescue our reasoning powers from their unhappy slavery and darkness. . . . It is the cultivation of our *Reason* by which we are better enabled to distinguish *Good* from *Evil* as well as *Truth* from *Falsehood;* and both these are matters of the highest Importance, whether we regard this Life or the Life to come."

A book like the present one, which discusses the views of many thinkers and quotes from their writings, owes much to the cooperation of publishers who own the copyrights of the books quoted. The author takes this occasion of thanking the following named publishers most heartily for their courteous permission to quote more or less extended passages from the books mentioned. Page references are noted in footnotes appended to the quotations in the text.

George Allen and Unwin Ltd., London:
  F. H. Bradley, *Appearance and Reality.*
  C. C. J. Webb, *Divine Personality and Human Life.*

American Sunday-School Union, Philadelphia:
  G. A. Barton, *Archæology and the Bible.*

D. Appleton & Company, New York:
  G. S. Hall, *Morale: The Supreme Standard of Life and Conduct.*

Bobbs-Merrill Company, Philadelphia:
  A. E. Wiggam, *The New Decalogue of Science.*

University of Chicago Press, Chicago:
  G. A. Coe, *The Psychology of Religion.*
  J. R. Geiger, *Some Religious Implications of Pragmatism.*

E. P. Dutton & Company, New York:
  J. Boehme, *Signature of All Things.*
  R. W. Emerson, *The Conduct of Life.*
  D. Hume, *Treatise of Human Nature.*
(These three volumes are all in Everyman's Library.)

Harper & Brothers, New York:
  E. D. Martin, *The Mystery of Religion.*

Henry Holt & Company, New York:
  E. S. Brightman, *An Introduction to Philosophy.*
  J. Dewey, *Reconstruction in Philosophy.*
  J. Dewey, *Human Nature and Conduct.*
  W. G. Everett, *Moral Values.*
  M. C. Otto, *Things and Ideals.*
  E. G. Spaulding, *The New Rationalism.*

Houghton Mifflin Company, Boston:
  J. Royce, *The Spirit of Modern Philosophy.*
  J. G. Saxe, *Poems* (Diamond Ed.).

Journal of Philosophy, New York:
  Articles in Vol. 17 (1920) and Vol. 22 (1925).

Alfred A. Knopf, Inc., New York:
  Willa Cather, *One of Ours.*
  J. C. Squire, Poems, *First Series.*

John Lane, The Bodley Head Limited, London, owners of
    English copyright:
    J. B. Tabb, *Poems.*

Longmans, Green & Co., New York:
    W. James, *The Varieties of Religious Experience.*
    R. B. Perry, *Present Philosophical Tendencies.*
    R. B. Perry, *Present Conflict of Ideals.*
    B. Russell, *Mysticism and Logic.*

Macmillan & Co., London:
    S. Alexander, *Space, Time and Deity.*
    B. Bosanquet, *Some Suggestions in Ethics.*
    B. Bosanquet, *What Religion Is.*
    H. Sidgwick, *Methods of Ethics.*

The Macmillan Company, New York:
    M. W. Calkins, *The Good Man and the Good.*
    J. B. Pratt, *The Religious Consciousness.*
    R. W. Sellars, *The Next Step in Religion.*
    S. S. Singh, *Reality and Religion.*
    R. A. Tsanoff, *The Problem of Immortality.*

University of North Carolina Press, Chapel Hill:
    R. Pound, *Law and Morals.*

Open Court Publishing Company:
    J. Dewey, *Experience and Nature.*

Oxford University Press, London:
    N. Macnicol, *Indian Theism.*

Charles Scribner's Sons, New York:
    W. McDougall, *Outline of Psychology.*
    G. F. Moore, *History of Religions.*

University Press, Cambridge, England:
    W. R. Sorley, *Moral Values and the Idea of God.*

Yale University Press, New Haven:
    W. E. Hocking, *The Meaning of God in Human Expe-*
    rience.

The chapters of this book have undergone numerous
revisions. In their present form none of them have been
published before. Earlier articles are, however, the
substantial basis of several of the chapters, and thanks
for permission to republish articles in revised form are

due to the faculty of Rochester Theological Seminary (for Chapter II, previously published in the *Bulletin* of the Seminary), to *The Methodist Review* (Chapter III), to *The Journal of Religion* (Chapter IV), and to Dean Walter Scott Athearn (for use of materials in Chapters VI and X, originally published in two issues of *The Bulletin of Boston University*).

The first form of Chapters IV, V, and VI was given as a series of lectures before the Providence Biblical Institute, meeting at Brown University. Chapters VII, VIII, and IX were delivered as Lowell Institute Lectures at King's Chapel, Boston. I thank Professor Henry T. Fowler of Brown University and Professor William H. Lawrence, Curator of the Lowell Institute, for their cordial consent to the use of the material mentioned.

EDGAR SHEFFIELD BRIGHTMAN.

Newton Center, Massachusetts, June 12, 1925.

CHAPTER I

THE LOGICAL BASIS OF RELIGIOUS BELIEF

1. RELIGION AS ISOLATION OR COOPERATION

WHEN we consider the religious values, we are thinking about a genuine aspect of human experience. There is no doubt about the existence of religion nor about the fact that men usually find value in their religious experiences. But there is much doubt about the interpretation of those experiences. It is, then, the task of every generation and of every individual to confront afresh the experience of religious values and to seek for a reinterpretation of their nature and their relations to the rest of experience. It is the aim of this book to suggest some ideas that may contribute to such reinterpretation.

In order to be clear from the outset we should have in mind a working definition of the two concepts which are central to our problem, namely, *values* and *religion*.

A value, in the simplest sense of the word, is whatever is liked, desired, or approved. But many "values" lead to conflict with other "values" and with the laws of logic; hence they are value-claims only, not true values, for they cannot be permanently approved in the long run. A true value, as distinguished from a simple value-claim, would be what is liked, desired, or approved in the light of our whole experience and our highest ideals, such as the logical ideal, the moral ideal, the æsthetic and religious ideals, and the total ideal of personality. Observation shows that only conscious persons can experience value or be valued intrinsically for their own sakes. Things, abstractions, and even ideals have only instrumental value; that is, they are means to the end of intrinsic value-experience.[1]

Religion is more difficult to define than is value. It will serve our present purpose to regard it as including the experiences of man's total personal and social life in approaching what he believes to be the Supreme Reality and the Supreme Value in the universe—Supreme, at least, so far as the destiny of the individual or the group is concerned; and also those experiences which are believed to originate with the Supreme Being or beings and which affect the destiny of man as an experiencer of value. Any such definition of religion sounds both complicated and hollow. It is, however, unavoidable that an inclusive definition shall be very broad. It must be a blanket capable of stretching over primitive cults, polytheism, pantheism, positivism, all the great world-religions, and the religious moods of individuals. As the discussion progresses, our concept will become more precise.[2]

Religious values, in some sense, have been a constant factor in human experience, but in modern times religion has had to fight for its life. This is a relatively recent event in its history.

Primitive man took religion for granted without reflection. His daily acts, his social relations, were inseparably bound up with his relations to unseen beings which determined his destiny. It did not occur to him to question the truth or value of his religious beliefs and practices. As religion developed, men became more clearly aware of the existence of different types of

---

[1]Chapter III of this book and E. S. Brightman, *An Introduction to Philosophy* (New York: Henry Holt and Company, 1925), pp. 136-165, contain further discussion of the nature of true value.

[2]See other definitions in E. S. Brightman, *op. cit.*, pp. 317-322.

religion among different tribes and nations. Then, too, within the great religions, as in Egypt, in Persia, in India, China, and Israel, there arose reformers who proclaimed a higher type of conduct and of worship and who exhorted the stiff-necked and the perverse.

But there was no serious attempt at a radical criticism of religion itself, its essential beliefs and values, until the rise of Greek philosophy. This criticism, much to the distress of Nietzsche, Mr. Dewey, and others, resulted in an affirmation of the soundness of the fundamental religious faith in God, immortality, and the objectivity of values.

Greek philosophy came to an end in 529 A. D., when Justinian closed the Neoplatonic school of philosophy in Athens. There ensued the Middle Ages, a long period (529-1453 A. D.) in which far more substantial intellectual work was being done than is commonly recognized, but a period nevertheless in which religious thought was largely confined to the elaboration of theological premises given by revelation and tradition rather than venturing an independent examination of the foundations of religious faith.

It would be a gross error, however, to regard the Middle Ages as homogeneous. The seeds of scientific investigation and critical thought were being planted in many minds. The Renaissance and the Reformation did not find the world wholly unprepared for the new perspectives and new problems which they brought to the mind. The seeds of free, critical thought, long germinating, now grew and bore abundant fruit. Much of it was wild; but out of the luxuriant productivity of the period since the fall of Constantinople in 1453, there have been matured the ripe fruits of the great scientific discoveries and philosophical systems.

Meanwhile religion has been profoundly affected by

the changes in the intellectual atmosphere. In such circumstances as prevail in the modern world, religion, like nations, must choose between two courses of action, namely, isolation and cooperation. That is to say, either religion is to regard itself as a unique power, self-determining and self-sufficient, or it is to acknowledge its membership in the total spiritual life of the race and thus impose on itself the duty of intellectual comity with science, philosophy, and art.

Whichever alternative religion chooses, it has to fight for its life. If it choose isolation, it must defend that position against internal dissension and external assaults. The Roman Catholic Church has shown incomparably greater skill in holding the position of isolation than have most Protestants who have chosen the same sort of strategy; but the story of Tyrrell and Loisy and other Modernists who have arisen within the Roman communion shows that even the skill of Rome fails to persuade many of her own most spiritual leaders, and that her fight to maintain religion in isolation from modern thought and extra-religious values rests in the end on coercion rather than on the use of spiritual weapons.

If, on the other hand, religion choose the second alternative, that of cooperation with the whole spiritual and intellectual life of humanity, it imposes on itself a far more difficult task than that of splendid isolation. It enters into the arena of life, rests its appeal not on tradition or authority but on human experience and intelligence, and on its harmony with the best achievements of scientific and philosophical thinking—the best achievements, be it noted! It becomes a member of the League of Values, with all of the privileges and responsibilities of such membership.

If religion is to survive, it cannot be by accepting

any and every philosophical system. To pursue that course would be to confess that religion was intellectually neutral. This would mean a return to the position of isolation and a reducing of religion to the level of mere emotion or mere conduct without ideas or ideals. Such an outcome is both intellectually and religiously intolerable. Religion should come to an understanding with the intellectual life of the times in which it lives.[3] It should become clearly aware of its relations to contemporary scientific and philosophic thinking. It should understand which philosophies interpret and which philosophies reject the values about which religion is concerned. Above all, it must show that the beliefs on which it rests may reasonably be held as true not merely in their own isolated right, but also when set into relation with the other work of the intellect, as well as with the total experience of life itself.

The attitude of extreme isolation refutes itself. It is in principle broken down by the advance of thought. It still maintains its hold on institutions and individuals; but if there be true values in religion, those values cannot be conserved by the policy of the isolationist who hid his talent in the earth, but, rather, by that of the cooperators who went and traded. Religion, if it be true, will thrive in commerce with the other values of experience. If it have profound faith in itself, it will not shrink from that commerce, but will welcome it.

2. RELIGIOUS BELIEF AND LOGIC

The origin and history of religion show conclusively that religious values are not originally produced by logical reflection. They are the outgrowth of hereditary

---

[3] See A. C. Knudson, *Present Tendencies in Religious Thought* (New York: The Abingdon Press, 1924) for an excellent discussion of many such problems.

tendencies, social situations, and other environmental factors, in all of which religious faith sees the hand of a God who dwells in and acts through that which we call nature and natural laws. Life, then, produces religion before critical thought begins. In this respect, however, our experience of religious values differs little from any other experience. Whether in sense perception, or in the growth of social institutions, or in artistic creation, forces other than critical intelligence are at work. No amount of reasoning could ever think a color or a sound into being if the reasoner had not experienced any sensations. Our customs and traditions are the outcome of instinctive, inventive, and imitative activity, not of well-calculated theories or deliberate social contracts. Poetry is not the conclusion of a syllogism. In all our experience, then, as well as in religion, there is a great deal that is not the product of reason. This is the valid meaning of Lotze's maxim that life is more than logic, and, too, of the Kantian doctrine that form without content is empty and content without form is blind. Reason always works with material that it does not create by mere reasoning.

There is, however, great danger of overemphasizing the nonrational or (as it is often ambiguously called) the irrational element in life. Reason does not create all of life, but it is the sacred duty of reason to interpret all of life. No irrational item has a right to declare its independence of reason. If reason were to agree that there was a realm about which it ought not to think, that agreement would be the self-surrender of the very nature of reason. Let the experiences of life be as nonrational in their origin as you please, it is always the task of reason to survey these experiences as a whole and to determine their relative meaning and value. The assertion of this duty is not merely in the interest of reason, but also in the interest of religion. It is religion that commands us to test the spirits and to interpret the unknown tongue. If the emphasis on life over against logic were to be carried to the extreme of meaning a life that is independent of logic, then life would become utter confusion. Reason certainly needs faith if it is to reach beyond immediate experience; but just as certainly faith needs reason, if it is not to abandon all claim to truth and value.

It follows, then, both from the situation in which modern thought finds itself and also from the very nature of all experience, that the values of religion need to be interpreted by logical thought. They cannot safely be taken as they come in every experience that claims religious value. If they are to be so interpreted, sound method demands that we begin with the most fundamental problem. We are to try to understand religious values, to give some reasonable and logical account of them. The first task of one who appeals to reason and logic is to show, if he can, what is meant by calling anything reasonable or logical.

3. COHERENCE AS CRITERION OF TRUTH AND REASONABLENESS[4]

On the surface it is evident that the reasonableness of any belief means its conformity to reason; but what is reason? Broadly speaking, it is the body of most general principles used by the mind in organizing experience and arriving at judgments accepted as true.

Hence if a man believes in God because of some divine revelation, we always ask him what his reason is for accepting this revelation rather than that, Mormonism rather than Christian Science, Hinduism than Moham-

[4]See E. S. Brightman, *An Introduction to Philosophy*, Chap. II, for a critical survey of various proposed criteria of truth.

medanism. Revelation is not the most general body of principles used by the mind. Revelation must be tested by reasonableness, not reasonableness by revelation. Revelation is a reason not ultimate but derived; it is not a criterion of truth but presupposes a criterion by which it is judged.

The plain man will find the next higher court of appeal in what may be called pragmatic considerations. He will say that he accepts his Christianity because of its results in his practical life, or in the history of the race, or in the success of missions. This pragmatic method is followed by the sciences in hypothesis and experiment; and it appears to have the sanction of the Jesus of the Gospels from the earliest recorded sayings of Jesus to John. But, after all, it is a servant of reason; it is not master of the house. That which is to be the arbiter of all our thinking must have at least a clear meaning. What, we must inquire, does pragmatism mean by practical life? No one who has read Rickert's *Die Philosophie des Lebens* can continue to feel comfortable in basing his beliefs on a practical life that is so very living and protean that it may mean everything or nothing. If we mean biological life, does not biology presuppose the logic of scientific method? If we mean ideal life, is it not, then, our task to define the ideals which lead us to accept a belief as true? Professor Moore has complained of "Some Lingering Misconceptions of Instrumentalism," and assures us that instrumentalism "appeals to a transfigured and glorified biology, loaded with all the conscious and social values which are denied to it by those who find it such a bugbear."[5] But it is clearly the business of logic to specialize in the "transfiguration and glory." If we

---

[5] *Jour. Phil.*, 17 (1920), pp. 514-519, esp., p. 516.

should press minds of various types to define the meaning of the proposition, "This is life," we should doubtless receive many interesting answers; but if we undertook to test religious belief by its fruitfulness for life as defined, we should have chaos, not reasonableness.

Not raw, immediate life as it comes, but life interpreted, organized, seen in the light of a transfigured glory, that is, a logical ideal, is our ground of belief. The task of the mind is the organization and interpretation of experience; the elimination of contradictions, the establishing of relations—in short, coherence—is our ideal. It is the Supreme Court of Reason, to which biology, cash values, and all particulars and fruits must appeal. In Kant's words, "Human reason is by nature architectonic; that is, it considers all knowledge as belonging to a possible system, and hence admits only such principles as at least do not prevent the particular knowledge under discussion from standing in some sort of system with other knowledge."[6] There is a place for pragmatic factors within the realm of coherence; but to find a place for coherence under the legislation of any other principle is impossible.

Any belief, then, is true if or insofar as it organizes, interprets, and explains experiences more consistently, systematically, and economically than any competing belief.

4. FORMS OF UNREASONABLENESS

All may not be willing to accept the criterion of coherence; but no one, least of all a pragmatist, could object to trying it, to see how it works.

If religious values should turn out to be incoherent, they would be untrue, and (at the present stage of our thought) would merit no further consideration. We

---

[6] *Kritik der reinen Vernunft*, 2d ed., p. 502.

therefore begin by asking what is meant by unreasonableness.

a. *Incoherence.*—It has often been said that religious belief is incoherent; that is, inconsistent with itself or with the facts.

The worst form of incoherence is self-contradiction. Is the idea of God self-contradictory? Kant called it "ein blosses, aber doch fehlerfreies Ideal," "a mere ideal, yet an ideal free from flaw."[7] It is hard to believe that Kant (out of fashion though he be) could have called a round square an ideal free from flaw! Attempts made to show that an absolute person is a self-contradiction strike us as logomachy which vanishes with a clear definition of terms. An *a priori* denial of religious belief is as risky as an affirmation of *a priori* knowledge.

Incoherence may take the form of inconsistency with the facts of experience. The chief facts that seem to contradict belief in God are those to which we give the name of evil. It is true that these facts contradict certain concepts of God; they contradict a God for whom pleasure is an absolute good and pain an absolute evil; or a God who multiplies the cattle of the righteous and blasts the crops of the unrighteous; or a God whose purpose is completely revealed to every prayerful believer. But, with all their difficulty, they do not contradict a God whose purpose is the moral education of free beings in immortal life.

b. *Noncoherence.*—While belief in the God of religion may not be sheer nonsense, and may not flatly contradict the facts, it may lack the capacity to unify and interpret experience; that is, it may be noncoherent, like the belief in a spiritual chimæra in the nth dimension. This belief is not self-contradictory; it contradicts no

---

[7] *Kritik der reinen Vernunft*, 2d ed., p. 669.

item of experience; yet every sane mind rejects it. Why?
Because, as we say, there is no "reason" for it; that is,
it connects with nothing in our real world of experience;
there is no evidence for it. Many honest minds regard
belief in God as of this sort. But it is surely ill-consid-
ered to say that there is no evidence for theistic belief;
the whole of experience is the evidence, and belief in
God is in some measure, at least, an interpretation of
the evidence. Perhaps it is not adequately coherent with
the facts; it is certainly not utterly unrelated to them.

Religious belief has, however, a property that greatly
offends the dominant positivism of the day. This positivism holds that only those beliefs are reasonable that
are verifiable; that is, that lead directly to the objects in
experience to which they refer. But the God of religious
worship is transcendent; he can never, for all his immanence, be an object in immediate experience (although
he may well be an object *of* immediate experience, which
is quite another matter). This makes him (so we are
told by positivists of pragmatic or realistic type) an
unverifiable, unintelligible thing-in-himself, a metaphysical monster outside the universe of discourse that can
rationally be meant by experiencing persons, and so,
thoroughly noncoherent with our experience.

Powerful as this positivism is, it may be doubted
whether it will receive a favorable decision in the
Supreme Court of Reason. The opinion of the Court
will, at any rate, have to reckon with the following
facts: The transcendent God of theism is not a *Ding
an sich;* for his being is through and through of the
nature of conscious experience: he is a Person. Further,
true though it may be that we live in a world of social
objects and of common experience, no theory can deny
the fact that every person experiences himself as himself,
however "social" the content of his experience may be.

Again, every proposition about society, or past experience, or universals, is a metaphysical proposition, which, equally with theistic belief, is incapable of positivistic-pragmatic verification; that is, it cannot lead directly to the objects in experience to which it refers. If God is a metaphysical monster, so is the Common Will. In present or future experience no such object will ever be met as all men, or their will, or God. Must we, then, reject the whole brood and breed of these monsters, or should we revise our concept of verification in the light of the way in which our mind actually builds its world? The pragmatic conception of verification appears to be arbitrarily narrow; it is only one special instance of the agreement of hypothesis and fact. Any hypothesis is valid which renders our experience more intelligible, whether the object to which it refers ever has been or ever can be an immediate experience of mine or not. It is not too much to say that current positivism is a dogmatic limitation of the function of reason. Its attempt to show theistic belief to be noncoherent is essentially a refusal to think the problems through to the end.

5. Forms of Reasonableness

All reasonableness is coherence; but it is important to remember that there are kinds and degrees of reasonableness. Rationality assumes different forms according to the type of structure that may be found in the subject matter dealt with. The kind of evidence or verifiability that it is reasonable to look for is therefore determined by the type of structure with which reason is dealing.

a. *Logical and mathematical.*—Within logic and mathematics we have illustrations of perfect coherence; the axioms and postulates imply the entire system of the science. Here is, indeed, coherence; but here is no knowledge of concrete and particular reality.

b. *Empirical.*—The causal sciences are a coherent explanation of the experienced data of sense. Coherence here is more than formal consistency; it is the finding of meaning and structure in content, and the devising and testing of hypotheses regarding the laws of this content.

c. *Belief in other persons.*—The present chaos in theories of consciousness makes one hesitate to say anything about persons; but, like Massachusetts, there they stand (or, as the functionalist, following the familiar figure, might prefer to say, like Kansas, there they go) ; and we must make something out of them. The conscious life of other persons is a different type of structure from the subject matter of logic or of the empirical sciences. Behaviorism is at our heels, and we must express ourselves: the simple truth is that a psychology of other persons is a metaphysical science. Social communication is a metaphysical fact. Originally social though my consciousness may be, the assertion that there are others in the same boat is metaphysical and open only to analogical proof. Yet the fact that there are other persons is most substantial knowledge, and is valid because it is the only coherent interpretation of the evidence.

d. *Interpretation of experience as a whole.*—When we undertake to give a coherent account of the meaning of experience as a whole, we are launched on what is the most unavoidable and the most precarious task of reason. Much confusion arises from demanding in our synoptic interpretation of reality the same type of coherence as is appropriate to some one of the subordinate types already mentioned, such as formal logic.

The remainder of the chapter will be devoted to considering in what sense theistic belief may be said to be a reasonable interpretation of experience as a whole.

6. In What Sense Is Theistic Belief Reasonable?

In this discussion, for the sake of definiteness, we are assuming a proposition which will be examined from numerous angles in later chapters, the proposition, namely, that the object of religious experience and the source of religious value is a real personal God, who is immanent in the world, but who also transcends it. Such a theistic God is more than a venture of hope for the future of humanity (Perry), and more than the common will (Overstreet). He is the ground of all existence and value. He is an ontologically real Person for himself. The problem of the logical basis of religion is, therefore, essentially concerned with the reasonableness of theistic belief.

In a discussion of this kind it is our duty to avoid unreasonable and extravagant pretensions either in behalf of or in opposition to the reasonableness of theism. Extravagant pretensions are regrettably characteristic of much theistic apologetic and of much anti-theistic polemic.

To suppose, for example, that in a matter concerning the interpretation of experience as a whole we have attained or can attain ideal reasonableness or complete coherence is either mere pretense or self-delusion. Kant was not infallible, but he should have taught us something.

It would be an extravagant pretension of reason for it to demand that theistic belief, in order to be regarded as rational, should be expected to attain the ideal of complete coherence, when our other reasonable beliefs about the real world do not attain it, and still are regarded as rational. There is a certain theophobia which causes minds to stagger at the belief in God, although they accept other beliefs which are logically as incompletely coherent as theism. Men will believe in teleology—but not in God; in human freedom—but not in God; in theism, so long as theism is taken to mean the possibility of progress, or the victorious struggle of good with evil, or the impersonal objectivity of values— but not in God; in a suprapersonal Absolute, no matter how meaningless the concept suprapersonal may be—so long as we do not believe in God! This theophobia arises from many sources: from fallacious theistic argu- ments, from resentment against dogmatism and eccle- siasticism, from the feeling that our deepest and most sacred beliefs merit the most critical examination, and from real difficulties in the concept of God. None the less, it is not good intellectual sportsmanship; it is, to be precise, not coherent, to accept one relatively but incompletely reasonable belief on the ground that it is the best that we can get and to reject another such belief on the ground that it is not completely proved. Much less is it good sportsmanship or good thinking to deny a relatively coherent and intelligible belief in order to substitute for it a less coherent and intelli- gible one. Is not Professor Perry's melioristic faith in progress in a universe from which moral and spiritual ontology is banished less reasonable, and more naïvely confiding, than faith in progress in a universe in which there is a God, and purpose, and freedom? Again, is not the suprapersonal a less rational concept than the per- sonal, and is there any reason for belief in the supra- personal which is not a better reason for belief in a personal God?

It is, further, an extravagant pretension of reason for it to suppose that it can organize and interpret its world without making assumptions and hypotheses about what lies beyond the here and now. The extreme empiricist holds that the mind really operates by trial and error, like a mouse in a maze; but the geological ages are not long enough to account for the construction of science, of ideals, and of philosophy, by "blind, empirical groping" (Kant). The extreme rationalist holds that syllogistic reasoning from intuitively necessary premises will yield us all we know or need to know. The emptiness of such a conception of the work of reason is pretty generally conceded to-day.

If a coherent world doesn't gradually happen to us by good luck, and if it wasn't forced on us by formal logic, how do we come by it (or by such an approximation to it as we possess)? To this question the answer may be put in many different ways. It may be said that there is a *nisus* toward totality, or that the spirit of the whole is operative in us, or that we cannot understand ourselves without framing an ideal vision or synopsis of a meaningful world, or that our faith in the rationality of the universe impels us to make assumptions and form hypotheses which we test by their ability coherently to articulate experience. That is to say, the only account of the mind's work that is true to the facts involves the recognition that reason cannot progress without making assumptions about a universe.

What then, does all this mean for the reasonableness of religious belief? The following propositions will summarize our position:

a. Theistic belief, being a belief about the meaning of the whole concrete universe, is not completely reasonable; a completely coherent account of all experience is not likely to be attained by finite beings.

b. Theistic belief is not incoherent; it is incompletely coherent.

c. If incomplete coherence does not veto belief in other fields, it need not in this field.

d. It is unreasonable to expect formal proof of theistic belief.

e. If theistic belief is relatively the most coherent interpretation of experience available, it is reasonable to accept it, unreasonable to reject it.

f. The reasonableness of theistic belief is to be tested, not by its absolute adequacy to solve every problem, but by its relative adequacy as compared with other world-views. Carneades was right in holding that probability is the guide of life; absolute rational certainty is not accessible to man. But it remains true that there is a vast difference between random guesswork and the probability of coherent thought. Only the most rational probability is intellectually respectable.

CHAPTER II

THE MORAL BASIS OF RELIGIOUS VALUES

1. Summary of Chapter I

In the previous chapter we discussed the logical basis of religious belief. It was shown that if religion is to assert the truth of its fundamental beliefs, it is called on to interpret their relation to the beliefs arrived at through other channels than religious experience and formulated by science and philosophy. This is true, we showed, whether religious values be regarded as independent of the other achievements of civilization or as interrelated with them. It was shown, further, that, while actual religion is historically developed prior to any critical reflection upon it, nevertheless it is the duty of logical thought to interpret the meaning and truth of every religious belief. The remainder of the chapter was devoted to a defense and explanation of coherence as the essential nature of reason, and so as the test of the logical value of religious beliefs.

2. The Problem of this Chapter

If our thinking thus far has been sound, religious beliefs are subject to the jurisdiction of reason. They are not, it is true, to be deduced as a conclusion from nonreligious premises, but they are members of the same mind that entertains nonreligious beliefs. Reason must see to it that all the beliefs held by one mind dwell together in peace and harmony.

This logical foundation is necessary, but (it must be confessed) it is pretty formal, in the logical sense of

32

the word. It notifies us that religion (whatever it may be) must not believe anything which violates other necessary beliefs, and, further, that its beliefs must have a coherent connection with the rest of our life; but it does not tell us what there is in religion that is distinctive or that makes it worth believing. That is to say, it does not define or interpret the nature of religious value.[1]

In the present chapter we aim to draw somewhat nearer to the interpretation of religious values, which is the central problem of this book, by the study of a type of experience closely related to the religious, namely, the moral. We shall leave to one side the question of origins, taking for granted the fact that our religious and our moral values have both gone through a long evolution, and admitting that it is very difficult to say just when either religion or morality began, or which emerged first. In the study of chemistry we should not be greatly concerned about the science of the early Polynesians; nor in determining our present duty should we be guided or disturbed by the moral thinking of those worthy savages. The present significance of religious and moral values is no more to be learned from a study of their remote origins than is the present significance of geology to be learned from a study of the opinions of the first pithecanthropus who noticed a difference between pudding stone and flint. Religion and morality are both, it is true, living processes of individual and social experience, and should be interpreted in their true historical perspective; but mere "origin does not determine meaning and value." Our aim, then, will be to inquire into the meaning of moral values in the best form in which we know them,

---

[1]For a definition of the term "value," see Chap I, § 1, p. 15.

with special reference to their relation to religious values.

That it is reasonable to assume a close relation between the two types of value is evidenced by the history of religion. About many of the greatest figures in the past of religion, such as Confucius and Buddha, it is hard to decide whether their teachings should properly be called religious at all, so predominantly moral was their content. Every important religion has had some sort of moral code and has taught something about the ideal aim of the good life. It is the opinion of many competent observers that the moral laxity of modern times is related to the lessening of religious devotion. It is also to be observed that the fiber of religion either becomes flabby or is abnormally and harmfully excited when religion forgets its moral basis. Antinomian fanaticism is obviously evil, but liberal sentimentalism is no better. When a distinguished clergyman is reported as saying, "The thought of duty should be banished from our lives; not 'I must' but 'I love to' should be the expression of blessed service," he shows an equal obtuseness to the love of duty and to the duty of love. The problem, then, concerns both theory and practice. Our task is to inquire into the nature of the relation which is implied by these facts.

In order to succeed in this task it will be necessary to examine the nature of morality. A moral man is one who does what he ought to do; a moral society is one that honors its obligations. Our study, therefore, will concern itself chiefly with the meaning of obligation and its relation to religious values.

3. THE MEANING OF OBLIGATION

Socrates taught that knowledge is virtue; Bacon, that knowledge is power. This generation has more knowl-

edge and more power than any generation since history
began, but it would be optimistic to say that it also
had more virtue. More than knowledge and the power
that knowledge brings is necessary to virtue. This more
is expressed in the saying of Jesus, "By their fruits ye
shall know them." Indeed, there is some knowledge that
follows, not precedes, virtuous living; "if any man
willeth to do . . ., he shall know." Hence, although
this generation has more knowledge than any that went
before, it is greatly in need of knowledge, namely, the
kind of knowledge that grows out of the experience of
virtue. Information about the facts of nature and
human nature will always be essential to good living,
but understanding and application of the principles of
obligation are more essential than any knowledge of
matters of fact. What-is is a brute mystery unless it
be related to some ideal of the ought-to-be.

Obligation, the subject of our present study, is a timeless subject that is always timely, and never more timely
than in an age that seems to be careless of many obligations. Whether one looks at the world of business, or
sport, or government, or religion there appears to be a
relaxation of the stern "Puritanic" sense of obligation.
The relaxation has different causes and takes different
forms, but it is almost equally true of the much-dis-
cussed younger generation and its parents. The tendency of the age appears to be indorsed by current psychology, which seems able to find a complex or a gland
that is quite sufficient to account for any delinquency
of young or old.

The approach to an interpretation of morality and
religion through the conception of obligation is not the
usual one at present, but it is one that seemed fundamental to Kant, and it has commended itself to recent
thinkers like Josiah Royce and Mary W. Calkins in

America, and W. R. Sorley and J. E. Turner in England.[2] It is not the only approach, but we shall try it for what it is worth.

That there is some relation of obligation to religion as well as to morality has been, as we have seen, an almost universal belief; but there has been difference about the precise nature of that relation. For the present we can only say that there may be some doubt whether all obligation implies religion, but that there can be no doubt that all true religion implies obligation.

Some word conveying the sense of duty, oughtness, or obligation seems to be found in most developed languages, and the experience that is described by the expression "I ought" is one that most normal human beings have had. A few profess not to have had the experience. These are mostly either the "glad hearts" of Wordsworth's Ode, "who do thy work and know it not," or sophisticated moral philosophers (as Miss Calkins has pointed out). Whatever the number of those who have never experienced obligation, it is sound method to ignore them in any study of normal moral experience; the duty-blind and the color-blind are alike incompletely endowed. They must be dealt with by people who are capable of understanding obligation; but they themselves are objects rather than subjects of moral legislation.

When, therefore, we ask what obligation is, we are asking about a universal experience of man. Our startingpoint is not any theory or tradition or authority, but it is a fact that is observable by everyone in his own per-

---

[2]J. Royce, *The Philosophy of Loyalty* (New York: The Macmillan Company, 1908). M. W. Calkins, *The Good Man and the Good* (New York: The Macmillan Company, 1918). W. R. Sorley, *Moral Values and the Idea of God.* Second edition (Cambridge University Press, 1921). J. E. Turner, *The Philosophic Basis of Moral Obligation* (London: Macmillan & Co., 1924).

son. When I experience an obligation I confront a unique fact in consciousness; an obligation is not a sensation or an image or a desire; it is simply the acknowledgment that I ought to do this or that. It may have intimate relations, as we shall see, to social standards or to our desires (expressed or suppressed); but a standard that is an obligation is different from a standard that is merely socially approved, and a desire that is an obligation is different from a desire that is merely intense and enduring. When I say, "I ought" I am referring to an experience as genuinely unique as is the experience of color or of sound.

In saying that obligation is unique we have not completely described it. It has the peculiar property of being a fact that claims to be more than a fact; that is, it claims to be lawgiving for experience as a whole. He who acknowledges an obligation and means it seriously would be talking nonsense if he did not intend to imply that he believed the principle of his duty to be equally and always binding on himself and all persons under similar circumstances. Kant's categorical imperative is no antiquarian theory; it is what all moral experience means. The person who experiences any obligation may then be said to be legislating; he is laying down a universal ideal or law, of which he may be but dimly aware, but which is the real meaning of his obligation.

It is the tendency of current ethical thinking to ignore or minimize or explain away this experience of obligation. The subordination of the principle of duty to the principle of value is very general. But the tendency in question goes much further. Moralists seem to be more anxious to show Kant's shortcomings than to grasp the truth in his theory; more zealous to discover the psychological, social, or evolutionary antecedents of obli-

gation than to interpret its meaning. The soundest
current textbook on ethics[3] fails to do justice by Kant
or by the ought-experience. Yet into this book, as into
every objective account of moral experience, there enters
a recognition of universal obligation. "We hold," says
Everett, "that there is at least one intuitive, or immediate and axiomatic, judgment concerning it (that is,
value) which may be expressed as follows: 'The good is
worthy to be chosen.' "[4] It is interesting to note that
this formula means that all persons ought to choose the
good, but that the word "ought" is omitted.

We have said that obligation is a universal experience,
unique and lawgiving, but the ethical theorists seem
to desire to explain this experience away rather than to
take it as seriously as it takes itself. Is obligation truly
ultimate or is it to be explained in terms of something
else? This question must be answered before our definition of obligation will amount to much.

There is a general assault in the intellectual world
against everything that pretends to ultimateness or
finality. The Absolute is unpopular. Social institutions are in the melting pot. The mind is in the making.
Space and time and atoms are less privileged than of
yore. Psychology, as the saying goes, has lost its soul,
its mind, and even consciousness itself. Scripture is no
longer infallible. It would be astonishing if moral obligation alone should escape challenge and analysis.

The assault on all absolutes is not due to mere anarchy
in the spiritual life. It is only an overemphasis on the
first half of the apostolic injunction, "Prove all things,
hold fast that which is good." Modern thought is fully
justified in bringing every belief to the bar of reason.

---

[3]W. G. Everett, *Moral Values* (New York: Henry Holt and Company, 1918).

[4]*Op. cit.*, p. 259.

It is, however, true that the net result of the attack on foundation principles is both theoretically and practically pernicious unless it be followed by a constructive, synoptic view of what remains after the battle is over. The battle of thought is never literally ended; but there is more to life than the quarrels of the intellectuals, and it is high time to raise the question about the point that we have reached in thinking about moral obligation. After evolution and Freud, relativity and higher criticism, pragmatism and realism, the War and the Peace, is obligation still binding, or have all obligations fallen prey to the Spirit of the Times?

In order to answer this question we must consider the chief current conceptions of obligation that are opposed to the one presented in this chapter. These views all agree that obligation is not ultimate; that it neither falls from heaven nor is a part of original human nature, but that it is really a form of something other than obligation.

a. *Custom as the Source of Obligation.*—Every problem is being approached to-day from the social point of view. The nature of obligation seems to lend itself to social explanation. Man is conscious of the demands of family and clan long before he is conscious of having a moral obligation toward himself as an individual; and when self-regarding duty is recognized, the standard type of individual to which one feels oneself bound to conform is a type approved by some social group. Hence there are many who regard the moral life as no more than a systematization of group-customs. The moral problem for such thinkers becomes a struggle between the desires of the individual and the *mores* of the group.

There is much that speaks for the truth of this view. Desire of social approval and fear of social disapproval are among the most powerful motives in the life of men, whether savage or civilized. The *tabu* is respected everywhere among primitive men. The "things that are not done" are wrong. A Hebrew writer could put into the mouth of Abimelech the words, "Thou hast done things unto me that are not done" (Gen. 20. 9), or could say of the outrage on Dinah that "such things are not done;" while the revisers agree with the King James translators in rendering in both passages by the words, "ought not to be done." Likewise, for the most modern man or woman of refinement, the thought that "this thing is never done" is a sufficient veto on many an act.

Nevertheless, the identification of duty with what is socially approved is not rationally justified. When Greek thinkers began to inquire about the difference between what was true by convention ($\phi\acute{v}\sigma\epsilon\iota$) and what was true by nature ($\nu\acute{o}\mu\omega$), they were on the track of the fallacy which underlies the idea that obligation is wholly due to custom. Some things are right merely because society agrees on a certain procedure in order to avoid inconvenience or rudeness; such are the code of etiquette, the rules of any game, and many of the laws of the land. Such also is the choice of Sunday as a day of rest, rather than Tuesday or Friday. But some things are true by nature, and any custom which ignores nature is a bad custom and ought to be changed. As our knowledge of nature increases, old standards and customs should be and often are revised; customs regarding the care of the body, the treatment and prevention of disease, the drinking of alcoholic beverages, the place of woman in society have changed radically with the increase of knowledge.

It is true that custom is the origin of some particular obligations; it is untrue that custom is the source of

the validity of any obligation. An intelligent understanding of obligation, derived in part, as we have seen,
from knowledge of natural law, has led and will lead
to a sharp criticism of custom, to a disregard of social
approval or disapproval. Prophets and scientists,
philosophers and saints agree that custom is not the
fundamental sanction of obligation.

The sociologist may argue that our consideration of
this point has overlooked one important fact, namely,
that the first dawn of moral obligation always occurs in
a social situation. He may rightly say that this is true
not only of the race but also of the individual. He
would then argue that all further development of the
sense of obligation, no matter what form it may take,
goes back to this social root and is an outgrowth of it.
There is no doubt, we may reply, that we first learn
of obligation from others; but this does not prove that
obligation is merely social. Doubtless also our knowledge of a physical world, of mathematics, and of logic
has a social origin; but to hold that all our knowledge
is mere convention and custom because it has a social
origin is to abandon ourselves to utter moral skepticism.
Yet this is what those must do who derive the binding
force of obligation from custom, if they are rigorously
logical.

We may conclude that custom is probably the source
of our first experiences of obligation, but that it is
not the source of the meaning and validity of any
obligation.

b. *Law as the Source of Obligation.*—Law is only codified custom enacted and enforced by constituted authorities; and it would require no special discussion were it
not both for the differences of opinion among eminent
jurists and for the practical importance of the subject.
Anyone who is interested in an expert treatment of the

problem should read *Law and Morals*[5] by Dean Roscoe
Pound of the Harvard University Law School, a learned
and compact little book.

Law, we have said, is only codified custom; but the
legislator must select the customs that he is to codify,
and must sometimes institute new customs. He must
repeal or revise existing law. An analogous duty belongs
to the judge in the application of law; very often he
must use his discretion. In the light of facts like these,
Dean Pound has studied the history of juristic thought.
He points out that there are three main theories, the
analytic, the historical, and the philosophical. "To
the analytic jurist," he says, "law was law by enactment, . . . to the historical jurist it was law by convention, and . . . to the philosophical jurist it was law
by nature."[6] Since the facts of legislation and judicial
interpretation cannot be explained wholly in terms of
prior enactment or custom, the philosophical jurist is
right. The authority of law must rest back on "nature."
Law itself cannot be the source of all obligation. Good
men recognize an obligation to obey law, but they often
are conscious of an obligation to change law, and sometimes to resist it. The right of rebellion cannot be
denied without arbitrary ignoring of history, but it cannot be affirmed without admitting that legislation derives
its authority from moral law, not moral law from
legislation. Our view gives to law a deeper and more
sacred sanction than any merely empirical account.

c. *Desire as the Source of Obligation.*—The theories
that regard custom or law as the root of obligation
may be called sociological; from these we may turn to
the psychological theories.

The most common psychological theory seeks to inter-

---

[5]University of North Carolina Press, 1924.
[6]*Op. cit.*, p. 117.

pret obligation as a form of desire.[7] Man's nature is an arena of conflicting desires. Some are relatively transitory, some deeper and more permanent. Morality, many believe, consists in the discovery of the desires that are or can be permanent, and the guiding of life so that the dominant desire will rule all other desires. The consciousness of obligation is, then, simply the form assumed by the dominant desire. "I ought" means only "I desire as my chief good." This point of view has been held by most thinkers in the history of ethics except the intuitionists and the Kantians.

Nevertheless, it is not true to moral experience. The warfare of obligation and desire, which all admit, is not correctly described by calling it a warfare between dominant desire and conflicting desires. No desire, however long-lived or dominant, constitutes an obligation merely because of its existence as a desire. Often we acknowledge obligations without any desire to fulfill them; often we have no desire to discover the obligations that we know we should find if we looked.

There is some ground for the assertion of a relation between obligation and desire. Obligation is, in large part, a principle for organizing and judging desires; and conformity to obligation ought to be a dominant desire. Yet it remains true that no desire, because it is a desire, and for no other reason, is therefore obligatory. The law of "I want," even when calculated with the utmost prudence, is not the law of "I ought."

d. *Obligation as Behavior-Pattern.*—The popularity of behavioristic psychology has led to some recent attempts to apply behaviorism to ethical problems, as by Holt (*The Freudian Wish in Ethics*) and Givler (*The Ethics of Hercules*). In view of the fact that

---

[7]Bertrand Russell's *What I Believe* (New York: E. P. Dutton & Company, 1925), is a vigorous defense of this view.

ethics and Christian teaching both emphasize conduct, it has seemed not utterly fantastical to interpret morality in terms of behavior. However, a little reflection will show that no behavior-pattern could ever express the meaning of the experience of obligation. Any behavior you please may spring from an inner life of evil motive; the fruits by which we are to be known can be understood only in relation to the roots from which they grow. The tap-root of morality is the sense of obligation, and it can be found only in the inner life of consciousness. Any conception of morality or of education (secular or religious) that lays exclusive stress on conduct, on external expression, is untrue to the psychological facts of moral and religious experience. Out of the heart are the issues of life; and in the heart, that is, in conscious awareness, is the seat of obligation. A behavioristic theory must say that obligation is simply the act of pronouncing the word "obligation" plus the chain-reflexes aroused by that word. It is not going too far to say that extreme behaviorism explains obligation by denying that there is any such experience.

e. *Obligation as Rationalization.*—Our survey of opposing views would be incomplete if it omitted the attitude of the psychoanalyst. No study of obligation from the psychoanalytic camp has come to my attention, but probably one has been written, or, if not, will be. It runs, or will run, about as follows: The "moral" man, so called, is suffering from an inferiority complex, or, at any rate, he finds his desires frustrated. In this unhappy state his subconscious finds him, and flies to his relief, whispering to him words about the dignity of being true to obligation, which soothe his wounded self-feeling and restore his self-confidence. For such a view the consciousness of obligation is a compensation or defense-mechanism which may be said to "sublimate"

man's frustrated desires.   An idea with such an origin
is called a rationalization.

There is truth enough in the psychoanalytic account
to make it seem plausible.   It is true that there are many
cases of defense-mechanisms to be found both within
and without the walls of hospitals for the insane.   It
is also true that loyalty to obligation sublimates—makes
sublime—the frustration of man's desires and restores
his self-respect.   But this account, after all, does not tell
us very much about obligation beyond the fact that it
performs a certain psychological function.   There is
nothing in psychology which tells us that a "rationalization" is always irrational.   Obligation may perform
just the function that the psychoanalyst claims for it and
still be just the unique and significant experience that
our theory asserts it to be.   Psychoanalysis may tell us
something about some of the functions of obligation;
it does not tell us anything about its validity.

f. *Obligation as Unique Complex.*—The theories previously discussed all agree in trying to explain obligation
in terms of something else, and thus in denying its
uniqueness.   Miss Calkins recognizes the uniqueness of
obligation, but nevertheless holds that it may be analyzed into something else.   It is, she thinks, "an especially unique and distinctive complex of experiences
usually disjoined."[8]   These experiences are, first, a feeling of compulsion and, secondly, a feeling of freedom
and activity.   In being conscious of duty or obligation,
then, I am conscious of being commanded and com-
mander at once.   This analysis is very interesting, and
all will doubtless recognize self-compulsion and free
activity as elements that are present in moral experience.
Nevertheless, question may be raised about the com-

---

[8] *The Good Man and the Good*, p. 15.

pleteness of the analysis. If obligation is made up of
compulsion plus activity, it is, to borrow the language
of chemistry, not a mechanical mixture of the two but
a compound. Just as water has properties that oxygen
and hydrogen lack, so obligation has a property that
compulsion and freedom lack. There may be compulsion and freedom without obligation. The soul of the
woman who follows the styles may be conscious of a
unique complex of compulsion and freedom without any
touch of moral obligation; the sense of being well
dressed (so the saying goes) gives a peace that religion
(and morality) can neither give nor take away. After
all, the essence of obligation evaporates in Miss Calkins'
analysis as truly as it does in the views which we have
previously examined and rejected. "I ought freely to
compel myself," means something different from "I do
freely compel myself." The former states my experience
of obligation; the latter is what I feel when I carry out
the obligation. The "ought" remains a unique attitude
that cannot be analyzed away. I may be aware of an
obligation without any desire to fulfill it, with no sense
of compulsion, contemplating it as coolly as one contemplates a triangle, and ignoring it as completely in
my conduct.

g. *A Restatement of the Meaning of Obligation.*—
After all this criticism of opposing views, it is desirable
to make a somewhat more positive statement of our
constructive view. There would be little point in attacking other views only to leave in their place a wretched,
isolated feeling, "I ought," with no more meaning than
the bare words. "I ought," taken by itself, is hardly
more than the shadow of the skeleton of the moral life.
Yet even this is not to be despised; the shadow implies
the skeleton, and the skeleton implies that there is, or
at least has been, a living organism. To change the

metaphor, our X-ray examination has revealed the faint outlines of a bony framework; what have these outlines, these "ought"-experiences, to do with our living obligations? Let us look at the moral organism more carefully.

(1) *"Ought."*—First of all, there is, as we have found, the unique element of the experience of "ought" or, "duty." It is like nothing else. It is uniquely, or as Kant says, categorically imperative.[9] Moral life cannot stop with mere contemplation of the uniqueness of duty; but it cannot exclude its rigorous commands. Jeremy Bentham was incensed at those who made the feeling of duty a substitute for thought about particular duties; and in his *Deontology* he excoriated "ought" as "the talisman of arrogance, indolence and ignorance, . . . an authoritative imposture." Bentham was right if emphasis on "ought" be no more than a dumb assertion of obligation. We must refute him by considering the further implications of this experience.

(2) *Moral Law.*—The ought-experience is not a mere feeling; it is also, as we have seen, a piece of legislation. When I say, "I ought," I always imply something more than the presence of a feeling in my consciousness, even than the feeling, "I am coerced and yet I am active." "I ought" means "I approve the principle by which I am now acting as the principle by which all rational beings everywhere ought always to act when placed under circumstances similar to mine." It was Kant's grasp of the universal element in duty that made him so certain that morality cannot be based on any moral

---

[9]That the uniqueness of "ought" is no peculiar doctrine of Kant's alone is evidenced by the emphatic way in which Sidgwick, the hedonist, says that "the fundamental notion represented by the word 'ought' (is) . . . essentially different from all notions representing facts of psychical or physical existence." *Methods of Ethics*, seventh edition (London: Macmillan & Co., 1922), p. 25.

feeling. His antithesis of feeling and law was doubt-less grounded on faulty psychology, but his certainty of law in the moral life expressed a fundamental and essential truth. Morality is not merely compulsion and control; it is compulsion and control in the light of a principle acknowledged to be universally binding.

(3) *Ideal of Personality.*—It is generally agreed that Kant's doctrine is an incomplete account of what obligation implies. His view of the moral law should be supplemented by T. H. Green's doctrine of the ideal of personality if we are to understand obligation. "I ought" is a verb that implies an object and the universal law is not that object. It would be absurd to say merely that I ought to realize a universal law; for the law in my experience always takes the form of particular ends to realize, particular goods to choose. I ought, then, to attain what is truly valuable. This aspect of obligation is not sufficiently explained when I have drawn up a list of the values of life, like Professor Everett's table of values—the economic, bodily, recreational, associational character, æsthetic, intellectual, religious.[10] These values, which we all acknowledge, are to be realized not loosely and separately but in a personal and social life which is an organic whole. Our ought-experience imposes on us the obligation, or, rather, expresses the fact that we impose on ourselves the obligation, of framing for ourselves as individuals and for the society in which we live the best ideal of personal living that our minds can frame. Obligation means the duty of forming and of realizing, as far as in us lies, this ideal. This fact, given in the very structure of moral experience, is one reason for the fundamental importance of the expression of the religious and moral ideal in the personality of Jesus Christ.

---

[10]*Op. cit.*, p. 182.

Our conception of the ideal will grow; it will be nourished by every influence that enters our experience. The imperative command of duty is satisfied if our ideal is as good as we can make it, and our realization of it as perfect as our powers permit.

It is this ideal that gives content to obligation; but obligation is not merely knowledge or recognition of the ideal. We cannot get rid of the uniquely imperative basis of ethics. Neither the "goods ethics" nor the "duty ethics," as Bowne[11] calls the two points of view, can be explained in terms of the other; Bentham and Kant sought in vain to do away, the one with duty, and the other with value as a unique essential of ethical theory. Each point of view is necessary; neither alone is sufficient. Either without the other is empty or blind.

A further remark on the ideal of personality should be added. The meaning of obligation is the imperative command to make the ideal real. We sometimes speak of ideal values, but a value that is merely ideal is really no value at all. The ideal of personality, in so far as it is merely a program of action that is not acted on, even in intent, is quite valueless. A value is a type of personal life, a form of actual experience that satisfies through its conformity to some ideal. Among many practical men the word "idealism" is a by-word and a hissing, because it is taken to mean mere contemplation of ideals without regard to their realization. A significant ideal is imperative; when we think it we must add, "I ought to realize this ideal." It is the fact of obligation that mediates between our ideal of personality and our life of real value, and commands us to judge the real by the ideal, to make the ideal real. Any tendency to slur over our experience of the imperative

[11]*The Principles of Ethics* (New York: American Book Company, 1892).

tends also to make our ideals empty dreams, cut off from life, or realized only as whim and fancy strike us.

(4) *Possibility of Attaining the Ideal.*—There is a further implication of our experience of obligation. Since it implies a law binding on all rational beings, it obviously cannot command the impossible, for this would destroy the rational nature of moral law. Hence, as Kant teaches, ought implies can; the moral law presupposes freedom; obligation extends only to the limit of our ability in the situation in which we find ourselves. It is therefore not our obligation to attain the full ideal at once; but only to attain as much of it as we can and such aspects of it as are relevant to the situation. It is, however, evidently commanded by the moral law that we should keep the whole ideal before our minds when a choice is being made, because otherwise a fair judgment of the bearing of the ideal on the situation is impossible.

(5) *Knowledge of the Situation.*—The foregoing discussion has shown that the small word "ought" has a rich content. "I ought" means (1) a unique imperative, (2) that formulates a universally binding law, (3) directed toward the realization of the highest type of personality, (4) and yet commanding only the possible. It is evident that (4) is meaningless unless we add (5), that obligation commands us to act in full light of the best possible knowledge of the situation in which we are and its consequences.

Emphasis on the moral situation is one of the important contributions of pragmatism to current thought. It is interesting to observe that a nonpragmatic analysis like the present one necessitates the same emphasis. If we aim only to understand what obligation means, we are driven to take the total situation into account just as inevitably as though we started with a pragmatic bias.

But our approach has an advantage over the pragmatic; the latter usually involves an overemphasis on the biological aspects and on immediate results, while the former takes the whole range of the meaning of moral experience into account and does not seek to reduce obligation to survival-value or meaning to action.

4. WHY IS OBLIGATION BINDING?

With our view of the meaning of obligation, we have the materials for an answer to the most searching question that may be raised by the moral skeptic, namely, Why is obligation binding? Why should this word "ought" rule our lives, when it conflicts with so many of our desires?

On our view obligation is binding because it is self-imposed, or, as Kant would say, autonomous. Obligation does not arise from the mere command of a foreign power like society or even God himself; we are bound to do what we recognize that we ought to do; and the obligation is binding, inescapable, because we have imposed it on ourselves. We cannot evade the jurisdiction of laws that we ourselves have made.

To some this will seem like a surrender of the foundations of morality rather than a strengthening of them. Society perhaps, these may say, does not create obligation; but how can it be said that God is not the source of obligation? Is he not the source of all being, of all value? What law can be binding save in dependence on his will?

The implied answers to the foregoing rhetorical questions are all, I believe, true. Nevertheless, although God is to be regarded as the source of the moral order, when he chose such an order he chose a world of self-respecting persons, whose moral life should develop from within, and who must themselves choose their own careers and obligations within the limits of possibility. Much is imposed on us by God; but it is the gift of God that we should impose our obligations on ourselves, and meet him as free person meets free person, face to face. There is at stake here the fundamental issue between Catholic and Protestant morality; the former denies and the latter affirms the principle of autonomy. Not in vain has Kant been called the philosopher of Protestantism.[12]

Further, obligation is also binding because it is rational. To acknowledge obligation is to be conscious of a rational law. Reason is the synoptic vision of the mind; it is the power to be self-consistent and inclusive, to take everything into account and to see everything as a whole. "Ought" is always a command to be rational, in this sense. He who violates obligation violates reason; he is not only a bad man, he is also an unreasonable man. For, to violate obligation is to do what we judge we ought not to do. The bad man thus either contradicts himself, or, at best, leaves something out of account that reason bids him to consider. The man who is reasonable must, if he has moral experience at all, be true to obligation.

Finally, obligation is binding because loyalty to obligation is essential to human welfare. True human welfare means the realization of the individual-social ideal of humanity. Heredity, habit, social convention and other forces conspire to keep the average mass of the race somewhere near the point of tolerable living. But if experience and reason may be trusted, it is clear that no external forces acting on man, and no psychological mechanisms of which we know can be trusted to work

---

[12]See M. de Unamuno, *The Tragic Sense of Life* (London: Macmillan & Co., 1921), p. 67, for a statement of a Roman Catholic standpoint.

uniformly for human welfare. Only the man who sees
the human problem in the light of obligation will keep
steadily loyal to the cause of individual and social welfare. Wordsworth's "happy spirit" is far too much a
creature of habit to be trusted to see the ideal needs of
man in the complex situations of modern life, and to act
faithfully in conformity with that ideal. After all that
can be done by suggestion and habit-training and gland
treatments and psychoanalysis has been done, there will
always remain the fact that man's personality is a unity;
and that it must govern itself as a unity by intelligent
loyalty to reasonable obligation. Moral education,
therefore, needs to lay more stress on personality and
moral reason, and perhaps less stress on the externals
of conduct.

5. The Social Significance of Obligation

Any theory of obligation which roots in the individual
and advocates moral autonomy must face squarely the
social problem. Only the individual person can say, "I
ought." No one can say to him, "Thou oughtest," save
in the mild sense of stating for him the result of his own
moral legislation. Socially speaking, such a doctrine as
this seems not merely individualistic; it seems anarchical. If society is a collection of self-legislating individuals, how can a genuine community arise? How is
real moral cooperation possible?

This is no purely academic question. Everyone
knows that there is a real clash between conscience and
the demands of society, both in time of war and in time
of peace. Further, there is a deeper clash between the
permanent welfare of the individual and of society. If
society is to prosper, the individual must sacrifice himself or be sacrificed.

It is, however, hasty to conclude that because obliga-

tion is imposed by individuals on themselves it is therefore anarchical or antisocial. On the contrary, the experience of obligation has great social importance.

The experience of obligation usually occurs in a complex to which we give the name of conscience. It is
important to distinguish between the emotional and
the rational conscience. As we ordinarily meet the feeling of obligation in ourselves, it has the form of a rather
intense emotional experience; but this emotional conscience is not the binding obligation of which we have
been speaking. Conscience becomes binding only when
we stop to think what it means, grasp something of the
principles involved, and impose its laws on our choices.
Now, it is evident that the emotional conscience may be
very arbitrary; and there is grave danger that it would
be antisocial. But the rational conscience, by its very
nature, is social.

Reason is, to some extent, shared by all normal human
beings. Every intelligent mathematical operation is an
instance of a process that is at once individual and
autonomous and also social in its meaning and outcome.
In principle, such is also the moral reason. When it has
its perfect work, it arrives at results that are true for
all and good for all. Moreover, the moral reason teaches
us to respect other persons, and treat them, as Kant
teaches, never as means only, but also as ends. What
principle is more significant socially than that of respect
for personality? More specifically, obligation commands us to attain the maximum value, the closest approximation to the ideal of personality in every situation; and this value, this ideal, if reasonable, must take
society into account and must assume a social form.
The human moral legislator-for-himself, the social legislator, and the divine legislator start each from his own
point of view; but they meet in the objective values that

each sees to be worthy of realization. Value is a social principle; for while it may be chosen by an isolated individual, the great values of life can be realized in their fullest and richest forms only by a cooperating community. He who is fully loyal to obligation is driven to social loyalties.

If all these considerations fail to convince, and the critic of obligation as a basic principle still regards "I ought" as too individualistic a basis for a social ethic, one other consideration may still be urged. There is only one ultimate alternative to a society of autonomous moral persons, namely, a society of persons who recognize no obligation but are ruled by force. It is thus that Hobbes conceived morality. But over against the view of human nature that Hobbes and Machiavelli hold —a pessimistic denial of the power and social outcome of individual obligation—there are Kant's view and Hegel's view, that see within the human individual a reason at work that is social in its meaning and can be, must be, trusted to work out right social consequences. On moral pessimism a moral society cannot be built.

This does not imply that all use of force is immoral. On the contrary, it means that society is under obligation to provide conditions which make the existence and development of moral persons possible. Hence nonmoral and immoral individuals must be restrained and often the moral man whose judgment differs from that of society must be compelled to cooperate against his will. Loyalty to obligation will thus lead to an unstable equilibrium between society as a whole and its constituent individuals until a perfectly moralized society of perfectly moralized individuals has been attained. Loyalty to obligation may cause much suffering and many tragedies on the way; but it is necessary to per-

manent and truly worthful social progress. Only the
loyal lead humanity toward the goal of perfection.

6. The Significance of Obligation for Religion

We are now ready to confront the problem to which
our whole discussion has been leading, namely, the
problem of the relation of moral to religious values.
Religion seems to move in a different realm from mere
morality and to breathe a higher and purer air.[13]

Religion seems to be no mere human goodness; it is
a power of more-than-human origin. "Religion," as
Fichte says, "consists in the fact that in his own person and not in that of another, and with his own spiritual eye and not with that of another, man sees, has,
and possesses God immediately."[14] Yet, on the other
hand, morality, like logic, also asserts its prerogative
to legislate for religion.

At first sight that legislation might seem to be pro-
hibition, or declaration of war. Just as obligation seems
to conflict with the demands of society so also it seems
to conflict with the demands of God. Conscience seems
to be individual, not social; human, not divine. To make
one's own moral judgment the supreme arbiter appears
to be rebellion against Cæsar and God alike. In addi-
tion to these problems, common to the social and the
religious approach, religion raises difficulties of its own.
If God be supreme, he must be the source and giver of
the moral law; then, human moral autonomy becomes

---

[13]See the very informing articles by A. C. Knudson on "The Significance of Religious Values for Religious Knowledge," in *Methodist Review*, 106 (1923), pp. 341–352, and on "Religious Apriorism"
in E. C. Wilm, *Studies in Philosophy and Theology* (New York: The
Abingdon Press, 1922), pp. 93–127; also an article by the same writer
on "Henry Clay Sheldon—Theologian," *Methodist Review*, 108
(1925), pp. 175–192.

[14]*Anweisung zum seligen Leben*, in *Werke*, Vol. V, p. 418.

meaningless. Further, critics of religion are often asking in these days how it is possible to reconcile the moral consciousness, and its demand for improvement, with the existence of a perfect God, who would obviously have made the world already as good as omnipotence could make it, and hence hardly capable of improvement by us impotent mortals. Religion, they think, means paralysis of morality.

Let us approach the problems with the hypothesis that, in spite of appearances, the moral experience and the religious experience are both fundamentally trustworthy; and, in the spirit of sympathy with each, seek for some solution to the apparent contradictions. If our hypothesis is that both obligation and religion are lawgiving in human life, then our first question should be about the relation of the two. Either morality is dependent on religion, or religion on morality, or each is (in some sense) independent of the other.

In any philosophical inquiry it is wise to begin with experience. There is no doubt that both morality and religion are facts of human experience. If we cling closely to the facts of experience, and subtract the additions made by faith and belief and reasoning, we shall be forced to admit that moral obligation is a more immediate experience than is the existence of God. I say "more immediate," for I do not believe that any experience is purely immediate and free from all interpretation; but most men will agree with the statement that less of either faith or reason is involved in acknowledging an obligation than in believing in God. We may go further, and say that our experience of values in general and of moral value in particular is an undeniable fact, whatever our further theories may be. Whether we believe in God or not, there is value and there is obligation. Whether God issues moral commandments or not, obligation is self-recognized and self-imposed. The principle of moral autonomy means that the binding law of obligation and the implied command to realize values do not depend logically or psychologically on belief in religion, and therefore that the whole realm of religious experience rests on the basis of loyalty to moral obligation, and cannot declare its independence of morality.

Friends of religion are often loath to recognize this fact. It seems to them a surrender of the supremacy of the value that they prize, and a rebellion against the sovereignty of God. Yet the facts of life speak strongly against this attitude. No faith or theology has permission to deny experience; and experience testifies that many men, great and small, who have been unable to accept the belief in God have nevertheless been loyal to obligation, and have devotedly added what they could to the sum of human happiness. Nor should the friend of religion regard this fact with aversion. On the contrary, it is one of the most significant proofs of the supremacy of value and of the existence of God if the universe is such that the recognition of imperative values is somehow native to the soul of every human being, whether his mind accepts or rejects the God of all values. Bertrand Russell's famous essay, "A Free Man's Worship,"[15] is a good example to show what I mean. Russell rejects God; he sees no hope, no future for the race; "slow doom falls pitiless and dark." Nevertheless, in man there are ideals, noble thoughts; and it is man's business to cherish these, "proudly defiant of the irresistible forces that tolerate, for a moment, his knowledge and his condemnation." Russell's facts are more important than his theory. His facts are a world

[15]In Bertrand Russell, *Mysticism and Logic* (London: Longmans, Green & Co., 1921), pp. 46–57.

in which moral persons bravely strive on, even when appearances are most unfriendly, a loyalty to obligation that will not be frustrated while it can breathe. His theory is of a purposeless, godless universe. Do not his facts cry aloud for a God? If the universe is as he understands it to be, the existence of meaning and value in human experience is a sheer miracle.

When God seems far away, and there is dense darkness about us, there is a pathway back to God that no human soul can lose so long as it remains human; wisdom and philosophy may be lost, faith in God and even faith in our fellow man may be lost, but no one will deny that in his innermost being there is a law that tells him, "I ought to be better than I am," or that in his daily life there are some experiences of beauty and goodness, of truth and wonder. Obligation and value are always there; and a world in which the law of obligation is universal and inevitable is a world in which there is strong likelihood of there being a God.

From the religious point of view there is a further reason enforcing the truth that the validity of obligation is logically prior to that of religion. Any religion that has developed very far holds to the belief that God is good. Judaism, Mohammedanism, Christianity, Zoroastrianism, modern Buddhist sects, and others agree that God is good and that he expects goodness from man. This means that we must acknowledge goodness before we can acknowledge a good God. Belief in a supreme personal creator is not belief in God, unless that creator recognizes moral obligation. Experience of the *mysterium tremendum,* the awful mystery, of which Otto has been telling is not religious in the ideal sense unless the mystery is good as well as awful. Otherwise, how could we distinguish a religious experience from experience of the *monstrum horrendum informe ingens* of our school days?

The Supreme Being, then, is God, not by virtue of his being a creator, nor by virtue of his power to inspire awe, but by virtue of his loyalty to obligation and his realization of values. Only a creator who is also a redeemer is a God truly worthy of the name; only a mystery who respects the moral law can be worshiped rather than dreaded. We are driven to the conclusion that recognition of obligation, that is, of the formal part of moral law, is prior to and more fundamental than our acknowledgment of God's existence or our experience of religion.

Having thus separated the fields of obligation and of religion, we need to supplement our result by considering their mutual relations.

We are working with the hypothesis that religion and morality are both fundamentally true. Then, if religion be true, it is evident that an obligation to be religious is an essential part of the moral life. This follows from the view of obligation that has been presented. If obligation commands us to realize the highest possible ideal of personality, and if religion be true, how can we escape the obligation to include religious values in the ideal and in its realization? From this point of view religion is a part of morality.

To this conclusion the average man tends to object. He will say that a man may, like Bertrand Russell, be moral without being religious. The answer to this criticism, however, is almost self-evident from the statement of the problem; it was not said that for every human being, unconditionally, religion is a part of morality; it was only said that if religion be true, it is a part of morality. The only man, then, who is not morally obligated to be religious is the man who believes that religion is not true; the acknowledgment of its truth carries with it the obligation to realize its value. That obligation cannot be postponed until some formal moment like that of joining a church or of avowing one's intention to be religious, any more than the obligation to be good awaits the moment of our joining the Ethical Culture Society. It is immediate and imperative.

A more subtle objection is sometimes raised by the theologian who fears to make religion a part of morality lest the uniqueness of religion be imperiled. That this is no empty fear is evidenced by the tendency of numerous thinkers to make religion no more than an interest in the conservation of other values or even than any social interest. But the view that has been defended does not mean at all that religion surrenders its uniqueness or becomes "mere morality." Within "the moral empire" there is room for beauty and all its irreducible qualities; for truth and the laws of logic; and also for religion with every unique mystery and splendor that it can contribute to life. If religion be a part of morality, it is true that loyalty to obligation is a precondition to being religious; but it also means that it is our obligation to realize all the rich meaning that religion can contribute to life. None of the wine of life should be spilled merely because it is our duty to pour into the cup.

The relation between obligation and religion has not, however, been completely stated when it is said that religion is a part of duty; for, after all, what our duty actually will be in any situation is dependent on the kind of universe this is. It is self-evident that no one can tell just what he ought to do to make this a better world merely by contemplating the formal law of obligation. Obligation must set to work with its eyes open, must take everything into account. In other words, it must face the whole universe as fully as it can, and consider, the universe being what it is, how the maximum values attainable in the present situation can actually be attained.

The tendency of current ethical theory is unduly to limit the scope of the moral situation. Pragmatists, Dewey in particular, have inclined to interpret it in biological terms. The moral ideal then becomes the perfect adjustment of the organism to its environment, including the other organisms with whom one has to do. This view, despite its pragmatic label, is abstract and artificial. What real human being has ever lived only for his biological organism and his physical and physiological environment? Experience is crowded with objects and values that are immaterial and that lead man's interest far beyond his biological fate. Moral obligation commands us, it is true, to ignore no facts; all that the biological pragmatists say is relevant and should be considered; but while it is necessary, it is not sufficient. Moral obligation extends beyond what the eye can see into the field of all that the mind can see; and what we ought to do is to be chosen from among all the possibilities that are revealed to us by our most complete view of the universe. It is the task of religion to prevent the moral man from any artificial narrowing of his range to the needs of his body and his bankaccount, and to expand his vision so that the spiritual possibilities of life will be real and vivid to him. It says, "If there be any virtue, and if there be any praise, think on these things."

The moral man who is loyal to obligation will therefore be driven beyond himself by his own autonomous command. Duty can never be discovered or performed by the man who only looks within. The best can be found only by him who is looking for the best; the "adjustment" that the biological pragmatists seek can be found only in an adjustment to the universe. Thus the moral law commands us to seek light from science and history, from philosophy and experience, from the church and Bible, indeed, from every possible source. "Prove all things," it decrees, "hold fast that which is good."

He who is driven beyond himself to seek light from every source, cannot stop short of God. There is a road that leads imperatively from obligation to God. In general, this fact has been recognized by religious thought, although it has not always been reasonably interpreted. It has been held, for instance, that moral law requires a divine lawgiver. That this traditional view is questionable follows from the autonomy of moral law. Obligation is binding not because a foreign power, even God himself, legislates for me, but rather, because I legislate for myself; and, if I am true to my own moral reason, I cannot avoid acknowledging my responsibility.

The rational way from obligation to God has been stated more cogently by Sorley in his *Moral Values and the Idea of God* than by any other recent writer. Briefly, the gist of his argument is as follows: We have sense perceptions, some of which are trustworthy and some not; we distinguish genuine perceptions from illusions and the like by building up a consistent system in which all true perceptions find their place. All of our percepts claim objective validity, and it is rational to trust those that are congruent with the consistent system as revealing to us an objective order of nature. Similarly, we have moral perceptions, which also claim objective validity; when we recognize an obligation we do not merely impose it on ourselves, but we judge that the universe is such that all persons similarly situated really ought to do as we do. Some of our moral perceptions are erroneous, but, as in the case of sense-perceptions, we are able to build up a consistent system out of the moral experiences, which it is rational to trust as revealing an objective moral order. This order can exist only in a Supreme Person, for only persons can experience obligation or value. In his argument thus incompletely sketched Sorley has made an important contribution to theistic thought that is worthy of more careful attention than it has received.

The way from obligation to God that was outlined by Kant in the third postulate of the practical reason also contains more than a germ of truth. Our conception of the *summum bonum,* says Kant, includes not alone morality but also happiness proportioned to that morality. Yet there is nothing about the moral law that guarantees happiness to him who obeys it. From these Kantian premises we may go on, modifying his thought, to point out that, as a matter of fact, loyalty to obligation is one of the deepest sources of satisfaction. Indeed, all of the ideal values bring an exalted happiness to the soul, although there is no logical reason why that should take place. The universe, then, is such that only the highest values actually satisfy; and this fact can best be explained on the hypothesis that the source of all being is a unitary Person who respects obligation and, in the long run, gives happiness to the virtuous.

One difficulty, however, remains to be considered. It was said that critics of religion are attacking the idea of a perfect God on the ground that if God be perfect there can be no moral task; the universe would be already perfect. This objection when analyzed falls into two parts: one connected with our ideal of democracy and the other with our ideal of progress. In behalf of democracy we are told that God cannot be a king; there is no more room for Oriental despots on earth or in heaven. We have socialized recitations and socialized churches; we must have a socialized and democratized universe. In behalf of progress, we are told that the fundamental fact is that the universe is capable of being improved, and that therefore it is not perfect, and cannot have an *ens perfectissimum* as its cause.

It is rather striking that many so-called modern ideas are as uncritical as their antiquated predecessors. In ancient times, it was excusable to ascribe to God the attributes of the monarch in the current form of government; it is rather trivial for an enlightened modern to take the constitution of the United States as a model for the constitution of the kingdom of heaven. The notion of a democratic God is often very obscurely conceived; it is not clear whether it implies the election of a God every four years by some cosmic electoral college, nor is there any definite provision for the contingency of a deadlock. We may as well face the fact that the universe in general and religion in particular contain some undemocratic factors. We all stand face to face with facts that we cannot prevent or control. Our very existence depends on a power not ourselves. If God is immanent in nature, as seems reasonable to believe, he is a God of force, not waiting on human preferences. We must accept the universe, whether it suits the majority or not.

In spite of these strictures on the current demand for a democratic God, it remains true that religion and democracy are close allies; but the fundamental laws of obligation and value are normative, not the subordinate and somewhat provincial ideal of democracy.

The relations of religion to democracy may be shown in various ways. However exalted and absolute be our God, the very thought of God as Father of all is essentially democratic, for it implies the brotherhood of man.

Professor Coe relevantly quotes a newspaper writer who remarked "that monotheism is inappropriate and inconvenient for nations that are fighting for nationalism."[16] Further, the goodness of God as revealed in our experience is shown to be democratic in that he respects the moral autonomy of every person. No theory can justly deny this basic fact of our moral experience. Also, if the universe be the kind of moral order that our study of obligation takes it to be, then every individual person is an end-in-himself. There are, then, many democratic as well as some undemocratic features in the idea of God; but in no event should any political theory be made the criterion of universal being. It must be remembered that democracy is futile if it does not rest on the obligation of the community to recognize and attain the highest values, subject to the actual laws of the universe as it is.

Belief in democracy is nearer to the heart of morality than is belief in progress. Belief in democracy in some form follows from the fact that every person is an autonomous moral agent and, as such, worthy of respect. Belief in progress has less substantial foundations. He who does his duty will, of course, work for progress; but it by no means follows that actual progress will ensue in proportion to the work done. The belief in the continuous progress of man on this earth is, as has clearly been demonstrated, a modern idea, and a very influential one.[17] But more than one voice has been raised questioning whether the concept is sound.

At any rate, the idea of progress that is to continue indefinitely on this planet is, to say the least, somewhat dubious from the point of view of geology and astron-

---

[16]*The Psychology of Religion*, p. 75.

[17]See A. C. Knudson, *Present Tendencies in Religious Thought* (New York: The Abingdon Press), pp. 23f., 51ff., 272ff.

omy; and it is considerably less important for religion than the idea of loyalty to obligation. Over against the prospect of continuous progress in this earth as the goal of humanity is the religious faith in immortality. This faith is not incompatible with zeal for progress; but in the light of this faith, the planet earth may well be regarded as a hotbed for immortal souls. There should be a certain amount of progress in the care of hotbeds, but the degree of progress in that respect is no measure of the real progress in the universe. Metaphysical progress, eternal development, is, I believe, a religious faith that follows from the nature of moral obligation; for the end commanded by duty will never be attained until every person has exhausted all of his possibilities of ideal-forming and ideal-realizing: that is to say, it will never be finally attained.

This statement forces to the front once again the problem of the perfectible universe implied by morality and the perfect God implied by religion. If by religion we mean the Christian religion, it is safe to say that this problem, of which so much has been made, is largely verbal. Christianity believes in a perfect God, but it has never believed that the universe is now perfect. Further, its conception of a perfect God has not meant that God was static, until God fell into the hands of the theologians. For early Christianity, God was a being in whose life something happens,—creation, atonement, joy over sinners that repent, the growth of the Kingdom. As Professor Swenson pointed out in discussion at a meeting of the American Philosophical Association some years ago, the God of Spinoza—timeless, changeless, all-inclusive—was not the God of Christianity, for Christianity essentially believes in the reality of change. Sinners, it holds, can be converted: "my Father worketh hitherto, and I work."

In harmony with the Christian view of man is the view revealed by moral psychology. Personality, we have been discovering, is capable of seemingly inexhaustible development. New experiences keep flooding in; new values are created, "out of three sounds, not a fourth sound, but a star." A static perfection is not perfect. The law of obligation always drives beyond what we are to more discoveries, higher values, new relations with others and with God.

The view of God that is implied by these facts is difficult to state satisfactorily; but at least we may admit that the actual facts of our world become much easier to interpret if instead of the utterly timeless God of the theologians we have a living God, for whom the evolution that is his favorite method is no mere form, but is a real experience. A God to be a God must know everything that can be known and be able to do everything that can be done; but a rational, responsible, personal God must be loyal to the conditions of rationality, responsibility, and personality, unless the cosmos is mere chaos. We have been too anxious in defense of abstract concepts of eternity, infinity, and perfection to be thoroughly alert to the interpretation of reality. A moral God, eternally active, eternally creative, eternally reasonable, is indeed a God who will forever and changelessly be loyal to the same fundamental principles of obligation and value; but he is also a God for whom progress is a real experience, and a God who is limited by the very conditions of his being.[18]

7. Conclusion of the Chapter

Religious values, we have shown, rest on a moral basis, just as religious beliefs must have a logical basis. True

[18]See Bishop F. J. McConnell, *Is God Limited?* (New York: The Abingdon Press, 1924.)

religion obeys the laws of reason and of obligation, as Rudolph Otto points out on the first page of *The Idea of the Holy*. The road to God lies through reason and obligation; but, as we shall see in later chapters, the values of religion make substantial additions to the values of logic and of moral obligation.

CHAPTER III

TRUTH AND VALUE IN RELIGION

1. Are Values Subject to Logical Investigation?

THE attentive reader will have noted that while Chapter I was chiefly concerned with the basis of belief, Chapter II dealt chiefly with the problem of value. Beliefs, of course, may be true or false. They are convictions about what is, and they may and must be tested by the standards of logical thinking. But values, many are inclined to assert, are purely subjective and so cannot be "true" or "false." They merely exist. This view regards values as cases of liking or disliking, approval or disapproval. A liking cannot be true or false, like a belief; you either like prunes or you do not like them. There is no "true" value attaching to prunes. Your liking or disliking is the sole answer to the question about their value.

Yet, if the definition given in Chapter I was correct, the study of values is more than a study of desires and aversions; it involves a reference to ideals, such as the ideal of coherence or of obligation, by which the desires and aversions are organized and criticized. Our study thus far has tended to confirm the assertion of ideal laws and structures which judge the desires of the natural man, and thus to establish the conclusion that values are subject to logical investigation.

2. Does the Value of Religion Demonstrate Its Truth?

The relation between truth and value would easily be

settled if every belief arising from a valued experience
were true. It is the tendency not only of a certain type
of pragmatism but also of the uncritical religious soul
to take the step from value to truth without hesitation.
Apologists for religion frequently avail themselves of
this tendency.

They often argue that the most satisfactory—perhaps
the only—demonstration of the truth of religious beliefs
lies in their value for life. But these same persons,
if they are fair, must admit that many mutually contradictory beliefs are valuable to those that hold them.
The nervous system may be soothed, the moral nature
inspired, the spiritual life quickened, by Christian Science, by Roman Catholicism, or by Buddhism. Now,
Christian Science, Roman Catholicism, and Buddhism
cannot all be true, unless truth is chaotic nonsense; yet
each of them appears to be more or less valuable to
many people. The *argumentum ad bonum* proves too
much; and we are driven to admit that valuable results
may follow from untrue beliefs.

If we explore further the relations between truth and
value, we have occasion to inquire whether the true is
always valuable. "In a sense" (as philosophers annoy-
ingly say) it is always valuable for a truth-loving mind
to know what is true. But "in another sense" it often
turns out that truth is not valuable. It may be dispirit-
ing, painful, crushing. To learn that one's earthly all
has been lost through unscrupulous agents, or that one's
trusted friend is false, or that one's fondest desires are
doomed to frustration, is to learn the truth. Such truth
does not add to what would commonly be regarded as the
value of life. Perhaps under the circumstances it is
valuable to know the worst. "Where everything is bad,"
wrote Bradley in his notebook, "it must be good to know
the worst; where all is rotten it is a man's work to

cry stinking fish.''[1] True enough; but if this were the only value we could look for in the truth about religion, it would be a wretched enough substitute for the hopes and promises of salvation. It would be a surrender of real religious value.

Assuming the truth of the essential principles of Christianity, the objective student of history will have to admit that those principles have not always borne worthy fruit in the lives of sincere Christians. Nietzsche was not wholly wrong when he said that the Christian virtues of love, pity, and humility produce a weak and slavish type of life; some Christians are weak and slavish. Nor is popular criticism wholly wrong when it asserts that religion breeds effeminacy; some Christians are effeminate. The friends of religion as well as its critics have denounced the evils that flow from certain factors in religion which, taken in themselves, are true and good. For example: the social expression of religion requires ritual; but ritual often leads to a deadly formalism that destroys the very spirit of religion. Religion is impossible without beliefs; yet loyalty to good and true beliefs may engender a type of excessive conservatism and traditionalism that easily becomes hostile both to tolerance and to growth. An exclusive and one-sided allegiance to religion often leads to a spirit that is jealous of culture and the arts, hostile to science, timorous and fearful lest these other values should undermine or replace religion. The reader of Andrew D. White's *The Warfare of Theology and Science* can scarcely suppress the reflection that religion has often behaved more like a spoiled and jealous child than like a man, confidently reliant on God and his infinite power. This catalogue of ills that sometimes arise from religion

---

[1]F. H. Bradley, *Appearance and Reality* (London: George Allen & Unwin, Ltd., 1908), preface.

is incomplete; but it suffices to suggest that true beliefs may have evil consequences.[2]

But have we been fair? Is it the truth from which these evil consequences have been derived, or have they resulted rather from a failure to apprehend the truth rightly, either in itself or in its relations to other truth? It may well be that this objection is sound; none the less there remains untouched this residual fact: that a true belief often has bad consequences if that belief is not rightly apprehended and rightly related to other truth. I may correctly believe that veracity is a virtue. But if I rely on that true belief as my justification for telling everyone I meet precisely what I think of him, my truth causes personal disaster and social havoc.

If we are to attain a just estimate of the relation between truth and value in religion, we must recognize a further qualification, namely, that religion should not be expected to produce all kinds of value. It has a work of its own: that of relating the total life of human individuals and societies to God by moral and mystical bonds. Religion claims sovereignty over the whole of life, but in no case does a man's religious spirit actually create the rest of his being. First the natural, then the spiritual; the task of the spiritual is to do the best that can be done in taming and developing the natural. Religion does indeed remake a man or a society; but it remakes *that* man, *that* society. It does not annihilate them in order to substitute entirely different beings. It lifts the real toward the ideal.

It is, therefore, an error to expect that religion will suddenly transform nature or the social order. The values and laws of religion do not abolish or supersede other values and laws, but they add a new potency to natural life and give it a new direction.

---

[2] See Chap. IV, § 3.

3. How May True Value Be Distinguished from Apparent Value?

Thus far we have seen that valuable results may in some instances follow from untrue beliefs and evil results from true beliefs; also that there are numerous types of value which it is not reasonable to expect religion to produce. It would appear evident that the relation between value and truth is not so empirically immediate as popular apologetics assumes. Nevertheless, there is an intimate relation between religious truth and value. Religion is, as Höffding says, essentially a belief in the conservation of values. The whole enterprise of religion is based on the faith that what is truly valuable is also real and eternal; and is not the clew right here—the *truly* valuable?

Must we not distinguish between the apparently valuable, just as we distinguish between appearance and reality in other realms of experience? This distinction does not imply that the apparent is unreal, but only that it does not adequately express the real. Anything, we may say, has apparent value if we enjoy or approve it, or find it precious or satisfying at the moment of experience. It is not so easy to define the conditions under which we assert the presence of real value. But is it not true that when we assert that any object is really valuable, we mean, first, that it not merely appears valuable at the moment but would appear so to an "impartial observer" who took all truth into account; and, secondly, that it conforms to those ideal imperatives which the mind recognizes as laws constitutive of true value? Such imperatives are the norms of logic, of ethics, of æsthetics, and of religion.

Religion is concerned with true value, not with apparent value. She will not, when she understands herself,

rest her case on the mere presence or absence of apparent
values. She will fix her eye on what James called "the
long run," and Spinoza "the aspect of eternity." She
will not boast that religion is proven to be true if the
Christian succeeds in business, nor will she curse God
and die if the Christian suffers from boils. She will
cherish the eternal values, in the faith that no temporal
expedients can redeem the time, since the eternal is
(as Royce held) the only true practical. If religion is
to be a power in the world, it will not be by conforming
to "worldly" standards, but by shedding the light and
power of the eternal on every worldly circumstance.
Not every successful "drive" nor every comforting belief
is a real value. Not every gracious religious experience
proves the truth of the doctrine that led to it. There
is the same need of "sterilizing one's intellectual instruments" (as Bowne put it) in dealing with our valuations as in dealing with what science calls fact. "Beloved, believe not every spirit, but prove the spirits,
whether they are of God; because many false prophets
are gone out into the world" (1 John 4. 1). The value
of an experience or belief is not a guarantee of its truth;
but the values, like the spirits, should be proved. This
does not imply that a mathematical demonstration is
necessary or possible; it does mean that religious faith
should be grounded in a coherent whole of truth, not in
the haphazard likes and dislikes of the moment.

4. A Difficulty in This View

This point of view might appear to mean that the
relation between truth and value is such that only the
man who is wise enough to grasp truth comprehensively
can experience true value. The ideal goal of complete
knowledge of truth and appreciation of value should
indeed never cease to attract and stir the human mind.

No one ought to be satisfied with knowing less than he can know. Yet this does not mean that the realm of value is closed to the humble and unlearned. If the source of all reality is a Supreme Person, God himself, and the universe is a society of persons, then God is immanent in all finite life. The Divine Person works in and with the human person. Whether the human being is wise or foolish, learned or ignorant, righteous or sinful, the divine purpose is always the same, namely, the redemption of the individual and of society. The supremely good God works with all his creatures to this end.

God, then, is working with every man. Religion arises when man becomes conscious of the will to cooperate with the God on whom he is dependent. In such a universe, what is the status of the unlearned and ignorant? Granted the minimum of intelligence essential to religion, and granted a good will toward God, a man may be quite innocent of science, philosophy, and theology, and yet may experience the sense of personal cooperation between God and himself, himself and God, which is the essence of religion. His theological beliefs (beyond the minimum) may be inadequate or even false; if his will is in harmony with the divine as he apprehends it, God is working good in him through, but in spite of, his false beliefs. We must take seriously the doctrine of divine immanence. But disastrous practical and theoretical error ensues when the man who thus experiences the immanent God uses his feeling of religious value to justify his false beliefs. Calamitous instances of this procedure are found by every teacher of philosophy and religion and by every religious worker.

The man who is seeking to think his religion through will endeavor to criticize and to understand as clearly as he may his faith that the truly real is valuable and the truly valuable is real. But he will not yield to the temptations of an easy-going, this-worldly pragmatism. He may incline to Royce's absolute pragmatism, but he will keep before his mind Bowne's warning that God does not pay every Saturday night—and when he does, very rarely in cash.

5. Transition to the Next Chapter

We are now ready to begin, in the following chapter, the more specific study of religious values. In the light of the conclusions of this chapter, we shall aim to avoid any hasty identification of truth with value; but we shall seek, rather, for the true values of religion.

Since value is, as is generally agreed, a conscious experience of persons, and has no meaning whatever apart from consciousness, we shall begin our study by devoting Chapter IV to "The Human Values of Religion."

CHAPTER IV

THE HUMAN VALUES OF RELIGION

1. THE PROBLEM OF THE CHAPTER

WE have now reached the point where we may begin the specific study of religious values. All value is the conscious experience of persons, and the study of religious values must begin with the empirical facts. These facts are to be found in the fields that are studied by history and psychology. At a later point (Chapter VII) an attempt will be made to describe the psychological factors that enter into the heart of religious experience, namely, worship. In this and the two succeeding chapters the aim will be to define and then to interpret philosophically the values of religion as they are revealed by the larger facts of its history. The special problem of this chapter, then, will be to inquire what contributions religion has made historically to the value of human life. For the purposes of this chapter we shall not ask whether these human values are "apparent" or "real," mere "value-claims" or "true" values.

We shall leave behind every apologetic motive together with every question or doubt; dogma, doctrine, and theology will be left defenseless and uncriticized. Not theory, but historical fact; not proof, but life itself, will concern us. If any belief be as true or as false as you please, in this chapter we are indifferent to that fact. Without probing nicely into questions of the logical cogency of anyone's creed, we shall concern ourselves only with the question about the value of religion in the life of man. What does religion do for human life?

Does it make life better or worse? Does it help or hinder the attainment of the other goods of life? In short, What are the human values of religion?

2. DEFINITIONS OF RELIGION AND VALUE FOR THE PURPOSES OF THIS CHAPTER

When we hear the word "religion," we naturally think of our own religion, that in which we have received our early training, or to which we have come by our more mature experience and reflection. But if we were to define everything that religion means to us, we might have difficulty in persuading others to recognize every factor in our conception as essential to religion; so that a merely individualistic definition will not do. We must seek one in which our religion is included, but which also finds room for what is truly religious in every religious experience or belief. The attempt to reach a valid general definition of religion is one that cannot be abandoned. Despite the obvious necessity of postponing a final definition to the end of one's investigation, a working definition is always needed at the outset, if we are to know where the field of our study is located.

The task of finding such a working definition is complicated by the fact that the word "religion" may mean either a mode of life or a scientific concept used to describe that life. Now, the religious mode of life might well exist, whether in primitive man or in our neighbors, without the use of a scientific concept of religion or even without the willingness to say, "I am religious." With reference to the scientific concept itself no agreement obtains. Pages 339 to 361 of Professor Leuba's *A Psychological Study of Religion* are filled with a collection of more than two score of definitions, to which might be added many more.

We may be able in this confusion to agree on at least

one essential trait of a good definition of religion. It must represent religion as something living and developing, and not as static and unchanging; it must, then, be a law of life. If you look for any traits which appear, in unchanged form, in the religion of the Bushmen of Australia, of Socrates, of Saint Paul, of Spinoza, and of ex-President Eliot, you will deserve to look in vain, because you will have forgotten that the essence of religion must be found in some law of life rather than in any dead uniformity. A sound definition will not be a Platonic idea, but an Aristotelian entelechy: not an abstract concept, but a functional principle.

Elsewhere the present writer has suggested that historical religion, whatever its differences, always expresses at least one common function or attitude. "Religion," his proposed historical definition runs, "is the total attitude of man toward what he considers to be superhuman and worthy of worship, or devotion, or propitiation, or at least of reverence."[1]

Attitudes toward our fellow human beings, then, are not (contrary to numerous current views) to be regarded as religious unless they spring from a deeper attitude toward a superhuman being of some sort; and attitudes toward the superhuman are not religious unless the superhuman power or powers be deemed worthy of worship, that is, be in some sense a source of value. In primitive thought this value is very crudely conceived as "mana"; to-day, a Rudolph Otto interprets it as "das Heilige" ("the Holy"). Yet a common function is performed by both of these beliefs, namely, a reverence for values and a faith in their conservation.

W. G. Everett, therefore, is near to the heart of the matter when he suggests that the experiences of religion

---

[1] *An Introduction to Philosophy,* p. 318. In our discussion we shall usually refer to "the superhuman" as God.

"have as their center of interest the cosmic fortune of values."[2] It is true that the Bushmen of Australia have very little interest in "the cosmic fortune of values." This element, then, must be regarded not as an actual factor always present, but as a limit which any life called religious is approaching or tends to approach.

The other element in our topic, that of value, still awaits definition. It has just reminded us of its existence by appearing in the expression "the cosmic fortune of values."

For the purpose of this chapter the term "value" is less in need of further definition than the term "religion." Whatever the psychologists or the metaphysicians may finally have to say about value, everyone will doubtless agree that by a value he means something that he prizes, something worthful, precious, desirable: something that meets our need, something that fulfills our ideal of what ought to be. Whatever for its own sake we thus prize is called an intrinsic value; whatever is only a means to the attainment of intrinsic value is instrumental.

It must be recognized that this distinction raises problems such as that as to whether there are many intrinsic values (as pluralism holds) or whether all reduce to one, such as the organic whole of personality, or of society, or of the universe. But, for our purposes, we may assume a practical and at least relative difference between the fact that we prize religion for its own sake and the fact that it ministers to the attainment of other values. We should note that the term used to denote the contrary of value is disvalue or evil. Whatever is unworthy, or hinders the attainment of what is worthful, is, either intrinsically or instrumentally, disvalue. If we are to deal fairly with the theme of the

[2]*Moral Values* (New York: Henry Holt and Company, 1918), p. 382.

"Human Values of Religion," it is necessary to consider also its possible disvalues. To this aspect of the subject we shall turn for a while.

3. The Human Disvalues of Religion

The critics of religion have always been alive to its defects, and none of its friends, however ardent, could maintain that the presence of religion in life is always wholly good both in itself and in its consequences. It might well be agreed that this would be true of a proper attitude toward the true religion. But in our present study we are interested in actual religious life as it appears in history, not in the ideal of propriety and truth. Let us proceed to enumerate some of the elements of disvalue that may be found to exist in historical religion.

During the previous generation Nietzsche made famous the charge that religion, or at least Christianity, was essentially slavish and hence bad. It is doubtless true that religion tends to accentuate the dependence of man on the superhuman, and the infinite superiority of the cosmic powers to the human individual. It is also true that Judaism, Buddhism, and Christianity, in particular, inculcate the virtues of love for all and pity for the weak and suffering. Nor can it be denied that these very virtues in excess sometimes breed a false humility, a substitution of tender emotion for strength of character, and more sympathy with inferiority than desire for excellence. The great products of the religious spirit, it is true, makes Nietzsche's charge of slavishness ridiculous, if it be intended to designate an essential trait of Christianity or of religion in general. But in the sense that a slavish spirit is a disvalue sometimes arising from religion the charge is not without foundation.

Again, it is said that religion breeds effeminacy, that it appeals to women and children, but that it lacks masculinity. Insofar as it attracts men, they are said to be effeminate types or to be rendered effeminate by religion. True it is that the rôle of feeling in many religious experiences characterizes those experiences as predominantly passive rather than active, and, insofar, as feminine rather than masculine (according to the traditional view of sex differences which is by no means proved). Nor can it be denied that in contemporary American religion the distinctively religious aspects of church life are often cultivated more devotedly by women than by men, and that men who move in a religious society where they are largely in the minority, more or less unconsciously resort to a kind of screen of effeminacy as an instinctive protective coloration. Even pastors occasionally succumb to this subtle influence. There is, then, a real evil here; although any impartial survey will make clear that effeminacy is no universal or necessary trait of great religious personalities. It is sentimental misrepresentation, and not historical fact, that has pictured Jesus in such a light. Every great religion makes a profound appeal to the powers of intellect and achievement, and so to what is regarded as the essentially masculine. The disvalue of effeminacy is a fact, but it is surely not inherent in religion, nor a necessary concomitant of it.

Many great religious reformers, like Buddha, the Hebrew prophets, and Jesus, have attacked another evil tendency which keeps recurring in religion: the tendency to formalism, to an overemphasis of external rites and forms, which, carried to an extreme, passes from noble and significant ritual, through excessive ceremonialism, into thoroughgoing externalism and idolatry, which substitutes the act for the spirit and the thing for the god. We shall not here seek to appraise the just claims of ritual in worship. We are only concerned to point out the manifest contradiction that excessive formalism introduces into religion. In purely formal acts, thought and feeling have vanished, the sense of relation to the superhuman is forgotten, and values are ignored. Here is a disvalue, springing from one aspect of religion itself, which tends to destroy real religion; to take it from the spirit and deliver it over to mere motor habit.

Another evil of religion, in some respects allied to formalism, yet different from it, is conservatism or traditionalism. Conservatism tends to perpetuate a tendency to formalism once established; it is not, however, necessarily formalistic, and seemingly tends to function to preserve religion rather than to bore from within as does formalism. Why, then, it may be asked, is conservatism not a value? Does it not preserve the sacred treasures of the past? Does it not cherish religion against destructive foes? Is it not humanity's guarantee against anarchy and barbarism in every field? In view of these challenges, he would be rash who would pronounce conservatism wholly evil. It belongs in the class of the mixed, to which Plato not infrequently made appeal. For along with the elements of worth which must be recognized there are also elements of a very different sort. If the spirit of conservatism attain full control, it will function to maintain the entire *status quo* unchanged. Beliefs, types of experience, and practices are to continue as they have been and shall be, world without end. The infinite has been sufficiently revealed, and the proper emotional and active attitudes toward the infinite completely categorized long ago. What is there for men to do but to continue in the enjoyment of the blessings bestowed upon them by the past?

Conservatism so magnifies the function of preservation of the best in the past as to lay its dead hand upon the present and deny it the right to live and grow. It becomes intolerance and wages a quasi-holy war against every tradition or form of life that differs, if only by a hair's breadth, from its own. The spirit thus engendered is far from that recommended by the ethical teachings of religion itself. Extreme conservatism, then, like formalism, amounts to a self-destruction of religion; but since it can point to so rich and many-sided a heritage from the past, the dangers of conservatism are much more subtle and slow-working than those of formalism.

If we find in religion all elements of human nature, we may regard the evils thus far mentioned as arising from the excess of some one element: slavishness and effeminacy, for example, from an excess of feeling, formalism from an excess of standardized action, and conservatism from all elements, it is true, but especially from an excessive respect for the intellectual achievements of the past. Since these forms of disvalue characterize religion itself as more or less evil where they prevail, we may regard them as intrinsic disvalues of religion. But we also find instrumental disvalues in religion; factors in it which operate to hamper or to destroy other values in life, such as the scientific, the philosophical, and even the values of moral progress. In calling attention to this fact we do not forget the services of religion to culture and to science. The point is, however, clearly to be made that despite those great services there has also been the other side of the shield; and even to-day very large numbers of the religious, both leaders and followers, are suspicious of or openly hostile to æsthetic and scientific activities or to any reform that means change in approved conventions.

4. Limits of the Human Value of Religion

It is not to be supposed that an exhaustive list of the ills that man owes to religion has been presented. The catalogue has been incomplete; it does not pretend to *a priori* necessity like the Kantian table of categories. It aims only to make clear that religion as it exists is not wholly valuable. As a further precaution, it should be noted that religion, even at its best, with these evils suppressed or eliminated, is not all of life, although it is related to all of life. As much injustice may be done to any cause by expecting too much of it as by belittling its true value. In order to avoid doing this injustice to religion it should be remarked that religion cannot (or should not) pretend to impart intelligence to the unintelligent, nor to solve economic problems, nor to guarantee human freedom from bodily ills. When one expects these results one may well depart from religion with a false estimate of what religion has actually accomplished in human history.

Religion, we have said, will not impart intelligence. A religious awakening may impart a new stimulus and zest to the intellectual life, or may vitalize dormant powers of mind. The great leaders of the Christian Church from Saint Paul to Saint Augustine, Luther, Calvin, Wesley, Cardinal Newman, Phillips Brooks, and Albert Schweitzer, have been mighty men of valor in the realm of thought. But all great religions have made their appeal also to the common man, however unintellectual and untrained he may be. Christianity, as Harnack is fond of pointing out, was something which the serving-maids of Ephesus could appropriate. There is indeed a certain minimum of intelligence below which religion is impossible; a mind must be able in some measure to grasp a few fundamental ideas about God and man and human conduct, that is, about "man's place in the cosmos," if religion is to take root in that mind at all. But observation of the individual differences among men indicates that there are wide variations in their native capacity. There is no reason to believe that religion creates new capacity, or supplies deficiencies in education. A religious experience, however satisfying, or a religious belief, however firmly and reverently held, does not of itself endow its bearer with any special insight into questions of scientific or historical fact. However true it be that the facts of religious history may never be appreciatively interpreted by a historian to whom religion is not real, it is also true that the religious must be supplemented by the scientific and historical spirit before it is competent to pronounce on questions of scientific and historical fact.

In the present age it is worth while to emphasize the fact that religion does not solve economic problems. Such problems are the burning ones of to-day; how much fiercer to-morrow's conflagration will be who knows? Has religion, then, no message for the social need? Most assuredly it has. It calls society to consider its Maker, to face the meaning of life, and to seek for true and permanent value, that which is eternal. The religious spirit, when true to itself, is the soul of every undertaking; nothing human will be foreign to it. It drives men on toward an ideal solution of every problem; is the pervading stimulus of the whole of life. It drives on, but it does not build the roads on which to travel. It creates the vision of a divine plan in life, but it does not furnish the tools and instruments for building a mansion here below in harmony with the divine idea. Religious idealism is, in this world, impractical and futile, unless it joins hands with scientific knowledge of conditions and means. Hence it is that the social and economic ideas of religious personalities are often fantastic and unreal. The soul of the new order must indeed come from religion, but the body must come from the sociologists and economists. Only in the union and appropriate functioning of soul and body will the organism live and grow. Religion needs science.

Finally, it was said that religion does not guarantee freedom from bodily ills. There will at once occur to the mind of the reader numerous objections to this statement. Has not religion often taught that a complete conquest of the body was possible? Is not its ministry often a ministry of the healing of disease? Have not history and modern instances abundantly proved its power over sickness and suffering? While all this is true, it must be admitted that for one person who has sought and found in religion healing for disease, there are many others, just as genuinely religious, who have continued to suffer; and in the end, all die, the just and unjust alike.

Whatever physical well-being religion may bring— and it is no doubt a greater force for bodily health than most men know—such a result is incidental, a by-product. It is a grateful shade cast by the tree on certain weary travelers in the hot season; it is not the very root and life of the tree. Religion is the total relation of the life to that Power which is called God; and the man who desires health as his prime aim, and God only on condition of his gaining health, does not comprehend the spirit of religion. The religious soul desires God unconditionally; this means the unconditional faith that what is supremely valuable will never be destroyed; it does not mean the unconditional guarantee of physical life and health.

In our attempt to understand the human values of religion we have thus far considered the evils, the disvalues, to which religion gives rise or may give rise, and have pointed out some of the things that religion may not justly be expected to do for men. Although doubtless the most precious possession of human life, it is not an Aladdin's lamp, nor, in itself, a panacea for all ills. With the recognition of the abuses and limitations of religion, we have advanced one stage in our journey toward the understanding of the human values of religion.

5. How Religion Meets the Ills of Life

The remainder of our journey will be concerned with the search for positive values. Since it is the human values of religion in which we are interested, we may well approach our problem from the standpoint of the nature of human life in general, then proceeding to inquire what religion is worth to it, rather than confining ourselves to the religious aspects of life. The former method is much more broad in its scope, and lends promise of a fairer final estimate of the place of religion in life as a whole. It cannot, of course, be completely carried out within the limits of a single chapter; but it may be applied to some extent.

If one surveys life with the thought of its value in mind, one is struck first of all by the ills from which life suffers, which seem to frustrate and even to destroy higher aims and purposes; and then by the needs of life, its fundamental longings and aspirations. We may fairly test the human value of religion by considering how it deals with life's ills and its needs.

Of the ills of life the most widespread and universally experienced is the fact of suffering. About this fact religion by its very nature is most profoundly concerned. If it is interested in the cosmic fortune of values, every item of experience that hinders or renders impossible the fullest attainment of value becomes a problem. Suffering not only appears to do this, but it is in itself a disvalue, an evil. The Judæan prophet who describes the fall of man in Genesis does so in order to account for the suffering of woman in childbirth and of man in the hard tasks of agriculture. The four noble truths of Buddhism are "the existence of sorrow, the cause of suffering, the cessation of sorrow, and the eight-fold path that leads to the cessation of sorrow." The author of the epistle ascribed to James defines pure religion as this, "to visit the fatherless and widows in their affliction and to keep oneself unspotted from the world."

Pain, suffering, sorrow, affliction—what does religion do with these tragic facts? It seeks to reduce suffering, yet recognizes that there seems to be an irreducible element of suffering in life, and it sees the problem of suffering in a world where God and value are asserted to be supreme. We are concerned with the value of the practical attitude which religion takes toward each of these aspects.

Most great religions to a greater or less degree are touched with pity for a suffering world, and seek to feed the hungry and relieve the distressed. The human value of all such palliative measures is so obvious that it needs no special discussion. But religion recognizes that its humanitarian function is not the last or deepest word regarding suffering. For, strive as we will, perfect medicine and sociology as we may, it appears that suffering can never entirely be removed from human life.

Where religion is brought face to face with suffering as an irreducible fact, it is not and cannot be dumb. To the problem it has given different answers. It has said that this suffering was a punishment for sin, or a means of discipline and grace, or mere illusion and error, or a burden which God will give strength to bear, or an obstacle which a steadfast will may overcome and disregard, or a reminder that this world is not all. Religious faith may speak in many tongues about suffering, but what it says, being translated, has always one and the same meaning. This is the meaning: suffering is not the brute mystery that it seems to be; it serves some purpose, even though we know not what; it will be overcome, even though we know not how. Religion, then, meets the suffering of the individual with faith, a faith that comes to concrete and practical expression in various forms, but always as an act of implicit trust. What other resource than this in the face of suffering is not presently exhausted and baffled? Does not religion, based on faith in the Eternal, give to life its only indestructible refuge in hours of agony, and rescue it from despair or suicide?

The last word of religion, then, is God. The mere hope or trust that the problem of suffering has a solution would not long sustain the spirit were it not for the confidence that the solution of the mystery is in the hands of the supreme Power in the universe. This confidence immeasurably strengthens and fortifies the soul. Whether the belief in God is true or not does not now concern us; we are now interested only in observing that it adds substance and force to the religious conquest of suffering.

Intimately connected with suffering is death, the mysterious, which releases man from suffering by destroying life itself. It is a solution of our first problem which only creates a greater. Suffering usually leaves it possible for the sufferer to appreciate some of the values of life; death makes all meaning and value impossible. Blank nothing is left; or so it seems. Death appears to be the negation of religion, for what can be "the cosmic fortune of values" when human persons, the most precious of all values, are snuffed out like a candle? But it is precisely the acuteness of this challenge that drives men to religion. Schopenhauer's classic essay "On Man's Need of Metaphysics" is based on the thesis that it is the fact of death which gives the strongest impulse to philosophical reflection and to religious belief.

Religion, in the presence of death, may assert itself by one of two attitudes: that is, either by the assertion that the fate of the right cause is assured, even though the individual perishes, or by the faith that human personality survives bodily death. So long as religion is religion it must refuse to accept the fact of death as final.

Many finely attuned spirits are inspired to high living by the first of the two attitudes mentioned. I and we may perish, but the truly good, for which our life was lived, shall never die. Bernard Bosanquet has said, "Wherever a man is so carried beyond himself, whether for any other being or for a cause or for a nation, that his personal fate seems to him as nothing in comparison of the happiness or the triumph of the other, there you have the universal basis and structure of religion."[3] These beautiful words express the idea which underlies the attitude that we are now considering. The individual may be so utterly devoted to his cause that he will gladly lay down his life in all literalness if but the cause live on.

For some the religious conquest of death is thus achieved. But for most this conception is profoundly unsatisfactory. To them it is not clear what the cause is that will continue to endure after the last human being has vanished and left no conscious trace behind. The denial of personal immortality appears to most

---

[3] *What Religion Is* (London: Macmillan & Co., 1920), p. 5.

religious believers equivalent to the denial of ultimate value in life. Faith in immortal life is an all but universal trait of religions. In the higher forms it is an expression of the belief that all personality must survive because it is the most valuable fact in the universe, on which the real existence of all other values depends.

Whichever of these two attitudes toward death religion may assume, it means to proclaim its conviction that there is something in man's life which death cannot slay. There are, it is true, wide differences of opinion today as to the actual effect on twentieth-century life of this belief in personal immortality. It may be admitted that with many the faith is but a weak and powerless shadow, and that with many others it is a morbid and unwholesome force, destroying perspective, blunting the sense of value, bewitching judgment, and obsessing the entire life. It may walk the streets of the New Jerusalem in fancy, rather than cleaning the streets of the earthly Jerusalem. But despite these serious evils, it is clear that the value of the religious attitude toward death far outweighs its disvalue. It gives each believing soul the faith that his life has before it an endless road of possibility and service; it adds to the dignity of the moral law the serious reflection that we and all whom we affect are forever going to keep meeting again in our own persons the consequences of all our acts; it gives hope when death speaks only of despair. In defying death religion at once comforts with the thought of hope and compels attention to the actual eternity of moral values in an immortal society. Such thoughts of eternity, when held by a restrained faith that is not too eager to fill in imaginative details, imparts sacredness and elevation to human life. Religion thus fortifies the self-respect of man and consecrates his social obligations.

When religion emerges from its most primitive forms

it confronts an ill of man's own making which becomes
one of its acutest problems. I refer to sin. A Baby-
lonian poem begins with the words,

> "I advanced in life, I attained to the allotted span;
> Wherever I turned, there was evil, evil.
> Oppression is increased, uprightness I see not.
> I cried unto God, but he showed not his face.
> I prayed to my goddess, but she raised not her head."

Moral evil must become a problem for religion,
because it is hostility to the values with the conservation
of which religion is concerned. Sin implies the volun-
tary cutting off of the individual from the whole; the
setting up of a realm of narrower special interest separated from the whole. The sinner thus is unwilling to
face all the facts, to confront the context and implications of his choice. He is complacent in the denial and
contradiction of his own noblest aspirations.

Religion meets this ill first of all by intensifying it,
by dwelling on its heinous character, for religion is never
willing to regard sin merely as the misfortune of a
divided self; it summons the sinner to a cosmic bar
and appeals to him to contemplate a divided universe
resulting from his sin; the unity of his own soul, the
social structure of life, and the harmony between man
and the universe have all been rent asunder. Religion
views sin as a cosmic tragedy. But religion, as soon as
it recognizes the existence of sin, offers some way of
escape. By sacrifice or penance or repentance, or by
some combination of these or other means, religion provides to the sinner some way of doing his part toward
healing the breach which his act has wrought, and
assures him that God has already done his part and that
the Almighty will then receive him once more. Thus
religion makes it possible to remold nearer to the heart's

desire the world which sin had shattered to bits. It restores to life as a whole the meaning which sin had destroyed or denied.

Another ill of life is ignorance, itself a prolific source of yet further ills. It is quite true that nothing can dispel ignorance save knowledge, and that any weakening or impairment of the mind's zeal in the search for knowledge would be a calamity to the race. As history shows, religion has sometimes operated as such a weakening force. But in the nature of religion it is difficult to discern any reason for this hostility. Religion, when performing its own function, does not seek to dispel ignorance by the folly of competing against science on its own ground. It does, however, have two characteristic ways of dealing with the fact of ignorance. On the one hand, it offers objects of faith which lie beyond demonstrable knowledge, but which present themselves, notwithstanding, as revelations of truth. It would be the height of presumption to pretend that by the way of scientific or philosophic speculation it is possible cogently to prove God, or immortality, or the cosmic supremacy of values. Since Kant such an enterprise has been foredoomed to failure. But religious life and experience give to the mind items of religious, as distinct from scientific, knowledge that do not dispel our scientific ignorance, but still give humanity the faith that our ignorance does not shut us off utterly from the truly real. "Religion," says Professor Hocking, "is the present attainment in a single experience of those objects which in the course of nature are reached only at the end of infinite progression."[4] Thus does religion sustain man in the infinite task of overcoming his own ignorance.

---

[4]*The Meaning of God in Human Experience* (Yale University Press, 1912), p. 31.

In another fashion too does religion cope with human ignorance. In the midst of his trials Job is upheld by the thought, "He knoweth the way that I take" (Job 23. 10). Indeed, one of the chief traits of the idea of God in all developed religions is that he is the one who knows all, who understands all, in whom is the key to every mystery, the solution to every riddle. The religious soul may be ignorant, perplexed, doubtful, but so long as it is still able to say, "He knows," it can still receive the comforts of religion. For Josiah Royce it was this reflection that constituted the essence of prayer. The underlying faith that there is meaning in all things, though we know not that meaning nor can surmise what it may be, is one of the most potent values which religion imparts to human life.

In considering the relation of religion to the ills of life we shall mention but one more instance, namely, limitation and weakness. In a sense this sums up all other ills; man's happiness, his physical existence, his good will, his knowledge, all are limited. He is puny, fragile, and powerless. For the Neoplatonists the original sin consisted precisely in this fact, that man willed himself to be finite, a separate individual, more or less dissevered from the one universe which should be an unbroken whole. Neoplatonism offers to the individual the possibility of reabsorption into the One by mystical ecstasy. Other religions, now in one fashion, now in another, assert that man by himself is indeed finite and impotent. But they agree that man need not continue "by himself," for very near and accessible to weak and finite man is the infinite power of the universe. Different religious standpoints interpret in different ways the nature of this nearness and accessibility: all agree that man is not left alone, since the resources of an infinite universe are friendly to him. Thus does religion meet this ill too, as it has confronted and conquered the other ills of life that we have considered.

6. How Religion Fulfills Human Needs

Nor is religion merely a good physician to cure the ills of life; she is also a counselor in health, showing man how to meet the deepest needs of his life.

Of the relation of religion to the physical and economic basis of life we have already spoken. It remains to consider the higher values. We shall limit the discussion to three of the most profound needs of the human spirit: the need for unity, for purpose, and for permanence.

Our natural life, at first, is a chaos; the infant's blooming, buzzing confusion, made famous by James, continues for most of us in our higher selves far beyond the limits of infancy. If our thoughts and impulses be compared to persons, our life is often a raging mob; it needs to be a disciplined army, or, better, a town meeting with a regularly elected chairman, observing parliamentary law. If they be compared to musical instruments, it is a shrieking discord; it should be a symphony.

Other interests than the religious, it is true, also aim at unity in human life, notably the philosophical. But the intellectual unification of human life at which philosophy aims is clearly an ideal goal, not an actual attainment. The religious synthesis is also, in a sense, an ideal; who is perfectly religious, who has exhausted the depth of communion with God? Nevertheless, there is a sense in which religion gives an actual unity to life that no other type of human experience can approximate. Religion is all-inclusive: it sets all our thoughts, feelings, and volitions in their relation to God, not merely as an ideal goal of life, but as a real and eternal Power, a Presence ever present. A unity in life may be orderly and systematic, like a complete card catalogue index in an office, or like the plans of a General Staff in wartime; or it may be powerful, like the will of a Napoleon; or it may be passionate, like devotion to the beauty of music or painting or a beloved person. Yet none of these offers any such complete unification of life as does religion, which seeks the harmony of the whole personality with the whole God. For this same reason religion, when she is true to herself, cannot ignore nor deny any of the other less inclusive interests of life. When she has done so she has lacked in comprehension of her own essential function.

Consider, further, how religion meets the need of life for purpose. Easy enough it is to have purposes; to have a unified purpose is not so simple. For what shall we live? America first? Certainly our country has the right to expect the unique allegiance of all its citizens; but as the supreme purpose of life "America first" has no advantage over *"Weltmacht oder Untergang."* Or shall the service of humanity utterly engross and satisfy us? Doubtless many who do not name the name of God are doing profoundly religious work in their service to humanity. But Bernard Bosanquet, in one of his recent writings, has remarked that when he hears one saying that he desires to serve, he is prompted to ask, "What on earth has he to offer to others?"[5] That is, humanity in the long run will not be best served unless its real needs are met. If religion is a real part of life, it is supreme; and only the purpose to serve God is in the long run inclusive enough adequately to sustain the server or to benefit the served.

Human life also needs something permanent, some-

---

[5]Bosanquet, *Some Suggestions in Ethics* (London: Macmillan & Co., 1919), p. 3.

thing on which it can depend. The evanescence of the worldly hope men set their hearts upon has ever been the theme of poet and philosopher. Men long for that which will not perish, and which will give meaning to the fleeting moments of our life. Our days are like a series of bubbles, shining and radiant, then bursting as soon as blown. It is religion that points man to the eternal in the world of change and gives him a solid anchorage. A life thus established has nothing to fear from change, for in the midst of time and circumstance it is at peace with the unchanging. To quote Bernard Bosanquet again, by faith "we rise into another world while remaining here."[6] "To be rooted and grounded in the faith" is an expression sometimes used to mean that one has a certain store of unchangeable dogmatic prejudices; it should mean that one has confidence in a God of unchangeable power and goodness.

7. Transition to the Next Chapter

In this chapter we have sought to describe the values which men have experienced in historical religion. We have also faced its disvalues and limitations, and have found that they are real enough, yet not essential to religion, while it is clear that they are far outweighed by the contribution which religion makes to assuaging the ills and satisfying the needs of human life.

It is, however, important to remember the standpoint which has controlled this entire discussion: we agreed, that is, to leave out of account the question whether religious beliefs are true or not. This question is still on our hands, and, now that we have seen more clearly how potent religion is, it has become all the more pressing. Religion has this potency, we have assumed, whether it be true or not; and our discussion has implied

---

[6] *What Religion Is*, p. 9.

that widely varying and mutually contradictory forms
of religion may serve the values of life. Buddhism and
Theosophy, Judaism and Christian Science and Mohammedanism, each may bring its faithful into a satisfying relation to the Infinite. But not all the beliefs of
all these faiths can be true, for they conflict. Does it
then (as many to-day appear to be saying) make no difference whether your religion is true or not, so long as
it helps you? Is the only important trait of a religion
the fact that it makes you happy, or well, or calm or
socially-minded? Is the real existence of God, or of the
future life, an unimportant and obscure question of a
pedantic theology, and do the human values of religion
remain untouched, whatever we may think about the
truth of our beliefs?

Professor Pratt's important book[7] on religious psychology suggests that the current attitude toward these questions is wrong. In discussing prayer, he points out that
"the subjective value of prayer is chiefly due to the
belief that prayer has values which are *not* subjective.
No, if the subjective value of prayer be all the value
it has, we wise psychologists of religion had best keep
the fact to ourselves, otherwise the game will soon be
up and we shall have no religion left to psychologize
about. We shall have killed the goose that laid our
golden egg." What is true of prayer would appear to
be equally true of our belief in God and the cosmic fortune of values; if we believe that our beliefs are not
true, it is futile to pretend that we believe at all. Religion would then become a silly game of psychological
self-deception. If we are to have any religion at all, it
must at least seem to us to be more than a comforting
fiction. If we are to retain the human values of religion,

---

[7]*The Religious Consciousness* (New York: The Macmillan Company, 1920). The passage in the text is quoted from p. 336.

it is only on condition that we see a reference in them to something that is not merely human and that is true no matter what we think. The subject of our next chapter will, therefore, be the more-than-human values of religion.

CHAPTER V

THE MORE-THAN-HUMAN VALUES OF RELIGION

1. The Problem of the Chapter

THE preceding chapter attempted to show that religion gives to the common life some of its choicest and loftiest values; but that a religion need not be "true" in order to be valuable. Myth, symbol, and doctrine have inspired and strengthened life; they may often enough be recognized as self-contradictory or impossible. What religion has not saints, heroes, martyrs, and miracles to its credit? It would, then, almost seem that if it is to function successfully, a religion does not need to be true; it needs only to be believed. But at the conclusion of the last chapter there persisted the thought that the religion to retain its power must be believed, and be believed to be true.

What belief can sustain life if it is known to be untrue? Can faith and unfaith be equal powers? Water-tight compartments are, indeed, psychologically possible, but within the religious compartment, at least, one must play fair with oneself; and if one is trying to make a unity of one's total life, how much the more must one's religion be examined in the clear light of every day, and all partitions broken down! What we have called apparent value will not suffice for religion. There must be true value if religion is to save its self-respect. The other interests of life—intellectual and moral—as well as the religious interest itself, agree in demanding that religious belief mean what it says or say nothing.

Now, if it does mean what it says, it asserts that the human values of religion are largely dependent on a source that is more than human, on which man's life feeds and from which it derives its value and glory. It speaks of a transcendent world; that is, of a realm which is not merely the human thoughts and feelings and volitions that man experiences when he is religious, but is superhuman, cosmic, and eternal. When the great religious personalities have named the name of God they have always meant a Being who, however intimately he affects their experience, is independently real.

Now, as soon as one begins to talk about the reality of God, or says anything about "superhuman beings" or "the cosmic fortune of values," factors which are essential to the very definition of religion, so soon one is launched on a sea of troubles. Rocks, reefs, tidal waves, and typhoons beset us behind and before. Religion is a blessing to life, it appears; but theology and metaphysics are abstract, difficult, never-ending, and sometimes in their outcome skeptical and destructive of religious belief; they seem to be a curse.

Here, then, is the problem of this chapter: Is it possible to retain the human values of religion without the confusion and difficulty attendant on what we call the more-than-human values, or are these more-than-human values worth so much that they must be retained if religion is to survive? Or, stating it differently, can we give a complete account of what religious values mean merely in terms of our psychological life, our actual and possible immediate experience, or does the meaning of our religious experience depend on our relation to a real order which is more and other than our human life? If we hold that religion is merely subjective, we have been bravely freed of the puzzles of metaphysics and the dogmas of theology. But have we thrown the child out with the bath? Would it be better for religion to keep her faith in objective and eternal values, and accept with composure her ancient task of negotiating peace with the intriguing diplomats of science and philosophy?

Stating the problem in terms of current thought, it would read: Is the objective reference of religious faith important and fundamental to religion, or is it a make-shift which biological and social forces have devised in order to protect the sensitive life of the merely human values? The aim of the present discussion is to call attention to the importance of this problem and to discuss certain of its aspects.

2. POSITIVISM AND RELIGIOUS VALUES

The problem which has thus been stated is one that occupies a very prominent place in recent discussion. Speaking broadly, we may say that there are two possible attitudes that are to be taken by those who acknowledge the value of religion: they are, the positivistic[1] and the metaphysical. The positivistic attitude holds that the meaning of religion relates wholly to immediate experiences of human beings, and to nothing else; the metaphysical attitude holds that religion is a relation of our experience to what is truly real and truly valuable, and that the full value of religious experience is grasped only where this relation is recognized. The positivistic view regards God and all objects of religious faith as wholly immanent in human life, and as having no other existence than as guiding principles of human life; the metaphysical view regards the religious objects and values as related to human life but

---

[1]The term "positivism" is used in this chapter to describe a general tendency in current thought. No one "school" is exclusively referred to.

as having also a cosmic, transcendent, and eternal existence. For positivism the God idea is only a symbol for certain facts of human experience; for religious metaphysics God is the real power controlling the universe and conserving its values.

The opposition between these two points of view has been made very clear in much recent discussion. The positivistic tradition has been carried on since Comte by many writers. The late sociologist, Durkheim, is perhaps the most prominent and prolific writer of this school. He regards religion as wholly a social phenomenon, a fact of group life. He would admit that religious ideas seem to be transcendent, and in a sense really are, for they point beyond the individual to the group. But they do not point beyond the group. God is a name for tribal or racial or world-wide human consciousness. Immortality symbolizes the value of the group; the individual may perish, the group remains. Worship, ritual, prayer, mysticism—all that religion means as an experience or an institution is but a parable of the authority of the group over the individual or of the devotion of the individual to the group.

This positivistic temper is very widespread and affects the religious views of many who in other respects differ widely from each other. A few instances will suffice to illustrate the point. Roy Wood Sellars has written of *The Next Step in Religion* which is to be the restricting of religion to "loyalty to the values of life" and the elimination of all supernaturalism, such as is involved in belief in God and personal immortality. G. Stanley Hall's book *Morale, the Supreme Standard of Life and Conduct* makes life entirely a matter of "superhygiene"; the goal of life is "the maximum of vitality, life abounding, getting and keeping in the very center of the current of creative evolution, and minimizing, destroying, or avoiding all checks, arrests, and inhibitions to it."[2]　In the chapter on "Morale and Religion" Hall pokes fun at the liberal Christianity which "clings tenaciously to the dogma of a personal objective God and individual immortality"; he urges "the substitution everywhere of immanence for transcendence," and seeks to account for all religious ideas in terms of subjective human needs.

Mr. Geiger, author of the monograph, *Some Religious Implications of Pragmatism* regards theology as "a science of social values," and expresses his meaning clearly in the following paragraph:

When theology acts on the positivistic cue furnished by the natural sciences; when it leaves off following the will-o'-the-wisp of "design" and "special creation" and "providence" and "attributes"; when it assumes once for all the reality of its subject matter as embodied in practical, concrete experience and concerns itself with constructing such a set of intellectual statements about this subject matter as will facilitate its control, we may expect the content of the divine to begin to assume an empirical and practical character approaching in definiteness and fruitfulness the great conceptions wrought out by the natural sciences.[3]

Religion, for such a view, is primarily an instrument of social control, not a relation to superhuman reality.

This American pragmatism is even more extreme than the view of Hans Vaihinger, who, in *Die Philosophie des Als-Ob*,[4] asserts that all our metaphysical ideas are fictions, but that we are bound to act *as if* they were true. In Vaihinger's view there is still the influence of the metaphysical; he would have us behave as if God were really transcendent, while the thoroughgoing posi-

---

[2]New York: D. Appleton & Company, 1920, p. 1.

[3]University of Chicago Press, 1919, p. 38.

[4]Tr. in the International Library of Psychology, Philosophy, and Scientific Method, published by Harcourt, Brace and Company, New York.

tivism of the age sees no value even in the belief in a
more-than-human. The closer we confine ourselves to
humanity and its needs, say those who hold to this idea,
the better off we are. We need social control: we do
not need cosmic support.

Many voices to-day thus join in the positivistic chorus,
which sings "Glory to man in the highest," and sees in
religion a purely human undertaking, humanly initiated
and humanly consummated. Thus religion avoids scho-
lastic theology, joins hands with empirical sciences, and
also (not the least of blessings) becomes quite democratic. For it overthrows God the king, and does not
dally long with the fancy of God as president. President and candidates are so numerous, and are so incal-
culable in their behavior that a presidential Deity might
be even more arbitrary and confusing than a regal one.
The truly democratic residuum is the apotheosis of society, the deification of the general will. This has come
to pass in many quarters, literary, philosophical, and
sociological, ever since Comte. Humanity is the only
Supreme Being worth mentioning.

3. METAPHYSICS AND RELIGIOUS VALUES

The positivistic current, however, is not the only vocal
philosophy of the present. The belief that religion is
essentially metaphysical, and its values more-than-
human, is held by many of its thoughtful interpreters.
A few illustrations will suffice to point out the tendency. Eucken, for example, is always contrasting the
merely human, the pettily human, with the Spiritual
Life which comes from without into human life and
ennobles it with the eternal values of truth and goodness and religion. Windelband finds the very essence
of religion in its reference to a reality which is beyond
experience, beyond this world of sense; so that he

regards Comte's religion of humanity as a mere caricature of religion. Hocking remarks,[5] "Religion would
vanish if the whole tale of its value were shifted to the
sphere of human affairs." G. P. Adams, in his *Idealism
and the Modern Age,* pleads for a Platonism which
makes the values of our human world depend on our
apprehension of superhuman values. Pratt's *Religious
Consciousness* (mentioned in the previous chapter)
points out that it is bad psychology to confine ourselves
to the merely pragmatic factors in the God-idea (as we
have been doing) because "it neglects altogether certain
real elements in the religious consciousness, whether
found in philosopher, priest, or humble worshiper—men
who through all the ages have truly meant by
'God' something more than the idea of God, something
genuinely 'transcendent' " (p. 209). Fitch's Lyman
Beecher Lectures on *Preaching and Paganism* argue, as
against naturalism and humanism, for supernatural and
superhuman sources of religious life. Rudolph Otto's
Idea of the Holy, the most important original contribution to philosophy of religion in recent years, is based
on the same thesis. Pringle-Pattison's *Idea of God,*
W. R. Sorley's *Moral Values and the Idea of God,*
A. C. Knudson's Mendenhall Lectures, *Present Tendencies in Religious Thought,* and R. A. Tsanoff's *The
Problem of Immortality* all hold to the objectivity of
values.

4. THE OBJECTIVE REFERENCE OF RELIGIOUS EXPERIENCE

It is evident that if the positivistic interpretation be
correct, we shall need a radical recasting both of our definition of religion and of the practical expression of
religious life. For it, religion is no relation to cosmic
powers, no concern about the fate of values in the uni-

---

[5]*The Meaning of God in Human Experience,* p. 9.

verse, but merely a human manipulation of certain psychological and sociological laws in the interests of greater social efficiency. To face the issues thus raised is imperative, is essential to the health of religion in the modern world.

If we examine the facts with this problem in mind, we are struck first of all by one outstanding and universal trait that speaks against positivism, namely, the fact that religious life is objective. By this I mean two things. First, religion reaches out for a power beyond the human person. In this it is like magic. Secondly, it is not centered in self, nor is it intentionally a mere desire for *my* pleasure or *my* success. In this it differs from magic, for magic always aims to subject the mysterious powers to human desires, whereas religion, especially in its higher forms, tends to regard the relation of the human to the divine, and the authority of the divine in human life, as in some sense an end in itself, saying to many of our desires, "Peace, be still." It does not merely use God; it worships him.

Hence, not all devotion is religion; not even all devotion to one's best self and highest aspirations. Or, rather, such devotion is religious only when those aspirations are regarded as points of contact with the eternal. To view the task of human life as the highest possible organization and realization of our instincts is not a religious standpoint unless those instincts are also viewed as, in some sense, an experience of God. The task which religion imposes on man under the actual conditions of life is that of finding in himself the clew to something more than himself. In this, religion is like every other experience of life. Just as sense impressions in us give us clews to the objective order of nature, so do religious experiences in us give us clews to the objective order of value in a reality deeper than nature.

Similarly, Sorley argues in his *Moral Values and the Idea of God* that our moral experiences give us clews to an objective and law-abiding value-order, which, in turn, can be real only in and for a personal God. In each case the ground for our belief in the existence of an objective order is the fact that there is experience given which is capable of being organized into a coherent system, in some sense common to all and accessible to all. The appeal is to reason.

It is not the present purpose to try to press the truth of such argumentation. Ours is now the humbler task of pointing out that religion, as James has said, holds to "The Reality of the Unseen." "It is," he says, "as if there were in the human consciousness *a sense of reality, a feeling of objective presence, a perception* of what we may call *'something there'* more deep and more general than any of the special and particular 'senses.' "[6] It has a vision of a more-than-human.

A positivistic critic would, however, find little satisfaction in this asserted objectivity of religion. It would appear to him to be an unsubstantial speculation, unverifiable, and hence untrue and worthless. At most he would see in this assertion a symbol for certain social needs and interests. We shall therefore now undertake to meet such a critic on his own ground, and inquire whether this more-than-human value in religion is intrinsically worthless, or whether it is the necessary source of all true value. If the positivist is wrong, man deeply needs the transcendent.

We shall first discuss religious objectivity as only one manifestation of the objective reference of all human experience; we shall then consider the relation of the more-than-human values to the human desire for cer-

---

[6] *The Varieties of Religious Experience* (New York: Longmans, Green & Co., 1905), p. 58.

tainty; we shall then seek to show in some detail how a few specific religious experiences attain objectivity and find satisfaction in more-than-human values; and, finally, we shall consider objections that positivists might urge against the metaphysical position.

5. OBJECTIVE REFERENCE OF ALL EXPERIENCE

Objective reference is one of the most universal traits of human experience. In every elementary philosophical discussion there emerges a semimythical figure known as a solipsist, who is supposed to hold the belief that he and his ideas—himself alone—are the whole world. But with such a figure no one else could communicate, nor could he express his views to anyone else. Perhaps because it would make books and lectures even more futile than they are now, every philosopher makes haste to point out that he repudiates solipsism. The most vicious attack that can be made on a philosophical opponent is to argue that his position is, in its logical consequences, solipsistic.

But it must be admitted that every logical refutation of solipsism reaches its goal by assuming at the very start that there are other persons and an objective order. Without this assumption we can make no sense out of our experience. We cannot deduce by any "linear inference," but we must assume, or presuppose, or perceive that there is something real other than ourselves. We see that our life belongs to a larger whole. Reason itself implies otherness, reality, objectivity; the notion of a world in which I am alone, without others, or in which we all are alone without something other-than-human is incompatible with the very meaning of reasonableness. In the words of W. E. Hocking, "Some passion for objectivity, for reality, for substance, quite prior to other passions, there is at the bottom of all idea; a passion not wholly of an unreligious nature, not wholly un-akin to the love of God."[7]

In thus emphasizing the general fact of objective reference as a support of metaphysics and a refutation of positivism, I am not overlooking the treatment of objectivity by positivists, nor am I asserting that the whole problem of religious values is solved by pronouncing the shibboleth "objective and metaphysical." On the contrary, it is clear that objectivity is the problem, not its solution.

Positivists and metaphysicians have alike been concerned to interpret objectivity. Positivists have dwelt on the truth that the only world we have is the experienced world; that all objectivity must be found in the interpretation of that world; that the unexperienceable belongs in the outer darkness with all *Dinge an sich*. The transcendent is unthinkable; and if the objectivity of religious values mean this, away with it! Thus current pragmatism and new realism, with all their differences, join in a common empiricism.

The metaphysicians, while willing to admit that our only business as thinkers is to make the world of experience intelligible, have frequently replied that there is an ineradicable dualism in the cognitive relation. The object to which perception or thought refers is never identical with my act of perceiving or thinking. Even in a world wholly made up of experience stuff there would be a transcendent reference in every cognitive act. When now I refer to my own past or future, I transcend my present psychical state by what Lovejoy calls intertemporal cognition. When I assert that another person is suffering the pangs of despised love, I mean that there is a fact in the universe that transcends my

---

[7]*The Meaning of God in Human Experience*, p. 123.

psychical state, and that can never be as it is in itself (namely, for the forlorn one) a fact in my experience.

The metaphysician (if he be an ontological personalist and a theist) might therefore say to the positivist: I grant that everything to which my thought refers is of the nature of experience (provided the term be allowed to mean all that personal consciousness includes), but at the same time I assert that my object is other than my experience. I assert that knowledge implies transcendence, and also that reason forces on us the assumption that my thought can successfully describe that to which it refers. But it does not merely refer to its own past or future or to other persons; it also refers to the world of nature and to God. If other persons have an existence (however psychical) that is not identical with my "experience of" them; and if nature is not my or our experience of it, may not the Supreme Object of religious valuation likewise have an existence that is other than "our" experiences, however noble, social, and morally useful our experiences may be?

If philosophy of religion is to advance, there must be a clear definition of such terms as experience, verifiability (what crimes have been committed in thy name!), objective reference, objectivity, and the like. The present writer desires to call attention to the recent cooperative volume of *Essays on Critical Realism,* edited by Professor Durant Drake. In this volume current epistemological doctrines, pragmatic and neo-realistic alike, are challenged, and the problems stated in a fashion that may turn out to be of significance for philosophy of religion, and in particular for the problem presented in the present chapter.[8]

Objective reference, we may conclude, is the essence

---

[8]See also E. S. Brightman, *An Introduction to Philosophy,* Chap. III.

of all knowledge; science, philosophy, and religion all point beyond themselves to a reality which they describe. Man always finds himself by finding something else. Pure subjectivity seems to be impossible. What we call subjectivity is the domination of life by false or partial standards of value and the selection of some aspects of the objective order to the exclusion of others which are more complete and more worthy. The most normal life is the life that is losing or at least forgetting itself in noble causes and is reaching out through these causes to worthy contacts with other persons and the cosmic order.

It appears that the center of gravity of the positivistic account of religion is subjective, even though social; for a social solipsism leaves humanity in the same incompletely rational state as an individualistic solipsism leaves the human unit. On the other hand, the center of gravity of the metaphysical account of religion lies always beyond the self. One who thinks objectively about religion will find in religious values an experience which points beyond the moment to other moments, beyond all moments of the self to other selves, beyond all society to nature, and through nature to God. Communion with the object to which our religious valuations refer will thus bring with it also an expansion of the personal consciousness and will satisfy its need for growth. The apparently abstract epistemological theory of objective reference thus turns out to lie at the very heart of the religious experience.

6. OBJECTIVITY AND CERTAINTY

Every human being desires certainty. Yet the very mention of this desire seems at first to be a mockery. Granted that we desire certainty, is not the only certainty this, that nothing is certain? Of what element in human life, save perhaps the empty forms of logical thinking, can we say that it is demonstrably final, beyond all need of revision, incapable of being assailed by time and second thought?   There are indeed many beliefs of which we are wholly convinced, to which we have committed our lives, of which we are, as we say, morally certain.   But when we consider the limitations of the human mind, the ever-changing stream of personal consciousness, the flood of new experiences constantly pouring in, how can we attribute absolute logical certainty to any of the beliefs we live by or build our civilization on?

Nevertheless, religious faith takes the form of the most assured certainty.   This certainty too often leads to the spirit of intolerant dogmatism which manifests itself as unpleasantly among persons who boast of their progressivism as among the static conservatives.   Religious certainty[9] does not mean that any religious dogmas are absolutely proved by logical reasoning.   It means, rather, that religion is a committing of the life to what is absolutely real, to a cause that cannot fail.

To no human belief or symbol can there attach the same sort of absoluteness that belongs to the being of God.   The legitimate certainty which religion affords to the believer is the consciousness that, though his creed may not perfectly apprehend the Universal Mystery, yet that more-than-human reality which his faith is seeking and in relation to which his religious life is lived is the actual Rock of Ages.   It is the real God rather than flawless formularies or absolute philosophies that men need as the firm foundation of their assurance in life. To think out the formularies and philosophies is an essential part of the human task, but faith in them is

---

[9]See F. J. McConnell's instructive book by that title (The Abingdon Press).

not religion.   Faith in dogma and faith in God are not equivalent attitudes.

7. How Religious Experience Finds Objectivity

Leaving these more general considerations, we now inquire how specific aspects of religious experience actually seek to attain these more-than-human values. First of all, the reader of the previous chapter will recall that the facts there discussed with reference to their human value were or involved belief in some superhuman being and that they were all concerned with the cosmic fortune of values.   From the analyses there made it would appear already to follow that the human values of religion depend on the values that are more-than-human; what we prize for our own life is attainable only through something divinely precious which comes from beyond our life.   In order to test and clarify this idea, let us examine a few concrete instances.

One of the most characteristic experiences of religion is communion with the Divine.   The sense of intimate personal relationship between the soul and God is both present in the most spiritual moments of the highest type of religion and even in one of its most primitive forms, namely, totemism.   When the totem animal is slain and eaten in primitive rites, divine power enters into human life.   When the psalmist says,

"Hear my prayer, O Jehovah,
    And let my cry come unto thee.
    Hide not thy face from me in the day of my distress:
    Incline thine ear unto me;
    In the day when I shall call answer me speedily,"

he is calling to God.   He seeks communion with One who is able to respond.   "My heart and my flesh cry out unto the living God."   The priestly writer tells how

Moses communed with God on Mount Sinai, but "Moses knew not that the skin of his face shone by reason of his speaking with him."

Can one fairly interpret such records positivistically? Is the social symbolism of the totem animal a perfect clew to the highest spiritual values? Can one regard the narrative of the mystical experience of Moses as no more than the self-exaltation of the priestly caste in ancient Israel? The narrative describes a man who was so absorbed in God that he paid no attention to his own symptoms; here is a genuine consciousness of God that is more than subjective and more than social.

Indeed, it is hard to see how one can read these or countless other authentic documents of the religious life without being convinced that Pratt is speaking of a central fact in religion when he says that it "holds out to the desperate man who has lost all hope in himself or in human help, the promise of supernatural and unfailing assistance."[10] Communion, however, means more than the hope of such assistance. It means companionship with an ever-present One who is the source of all companionship and gives sacred meaning to every human association. It means sometimes intellectual contemplation, sometimes mystical worship and adoration.[11] But in every case this companionship means that the human life is reaching out beyond itself to another life where all that is good has its home. Religious communion with the divine means, at its lowest valuation, that man longs to be better than he is; fully appreciated, it is seen to mean far more, to carry with it a sense of man's incapacity by himself and of his need of God.

In our day religious experience very commonly takes

---

[10]*The Religious Consciousness*, p. 158.
[11]See Chap. VII of this book.

a social form. Men find God by serving their neighbors. As we have seen, the positivists go so far as to
find God nowhere else than in human relations; humanity, or the love of humanity, in their opinion, is God.
But it is not entirely easy to see the practical superiority
that is claimed for the positivistic over the metaphysical
way of interpreting religious values. Religion in its
genuine historical forms always regards the social problem as in part metaphysical, and never regards the
social as ultimate. The dependence of all human beings
on God is metaphysical. It means that human society
is not the highest object of man's devotion.

On the other hand, this metaphysical belief reinter-
prets social experience. It makes the relations of human
beings to each other not less but more intimate. The
faith that the ideals of the moral and religious order
are more real and objective than the rocks and the light-
nings is the most cogent of all reasons for seeking to
make those ideals real in human life.

Religion has too often fallen short of manfully carry-
ing out the task her ideal imposes on her. She has been
guilty of ecstatic visions that have lulled the soul to
blissful dreams of heaven instead of heeding the message of her own social prophets. She has at times
fallen victim to an extreme other-worldliness which was
quite satisfied to let slip opportunities for making this
world what it ought to be.

But it is a tragic misunderstanding to suppose that
one must either choose religion and other-worldliness
along with it or else reject religion and substitute for
it a wholesome regard for the affairs of this world. The
prayer of religion has always been for a union of the
real and ideal, of this world and the other: "Thy will
be done as in heaven so on earth." The religious motive
for service thus contains every factor that enters into

the humanitarian and adds to it supernatural sanctions and the guidance of a supernatural goal. The cup of cold water "in my name" is different from a mere cup of cold water. If the meaning of "in my name" be appreciated, the act of generosity is more likely to happen again and gives a more permanent benefit to the recipient. It unites the two persons concerned by an invisible and holy tie. In a human relationship the spiritual life that is expressed is at bottom the most significant, indeed, the only significant thing about it. In the human a more-than-human meaning is found.

True it is that for the majority of human beings the economic and social conditions of life are such that this spiritually significant experience is almost entirely strangled. All the more reason that the spiritual values should be cherished as a sacred trust by all who can now appreciate them against the day for which all good men are working when every human being may participate in them. If this be not faithfully done, there is no small danger that we may give ourselves so utterly to the improving of environmental conditions that the emancipated worker in the industrial democracy of the future may in reality be no better off than the wage-laborer of the present. True wealth lies always in the values of conscious experience. Where there is no vision the people perish as certainly as when they must make bricks without straw. Or, if the reader insists on the American Revisers' version, "where there is no vision the people cast off restraint",—an ominously appropriate warning to civilization that in the end social order and social progress depend on loyalty to moral and religious values. An age mainly interested in the instruments of readjustment too easily forgets the spiritual end of life.

Let us take one more instance, namely, that of the

belief in immortality. This belief is a peculiarly rich field for the positivist. To him it means only that the social influence of the individual is endless (immortality of influence), or that the group (such as the nation) or the group-mind is thought of as never dying (immortality of the social mind), or that immortality is but a symbol for the permanence of the social values. Of these forms of positivistic interpretation the last is nearest to what religion has intended by its faith in immortal life. It has always been profoundly interested in man's influence on his fellows and the preservation of the highest forms of historic life. But when it was speaking of these things, after all, it has not identified them with immortality. As was indicated in Chapter IV, faith in immortality is religion's reply to the apparent destruction of all value by death, for religion cannot admit that what is truly worthful can perish.

Religion, then, assuredly means to say that true social values are permanent. In this positivism is right. But what does positivism mean by permanent? It can mean only the preservation of values by the successive generations of human society on this earth. This means, in the first place, that every human person is a means to the experience of value in other persons; every generation a means to the experience of value in later generations; that is, every human being is a means only, none is an end in himself. This view which seems so altruistic when first presented turns into a cynical denial of true value; it makes every generation a bonfire to warm the hands of the next, which in turn is fuel for its successor. The tragedy is that no one remains to be warmed without being destroyed; and add to this the probability that the whole bonfire itself will doubtless some day be extinguished. Such permanence of values is no true permanence. As astronomical time goes, it is only a fraction of a cosmic second. The positivist will probably reply that the average man's watch is in the bondage of relativity and that cosmic time does not enter into his appointments. But is not the saying of Koheleth truer to the depths of man's nature, that "he hath set eternity in his heart"?

Shall we not, then, conclude that all of the positivistic accounts of immortality fall short of doing justice to the true religious function of that idea? Religion needs an objective conservation of objective values; hence only actual personal immortality will satisfy it. If it be argued, as some have done, that values may be conserved in some mysterious manner without the eternal life of human persons, religion would indeed in her heart of hearts murmur, "Thy will be done." But it is exceedinly difficult to fathom what would be gained either for religion or for insight by forsaking a fairly intelligible view based on our actual experience that value is dependent on personality for an utterly blind faith which abandons contact with experience and hopes against reason and evidence. Faith in immortality is the former; dreams of impersonal conservation of value are the latter.

Everywhere, then, religion asserts itself to be more than a useful and comforting set of beliefs that will help the individual and society to function more efficiently. All creeds and faiths that have taken root in history point to some revelation of truth, of eternal, more-than-human values, by which the human is saved and glorified. Even early Buddhism, atheistic as it was, consisted in an utter devotion to objective values and truth. If the benefits of religion are to accrue to a human soul, that soul must have its face set toward Jerusalem and must view all things under the aspect of eternity. Our study thus far compels the conclusion that religion is essentially metaphysical and that Windelband **was** right in calling positivism a mere caricature of religion.

8. POSITIVISTIC OBJECTIONS TO THE METAPHYSICAL INTERPRETATION OF RELIGIOUS VALUES

In spite of the apparent cogency of our conclusions, it would not be fair to leave the matter thus. Hitherto we have been analyzing religion sympathetically with but little regard to critical objections. We shall now face the more important of the positivist's objections and consider whether they are fatal to religion's claim that her values are truly more-than-human.

It should be borne in mind that the assertion of the metaphysical position does not imply that positivism is wholly wrong. There remains the truth that even false religious beliefs have been of great value to believers, and that there is some error in almost every human credo. It is also true that all religious beliefs have a social function and that many positivists are veritable prophets of the higher social values. Furthermore, an examination of almost any positivistic argument will show that it is concerned with some genuine item of religious life.

The metaphysical interpretation at which we have arrived has resulted from a study of the facts of religious experience. The familiar positivistic attack on the objectivity of value also grows out of an analysis of experience. To say that anything is of value (so this argument runs) is to say that man desires it or is interested in it. To be of value thus means to be desired; and the value of anything consists in its relation to my consciousness of desire. To say that the kind act of another is of value to me is equivalent to saying that I like it or that it supplies some need of mine. The valuable is the satisfying. It may appear that our standards of value often criticize and oppose our desires instead of fulfilling them. This, however, is due to the fact that we seek for the maximum satisfaction of desire; and an end in life which satisfies any large group of our desires will necessarily conflict with some of our less inclusive and more random interests. Such, in bare outline, are some of the traits of a theory of value like that defined by Perry in his *Moral Economy*.[12]

It is clear that, if this theory be correct, all values are subjective in the sense of being dependent on consciousness. If this were all that subjectivity meant, every sound psychologist would have to hold to subjectivism. It surely is true that value is, in some sense, what satisfies consciousness and that value has no meaning or existence apart from consciousness. An entity of which no one is conscious is of no value except as an object of possible consciousness.

But we must go further. The problem assumes this form : Does the psychological truth of value-subjectivism in the sense defined compel the mind to accept metaphysical subjectivism? Because value is relative to consciousness, must we be positivists? It is startling to find a "panobjectivist" like Perry and some of his neo-realistic colleagues holding to a thoroughly subjectivistic theory of value, and joining hands with positivists.

In all discussion of the objectivity of value, Plato's figure hovers near. Plato, we remember, did not find any incompatibility between recognizing the presence of desire in the value-experience and believing in the transcendent and eternal Ideas. Indeed, even in the theory under discussion, it is obviously presupposed that there

---

[12]For a fuller criticism of this view see E. S. Brightman, "Neo-realistic Theories of Value," in E. C. Wilm, *Studies in Philosophy and Theology* (New York: The Abingdon Press, 1922), pp. 22–64.

is something in any valued object which is capable of satisfying the desire of the one who values it (if his value-judgment is a true one). We must test the positivist's theory by its adequacy to interpret experience. The chief actual experiences of intrinsic or immediate value with which every theory must deal are what we call truth, beauty, and goodness (leaving to one side religion, which is the point at issue). The critic of positivism will admit that all of these are objects of desire for the mind that is true to itself; but he will question whether the full meaning of the value of any of these objects is expressed when we call it "the desired" or "that which satisfies desire." Truth, for instance, is not merely the desired, but it is that which conforms to the ideal of complete logical coherence and thus furnishes insight into the nature of reality. Truth satisfies, or ought to satisfy, but truth is not likely to be found if satisfaction is our prime aim. It is to be found only by acknowledging and acting on the laws of truth itself. When we do this we find a spiritual and ideal value in truth.

Is it not, therefore, nearer to the facts of life to say that true satisfaction is what we experience as a by-product when we seek to obey the ideal laws of truth or beauty or goodness? If this be so, all our valuations imply some sort of objectivity of value, as truly as does religion. Positivism overlooks or inadequately explains this objective law, or imperative ideal, which assigns values a very different place in the scale than would desire taken as sole standard. The very loyalty to intellectual values by a man like Perry appears to illustrate and confirm this remark, as does the enthusiasm for social progress among positivistic pragmatists. Through ideals we discover reality.

Is there not, however, some hope of a synthesis

between the truth in the positivistic theory of value and the metaphysical claims of religion? Positivism is emphasizing one of the dearest truths of religion, namely, that all value is personal and that apart from personality there is no value. Yet, although positivism says, "No value apart from relation to consciousness," religion says, "No value in my domain which does not refer to other-than-human consciousness." Is this an irreconcilable difference? It is, if positivism insists on its exclusive right and religion on its; there then arises a hopeless conflict between immanence and transcendence. But if each is willing to think further, both may find in personal idealism a synthesis that overcomes the conflict.

All values, such idealism would say to positivism, are indeed satisfactions of some consciousness, but they are more than satisfactions; they are laws, standards, ideals, norms, which prescribe to consciousness how it ought to experience, what ought to satisfy it. The *sollen*, as Rickert would call it, is fundamental. To religion, idealism would say that it is true that all human values point to a more-than-human. But what is the more-than-human? For idealism it is a realm of consciousness, a person. Only for persons can ideals, obligations, values, be real. In One Supreme Person, God, is the objective reality of those values which truly satisfy human life. If the nature of this Person is love, as Christianity believes, the Divine Person is ever drawing human persons to himself and giving to them their highest satisfaction only in communion with his will and its standards. Such a view, recognizing the thoroughly personal status of values, appears to do fuller justice to the facts of religious experience than does positivism, while at the same time it agrees with the psychological insight in the positivistic position. So much, then, for the positivistic objection that value is always dependent on desire.

A different objection to the recognition of more-than-human values may be urged. It may be said that objective values are meaningless fictions of the speculative imagination. Who has ever formed a clear conception of what is meant by the Platonic Idea of justice, for instance, as an eternally existing somewhat? The universals are to be found not apart from, but in, the particulars, says Aristotle; and nominalists and pragmatists have protested against abstract general ideas in favor of the concrete and particular.

But to cite this sort of objection as valid against all belief in the objectivity of value is not fair. Our observations in the foregoing paragraph have sought to make clear that the religious interest in objective value is not an interest in some quaint thing like an existing universal or a mysterious value-entity. It is merely an interest in finding an origin for our religious experiences in a real order beyond ourselves. Faith in a personal God supplies this need in a fashion at once more intelligible and more adequate to express the religious relation to God than would belief in any impersonal objective values. The more-than-human, then, is not a less-than-personal.

But a great issue like that between the interpretations of religion as merely human and as more-than-human is not settled by considering one or two arguments. If the positivist is silenced in one quarter, he returns to do battle in another. He may grant that it is possible, as we have been holding, that there is a divine order of value with purposes and standards for finite life. But he will insist that it profits little to suppose the existence of such an order if we are incapable of knowing its nature and laws. History is indeed full of assertions of the possession of such knowledge by religious believers. But dogmas collide with one another, pretended revelations are mutually contradictory, conceptions of God and his will are in a perpetual flux.[13] The confusion and conflict are real facts. They make it impossible to deny that there is a very large element in all our religious conceptions which is merely human and subjective.

But is the positivist's case here conclusive against the objectivity of religious values? If so, it is equally conclusive in principle against all truth whatsoever. In what realm are there not differences of opinion, imperfect and more or less contradictory apprehensions of truth, development in our grasp of it? Further, in what realm is it not true that our only rescue from chaos is in ideals—ideals always partially and incompletely realized? Only an ideal of a cosmos, a world of law and order, enables us to distinguish our fancies and imaginations from the perceptions of real objects. Yet the ideal of a perfectly ordered world, in which all relations and causes are transparently clear, has not yet been attained by science. It remains precisely an ideal, by which we test our fragmentary knowledge, recognize unsolved problems, and gradually build up an increasingly clear grasp on the real world of nature.

Now, the function of ideals in religion may be similar to their function in science. The ideal of objective religious value is the principle by which the mind tests and seeks to organize its religious experience. Without the acknowledgment of this ideal religious values are

---

[13] The lack of definiteness in thought about God is illustrated by a book like C. A. Beckwith's *The Idea of God* (New York: The Macmillan Company, 1922), and even more vividly in the article by A. E. Haydon, called "The Quest for God," and published in *Jour. Rel.*, 3 (1923), pp. 590–597.

subjective chaos. If it be acknowledged, the facts of religious history and psychology are seen to have a common goal. They acquire a unity and direction otherwise lacking to them.

We may then fairly reply to the positivist that, as far as imperfection, contradiction, and change are concerned, knowledge of religious values is in the same sort of logical boat with our knowledge of nature. No human knowledge is perfect; but our imperfect knowledge presupposes and is judged by an ideal perfection. Religious knowledge, then, is subject to no uniquely fatal disability in this respect.

Another objection, in some respects more serious than the foregoing, may still be urged against the belief in the objectivity of values. However plausible the case for more-than-human values may be, the positivist insists that it must be merely plausible and fallacious, in view of the fact that values are so patently a creation of the human mind. If this statement appear too sweeping, who can deny that some values, at least, are products of creative imagination? This difficulty is well stated by Mr. C. C. J. Webb, himself a believer in objective values. He says "that the artist is indeed ready to use the conception [of Divine Personality] for his own purposes, if it be expressly recognized as a product of imagination and as free for him to manipulate as he will; but, if it be granted an independent and objective validity, he is apt to regard it as suggestive of a tyrannical Power, cruelly or fiendishly denying its rights to that impulse of self-expression which is his very life and holier to him than any repressive law can possibly be."[14] Thus, if

---

[14]C. C. J. Webb, *Divine Personality and Human Life* (London: Allen, 1920), p. 91. For the problem involved, consider again the subject matter of our Chapter II, "The Moral Basis of Religious Values," in which the principle of autonomy is emphasized.

art be a value, then value-experience is no mere reading off of an objective order. It is the creation of a realm of spiritual beauty in and by human life. This appears true of all forms of creative art, and not of art only, but also of other values, such as friendship and invention; indeed, it is hard to conceive of any values from which it would be entirely absent. Personality is creative.[15]

Now, it appears that the objectivity of values excludes human creativity and genuine novel values. Further, the belief in value-objectivity has, or seems to have, practical consequences that are very serious. The pragmatic meaning of belief in the objectivity of values is said to be a consecration of the *status quo*. This sort of consideration greatly impresses a man like John Dewey. He, and others like-minded, reason that the believer in religion as an expression of transcendent, eternal values not unnaturally prizes the attitudes toward God which function in his own experience. The next step is to assess his attitudes and beliefs and those of the group to which he belongs as the supremely worthful religion, than which no better can be conceived. Then he identifies these beliefs with the eternal will of God and the structure of the universe. Taken with bitter seriousness such a view inevitably results in stagnation and dogmatism. If one has the eternal truth, what more is there to learn? It is no wonder that this sort of thing calls forth the socialistic battle-cry, "Drive the gods from heaven and capitalism from the earth!"

Thus our metaphysical theory is charged with the two-fold defect of excluding creativity and of dooming life to stagnation. That some who hold to the objectivity of values suffer from this defect cannot be denied. Illiberal dogmatism too often accompanies religious life. But when this is said it by no means follows that the

---

[15]See Chapter IX, "Worship as Creativity."

main criticism is valid. If our suggested idealism be true, the objectivity of a value does not reside in the decrees of any Council or the dogmas of any church.

Decrees and dogmas are but attempts to describe the eternal truth; yet that truth must be more than any human account of it. To say that value is objective, then, means more and better truth than any human creed has expressed. It means that the Supreme Person imposes on himself ideals, standards, obligations, which ought to be the laws and satisfactions of every finite person. But these ideals are laws of personal consciousness, hence, laws of creative life. If the more-than-human values are of such sort, the very principle of free creativity, which seemed to contradict objective value, may be very near to the heart of what is most objective. Only an impersonal or a static conception of value would exclude such creativity from being part of the order of what is objectively worthful. Indeed, if the universe is morally constructed, freedom in some sense must be a genuine and precious fact, precious not merely because it is humanly desirable, but also because it points to an objective law of the very structure of the universe—the law that persons ought to create. If the real laws of being are imperatives challenging the world of finite persons to be a perpetual exploration of the infinite, based on faith in its reasonable goodness, it is clear that petrification of any cross-section of the temporal order can occur only when the real nature of values is misunderstood.

The attentive positivistic reader of Chapter IV will, however, be able to summon up a further objection. In that chapter attention was called to the noteworthy fact that the human value of religion apparently does not depend on the truth of the beliefs implied by the values. A belief, we there found, does not have to be true in order to be useful; it has only to be believed firmly enough. Signs and wonders are performed by all religions; all religions contain some elements which enhance the value of life. Therefore, concludes the positivist, all are subjective.

The fact to which he calls attention is perplexing, but it does not lead so obviously to the positivistic conclusion as the uncritical observer might suppose. Perhaps our metaphysical hypothesis can explain it more adequately than can positivism. Let us suppose that personalistic theism, which we take to be the most rational interpretation of religious values, is really as true as it seems to be. Then, there is a reasonable account of the value of erroneous beliefs. First of all, it is, to say the least, edifying to consider that the power of God can and does work helpfully with men who err in their judgments about him. There would be no hope of man's ever finding God if beliefs with an admixture of error could not lead the soul to God. But this edifying reflection does not carry us very far. More significant is the fact that in the most diverse religious beliefs there are forces which lead toward truth and reality, even though they may be imperfectly understood by the believer.

In other words, personalism is a functional or teleological philosophy of the history of religion. Such an interpretation sheds a flood of light on the unity of function underlying the diversity of beliefs. This function transcends all biological or social adjustments; it consists in the fact that the most contradictory religious beliefs may lead the race gradually nearer to God. Any belief may, to some degree, fulfill this function provided there is in it a spirit which the Eternal Spirit recognizes as aspiration toward true value. Hence, the ultimate source of power in religious belief is ontological, not merely psychological; or, rather, let us say, there can be no psychological or social fact without ontological roots.

Erroneous beliefs are therefore of human value, in the last analysis, not merely because they are intense convictions, but because they stand in living relation to the purpose of the personal God. The function of the religious educator, then, is not to destroy but to fulfill the religious beliefs which he finds in those whom he is educating. In all sincere human error there is a gleam of truth that may lead the life toward God. At any rate, the positivist cannot assert that his interpretation of this error is the only reasonable one.

The most ancient and the most pressing objection to the belief in more-than-human values remains to be considered, an objection which impresses every human being, namely, the fact of evil in life. It is all well enough, we may be told, to prate of a real world of eternal good as an explanation of our experiences of value. But experiences of value are not the whole of life. Not always do we enjoy the beatific vision. Not always are we triumphantly sustained by faith in a true and moral and beautiful order that elevates us to itself by superhuman power when we reach toward it. Such experiences are selected facts, occurring in their pure forms only occasionally in the best of lives and entirely absent from the consciousness of great masses of the race. Instead of eternal values, struggle for the bare necessities of life, trivial desires and petty interests occupy the mind; or, worse still, there are torturing agonies of flesh and spirit and sins of the evil will. Such are the elements of the true picture of the human race which, we are told, must supplant the Utopian dream of an eternal world of light and goodness.

If anything is objective, the positivist would urge,

in the light of the instruction of experience we might well infer that evil is. Demons, spirits of ill omen, Satans and devils—these are nearly as universal objects of religious belief as is God himself. Whether we confront life as a whole or its distinctly religious part, we seem to find reasons for regarding the bad as equally universal, real, and objective with the good.

It must first of all be repeated that religion has never undertaken to blink the fact of evil. If the reader recalls the previous chapter, he will remember that the human value of religion was found to consist largely in the manner in which religion solved the tragic problems set by suffering and sin and death. Religion, we said, far from minimizing the evil of sin (for example) at first intensifies and accentuates it by regarding it as no mere calamity within individual life or even a human society, but as a cosmic tragedy, a separation of the life from God. Reference to the fact of evil cannot take religion by surprise. From the very first, religion has offered some sort of solution of the problem of evil.

This is not the occasion to undertake a full examination of the problem of evil nor of those modern realisms and pragmatisms for which it is no problem. But a few general considerations may not be out of place. First of all, it seems clear that the good is basic and normative, while evil is a deviation from the good. The nature of good or value may be defined without any reference to evil, or without implying that anyone ever fails to attain the highest good. On the other hand, you cannot define what you mean by evil without reference to the good. Evil is always in-consistency, disharmony, absence or repudiation of or inattention to the good. Evil implies good as a necessarily prior concept; but good (contrary to many popular ideas) does not presuppose evil.

"The evil is null, is nought, is silence implying sound;
What was good shall be good, with evil so much good more;
   On the earth, the broken arcs; in the heaven, a perfect
   round."

One does not need to take every syllable of Browning
with painful literalness in order to discern in his words
a profound truth—the truth, namely, that there is not
the same reason for asserting the objectivity of evil as
of good.

   This, of course, does not carry us far toward a solution. Whatever has been said on the problem of evil
has always left questions, facts unexplained, seemingly
irreducible mysteries. Is this, I wonder, a fatal barrier against religious faith in the reality of values? It
does not seem to religion itself like such a barrier. Nor
does logic require that it be so regarded. What theory
about ultimate questions completely solves every problem? Certainly, the presence of a surd does not invali-
date the objectivity of a system. Evil is a problem not
wholly solved; so is the relation between mind and
body, so is freedom, so is error, so is the value of π, and
so, too, is the experience of value itself. But is it not
more reasonable to regard the existence of evil as an
unsolved problem in a universe in which the deepest
reality is good and wholly worthful than either to adopt
a dualism that regards good and evil as equal powers
or to join with the positivists in abandoning the objectivity of good and thus to evade the whole cosmic problem of evil?

   Any doctrine of the fall of man and the origin of
evil, whether from Plotinus or Saint Augustine or Mrs.
Eddy, leaves us still questioning why in a divinely
ordered universe such things must be or could be. But
any doctrine of the rise of man and of the origin of
value which denies the objectivity of value, as do so

many current philosophies, leaves a more serious problem than the existence of sin in a universe of free persons, namely, the problem of how a universe without mind or value could produce mind and value.

The last word of religion is faith and hope in God, but a more rational faith than that of the positivist who accepts his human values without trying to understand their more-than-human relations. Our personal idealism interprets the experiences of religion as well as man's other experiences. But the reader should not suppose that the view here presented is demonstrably certain. It is, however, only fair to say that our metaphysical personalism gives an account of the religious life that is truer to experience as a whole than is positivism and further is able to refute positivistic attacks.

9. THE CONCLUSION OF THE CHAPTER

We are now prepared to state briefly the net outcome of the present chapter. Religion, in its beliefs and attitudes, we have found, meets a wide range of the deepest needs of life. It offers men a source of inner satisfaction by its faith that the values which it experiences have an origin and meaning which is more-than-human. It is true, we have found, that the attempt is often made to deny this superhuman factor and to explain all the forms of religious life as merely subjective or social phenomena. But if we contrast this positivistic attitude with the metaphysical account of religion, we find that the former denies or abridges nearly everything that is really characteristic in religion. Religion is metaphysical; it is a relation to the supernatural. It is supernaturalism, not as belief in arbitrariness, lawlessness, and capricious interventions, but in the more sober sense which holds, negatively, that the realm of nature visible to the sense is not all that is real or that needs to be explained, and, positively, that the realm of values, especially of those values revealed in religious experience, is objectively and eternally real. Religious thought has in most cases although not in all tended to interpret this realm as the conscious experience and will of one Supreme Person, God. Any experience or belief which includes no reference to the more-than-human is improperly called religious, whatever use it may make of religious terminology or of emotions otherwise associated with religion. Such a judgment, at least, would follow from the results of this chapter.

CHAPTER VI

RELIGIOUS VALUES AND RECENT PHILOSOPHY

1. THE PROBLEM OF THE CHAPTER

RELIGION, we have found in the previous chapters, claims more-than-human value. That is, it is essentially metaphysical, not merely positivistic; its God is immanent in the world of our experience, it is true, but he transcends that experience and could not be the object of worship, as religion has experienced worship, unless he were more than human. Positivism, we have held, does not do justice by the religious experience.

The interpretation of religious ideals and values at which we have arrived is not unchallenged in the intellectual world. Our discussion of the positivistic tendency in modern thought has already made this clear. In the present chapter, we aim to consider in more detail competing interpretations of religious values offered in some of the major philosophical systems of the present time, in the light of the ideal of reasonableness outlined in Chapter I.

The status of religious values is a burning focus of discussion to-day. Religious experience in most of its forms, certainly in all of its Christian forms, whether in worship of God or service of man, is very certain that it is dealing with values that are objective and eternal. When the religious soul prays, it intends, as we have seen, to commune with a real God; it does not mean merely to heighten the efficiency of its life by the use of subjective psychological laws. When it gives a cup of cold water it does so "in my name"—that is, it links

137

its service and the person served with the real God. Religion, then, is essentially metaphysical; it is a relation
to a reality other-than-human.

But there is a very prevalent belief to-day to the
effect that the testimony of religious experience is fallacious; and that religion is simply a complex of beliefs
and emotions that have grown up around certain aspects
of group life. On this view, religion means devotion to
human society, loyalty to social ends, group consciousness. Religion, we are told, consists in keeping the
Golden Rule. God and immortality are but names for
the ideal worth of society. Many currents of thought
share in this belief. For example, positivistic philosophy before and since Comte, sociological study of religion of the Durkheim school, much pragmatism, Ethical
Culture Societies and the like, tendencies in literature
to the deification of man, the neo-realistic rejection of
a moral and spiritual ontology, the view that social
problems alone are vital and that we should devote all
our energies to reforming the industrial order instead
of losing our way in the mazes of a metaphysical God.
Indeed, the predominant current of thought outside of
distinctly Christian circles is in the direction of what
may be broadly designated positivism, that type of
philosophy historically derived from Comte, and holding
that human knowledge is confined to the realm of our
sense experience.

2. A RESTATEMENT OF THE GENERAL ISSUE: POSITIVISM vs. METAPHYSICS

Here then is the problem: Is the religion of to-morrow
to be metaphysical or positivistic? If metaphysical, it
will believe that righteousness and beauty and truth are
eternally real in the personal God whom it loves and
on whom its hopes are based. If positivistic, it will

find all its value and all its hope in what humanity can do for itself. Either mankind must regard its life and destiny as a cooperative undertaking of the human and the divine, in which each plays an essential part for the realization of eternal values; or else man's world must be viewed as merely human, the very concept of the divine being only a mirroring of what humanity longs for.

These alternatives are no mere airy, fine-spun cobwebs of speculation that the first real broom will flick away to the dust-heap. They reach (as we have been trying to show) into the deepest needs of the human soul, into the sources of life's hopes, and life's meaning; and the choice of one alternative or the other will probably do more to affect the total perspective of a person's outlook on life than any other one choice he can make. The problems involved are individual and social, affecting in the end economics, art, jurisprudence, education— indeed, every human activity. The influence on education is made especially clear in a sentence from Hoernlé's report on a Congress of Philosophy held at Oxford. Writing in *The New Republic* for December 15, 1920, he says, "The waning influence of religion, in its traditional forms, on the modern world and the consequent problem of moral education on a nonreligious basis provided the occasion for a fresh discussion of the relation of morals and religion." It is significant that the net outcome of this discussion was a reaffirmation of the need of a religious basis for morals.

In this chapter we shall raise the question as to the adequacy of various philosophies to interpret religious experience. This putting of the problem is based on the idea that the task of philosophy is to interpret life as a whole. Experience, we assume, is fundamental; theory is relative to experience. A theory must be judged in the light of its adequacy to account for experience; experience cannot be ignored in the interests of theory. More explicitly, philosophy must be judged (in part, at least) by its adequacy to account for religion and experience can never be fairly appraised by a philosophy that has not taken religion into account in constructing its world view. As Mr. S. Alexander, the English realist, has recently written, "A philosophy which left one portion of human experience suspended without attachment to the world of truth is gravely open to suspicion; and its failure to make the religious emotion speculatively intelligible betrays a speculative weakness."

The principle, accordingly, whereby we shall test the various systems in the present study is that which we have called (in Chapter I) coherence. It may also be called the principle of inclusiveness. A system that includes in its interpretation a broader range of religious life, a greater number of facts of religious experience, is, insofar forth, truer than one which includes and accounts for a narrower range of facts. This does not necessarily imply that the adequacy of a philosophy to include the facts of religion proves its equal adequacy as a philosophy of science. The present investigation is to confine itself to the religious problem. On this basis we shall treat in order the systems known as instrumentalism, neo-realism, absolute idealism (or speculative philosophy) and personalism.

3. INSTRUMENTALISM AND RELIGIOUS VALUES

By instrumentalism is meant John Dewey's type of pragmatism. Dewey is probably the most influential figure in American philosophy to-day, and is so recognized by his colleagues. He is a philosopher in the rigorous and technical sense and also in the broad and humane sense. For him philosophy is both science and art; theory and life are not separate in his thinking, as in so many systems. Nothing human is foreign to him: every burning issue of the age attracts his attention. No question is excluded from his philosophy on the ground that it falls within the field of economics, or politics or pedagogy. His influence on current thought and practice, especially in the educational field, is very great.

In February and March of the year 1920 Professor Dewey delivered a series of lectures at the Imperial University of Japan in Tokyo, which he later published under the title *Reconstruction in Philosophy* (New York: Henry Holt and Company, 1920). This statement of his position will serve as our chief source for this discussion, since it is his clearest and most concise formulation of it. Reference will also be made to his later writings, such as *Human Nature and Conduct* (New York: Henry Holt and Company, 1922) and *Experience and Nature* (Chicago: Open Court Publishing Co., 1925). The latter work is perhaps to be viewed as Dewey's *magnum opus,* since he wrote it as the first lecturer on the Paul Carus Foundation, to which position he was chosen by a committee of the Eastern and Western Divisions of the American Philosophical Association. Some reference will also be made to other instrumentalists, influenced by Dewey.

Dewey's plea for "Reconstruction in Philosophy" is based on a genetic account of philosophy. Philosophy, he tells us, arose out of a very definite social situation. There was a time when man's life was concerned either with securing food and shelter or with fancies, feelings, and desires. Then the desires that recurred in social experience became the basis of group tradition, out of which ways of life, poetry, cult, and doctrine, emerged.

Here, then, is the root of morals and religion. But man cannot always live in the world of his desires: he gradually acquires "matter-of-fact," positivistic knowledge. His desires are checked by the brute facts of experience. At first only his particular desires would be felt to be frustrated. But as matter-of-fact knowledge increased it would come into conflict with the whole spirit and temper of traditional and imaginative beliefs in morals and religion. This happened in the Sophistic movement in Greece; and the fact that Socrates approached the problem from the side of matter-of-fact method was the real cause of his being made to drink the hemlock. Plato, however, threw the weight of his influence on the side of traditional emotionalized belief; not by acceptance of raw tradition, indeed, but by developing "a method of rational investigation and proof which should place the essential elements of traditional belief upon an unshakable basis" and should, by purifying them, add to their power and authority. Metaphysics becomes a substitute for custom as the source and guarantor of the higher moral and social values. This, according to Dewey (whose ideas and language we have been following closely), was the origin of philosophy; and its origin has determined its meaning and value.

Philosophy, then, is sworn in advance to the mission of extracting the moral essence of tradition in a fashion congenial to the spirit of past beliefs. Philosophy has never been unbiased and free. She has always been apologetic. She has been a handmaid not of theology alone, but also of the traditional *mores*. In order to fulfill her apologetic mission, philosophy has made parade of the apparatus of reason and proof. But the emotional and social subject matter of the beliefs with which she was predestined to deal (and to agree) did not admit of logical demonstration. Hence, the history of philosophy has made a show of proof, of hairsplitting logic, of the externals of system, all resulting in futile abstractions.

Since philosophy was aiming to support a tradition that was pervasive and comprehensive in the group life, she had to create an interpretation of reality that should be absolute. Thus arose the distinction of empirical and noumenal, positivistic science being assigned to the former, a perishing and imperfect world, and ultimate standards to the latter, which alone is ultimately real. At bottom, when philosophy has talked about truth and reality, she has not meant truth and reality at all; she has meant merely to symbolize the permanence and absoluteness of the essential social purposes, aspirations, and traditions of the group to which the philosopher belongs.

Dewey's prophetic inspiration is therefore iconoclastic; he would do away with delusion, and make philosophy overtly espouse the function that has always been hers behind the veil of metaphysics. A reconstructed philosophy would abandon all search for metaphysical ultimates, and concentrate on the task of clarifying men's ideas as to the social and moral strifes of their own day.

The preceding paragraphs give the substance of Dewey's first chapter, ideas which the remainder of the book expands with historical and scientific learning and the zeal of a reformer, a new lawgiver, proclaiming, Thou shalt not make unto thee any metaphysics, but thou shalt love society with all thy mind and with all thy heart. As Sterling P. Lamprecht puts the same idea, "it is both bad logic and bad practice to tie up the validity of ideals with ontological speculations."[1]

---

[1] In a review of Leighton, *Religion and the Mind of To-day*, in *Jour. Phil.*, 32 (1925), p. 135.

It is evident that Dewey's little book, which may be regarded as one of the most significant pieces of philosophical writing in America in its decade, is thoroughgoing positivism, more pragmatic and less sentimental in its treatment of religion than Comte. Religious faith in an objective personal God and personal immortality is part and parcel of the metaphysical midnight which disappears when the sun of positivistic science rises. It does not need to be refuted in detail; it sinks with the ship that bears it. And with it sinks substantially all of the human value of religion; there being left, so to speak, nothing but the religion of human value. For, like Comte, Dewey leaves a function for the religious spirit; in the positivistic future it will furnish an imaginative background to scientific dealing with social problems. In that day, saith Dewey, "science and emotion will interpenetrate, practice and imagination will embrace" (p. 212); and this will be religion. This is Dewey's final word—the recognition of a need for religion in life, if religion be only imaginative emotion. In *Experience and Nature* he reasserts the ideal of intelligence as critical method as "the reasonable object of his deepest faith and loyalty," and hastens sensitively to defend himself against the charge that even this is "romantic idealization."[2]

In *Human Nature and Conduct*, however, it must be said, a very different level of thought about religion emerges. Here Dewey tells us that "the ideal means . . . a sense of these encompassing continuities with their infinite reach"; speaks of religion as "a sense of the whole" and as "marking the freedom and peace of the individual as a member of an infinite whole," "a consoling and supporting consciousness of the whole

---

[2] *Experience and Nature,* pp. 436-437.

to which it [every act] belongs and which in some sense belongs to it." Religion is, then, "joyful emancipation." "In its presence we put off mortality and live in the universal."[3] In these utterances Dewey is plainly asserting the more-than-human values of religion. He is striking a note irreconcilable with his own positivism. He seems to experience a temporary flaring-up of his own early idealism. At any rate, it can be paralleled in no other of his recent writings that I have seen, nor can it be fitted into the scheme of a positivistic instrumentalism; or if it can be, then positivism is metaphysics and instrumentalism is idealism. If we take him at his word in *Reconstruction in Philosophy,* he means to be positivistic, not metaphysical.

It would appear evident that this new-positivism has tried to apply the criterion of inclusiveness; that is, it has tried to give an account of all sides of experience. But has it done justice to all sides? An interpretation which would compel the abandonment of every essentially religious idea in all of the great religions, while leaving the methods, presuppositions, and results of science uncriticized invites inquiry and investigation. It appears unfair to great realms of experience. Has Dewey's positivism successfully destroyed traditional religion? Must we abandon God for democracy's sake? Before committing ourselves, we should examine Dewey's positions carefully. Several points merit attention.

First of all, it is to be noted that the point of Dewey's whole argumentation turns about the assumption that positive science is true and that moral and religious tradition is false. The former states matters of fact; the latter only formulates group habits and desires.

---

[3] *Human Nature and Conduct,* pp. 330–332.

But why is it certain that the scientific method and tradition are exclusively true, whereas the religious are false? Is it because the religious are based on desire? But is not scientific knowledge also a product of curiosity and desire? Until desire arises science is impossible; fragments of fact may be forced into our life in spite of ourselves, but science must be a welcome guest or she will never enter. Or is it because religion is a social tradition? How long, then, could science survive without social tradition? Is it because religious truths are not absolutely demonstrated? Unfortunate suggestion! What room has science for absolutes? The world of science is a world of working hypotheses. Is it because religion won't work? Assuredly it will not work if one refuses to make the initial working hypothesis about God and the human soul that religion makes: but why refuse?

Hypotheses, Dewey tells us, are of value only as they render men's minds more sensitive to life about them. Now, it has seemed to be the peculiar function of religious faith to perform precisely this service. We seem forced to say that Dewey scarcely gives religion a fair chance, but proves the supremacy and exclusive truth of scientific method by his initial assumption; the assumption, namely, that the whole real world with which we have to deal is the world of sense experience or "matter-of-fact," as he calls it. This assumption is precisely what religion challenges. Proof by assumption is not proof. In order to interpret life at all we must, it is true, make assumptions, devise hypotheses; but assumptions should not be made arbitrarily. They should grow out of experience, function in experience, and take the widest possible range of experience into account. The Dewey assumption fulfills these conditions only for one who begins and ends by knowing, in some mysterious and authoritative way, that religion is not at all what it has seemed to be, a real relation between man and God.

Has not Dewey achieved his banishment of metaphysics and metaphysical religion largely by the creation of an artificial dilemma? According to his view, our interpretations arise either from desire or from matter of fact. We have hinted grounds for dissatisfaction with this dilemma. On Dewey's view, religion is always and only a product of desire; science is always and only matter of fact. Religion always leads to error, science always to truth. This dilemma not only ignores the desires of which every science is the realization, but also the matters of fact, the real experiences, out of which every religion has grown.

The imperfect disjunction, either desire or matter of fact, appears to be in part, at least, the expression of a very prevalent tendency of thought to-day. For many minds there appear to be only two views on any given subject—the traditional view and the modern view. The traditional view is always false and evil; the modern true and good. Such a standpoint tends to blur the really important distinction, which is not that between utterly novel science and outworn beliefs, but that between the positivistic and the metaphysical interpretations of experience, each of which has its traditions, and each of which is constantly developing novel forms and points of view. The result of this is that a positivistically minded critic will often attack some antiquated religious belief and then, rendered confident by the victory over a man of straw, will infer that he has destroyed religion. Religion is more than tradition, just as science is more than tradition. He who does not recognize this fact is in danger of failure to face the real problems in any fair way.

Dewey, of course, could reply to all this that his real objection to tradition is not merely that it is traditional but that some tradition has its origin in desires and emotions rather than in matters of fact. Suppose we agree with Dewey, and consent to live in a world in which there is nothing but the objects of positivistic science, that is, the facts of sense experience. In such a world, we must then urge, there is no goal or purpose for human life, no reason for doing one thing rather than another. Moral obligation and conscience do not exist. Loyalties and faiths, even when "critical intelligence" is their object, are, as Dewey uneasily suspected someone would say, mere "romantic idealizations." If desire has no legitimate guiding function in life, there is nothing which would stimulate our initiative: not even the sanctions of pleasure and pain are an adequate ground for action in a world of which you can only say, bodies fall, fire burns, ice melts, and diamonds cut glass. Of the purely positivistic world, with desire eliminated, such propositions, and such only, are true.

But obviously, by the elimination of desire as a ground for religious belief, Dewey does not mean to go to any such extreme as this. A world of mere fact which man was passively contemplating would doubtless chill his blood. His characteristic attitude toward life is one of "creative intelligence," of "reconstruction"—not in philosophy alone but in every field. The business of thought is, on his view, to discover humanity's ills and learn how to remedy them. "Growth itself is the only moral end";[4] we might say that his motto is, Move on. He earnestly desires progress.

Thus it appears that desire, crushed to earth, will rise again. When desire was the root of traditional morals

---

[4] *Reconstruction in Philosophy*, p. 177.

and religion, it was a root of bitterness and of all evil, poisoning the springs of philosophy and necessitating radical reconstruction. But now it reappears, and in far more tyrranical rôle, for now one desire, and one only, is the supreme good and the end of life, namely, the desire for change. For the scientific spirit, as Professor Dewey interprets it, "the world, or any part of it as it presents itself at a given time, is accepted or acquiesced in only as *material* for change."[5] Growth, we have seen, is the only moral end; that is, change. Science and philosophy alike are subservient to this one dominating desire, which must not have "perfection as a final goal," or any "fixed ends to be attained." If we are fairly representing Dewey's thought, his principle is that intelligence ought to be completely in the service of desire, desire for change.

A curious situation indeed: traditional religion is to be rejected because it was based on desire, in order to substitute for it a philosophy based on desire. In the end, therefore, it would appear that Dewey's hostility to religion is really not due to the genesis of religion in the life of desire, but, rather, to its metaphysical character, that is, to the fact that it ventures to have faith in an eternal reality which lies beyond the realm that our desires can manipulate at will. The question at issue is this: Can human life find something real and eternal to worship and to contemplate, or are its needs fully met by a program of action? This putting of the question would appear to meet instrumentalism on its own ground squarely. Dewey's whole view is based on the principle that men need hypotheses which will render their minds more sensitive to life about them. Now, if there is a spiritual life about us, the life of God, we

[5] *Ib.*, p. 114.

must assume attitudes toward that life by appropriate hypotheses, by acts of faith.

Dewey and his school fear a type of philosophy and of religion that is unrelated to the world of actual experience; but in their fear of the extremes of metaphysical extravagance they seem to have forgotten that all real thought requires hypothesis and interpretation which carry us beyond the experience of the moment, and even beyond any possible experience of our own, if we are to make sense of that experience. The interior of the earth, past history, the future, the feelings of others, all lie in a realm that can never be my present experience.

In ideal values, too, there is a meaning which carries us beyond the actual into the imperative. Obligation, we have seen in Chapter II, is a fact that is more than a fact. But when Dewey talks about ideals one finds that he assumes their imperative character, yet without making any provision for it in his thinking, for he wants philosophers to make clear to a troubled humanity "that ideals are continuous with natural events, that they but represent their possibilities."[6] All of this is true so far as it goes; yet it falls short of furnishing any clear criterion for selecting among these possibilities. The lack of a criterion that goes beyond the mere assumption that biological and social life ought to be preserved and developed is what makes pragmatism, in spite of itself, impractical. Its refusal to acknowledge the further implications of the "ought" which it loyally obeys gives it

---

[6]Quoted by M. C. Otto, *Things and Ideals*. (New York, Henry Holt and Company, 1924), p. xii. Otto's book is a vividly written exposition of the practical and positivistic point of view. The essence of the book is found on p. 129, where the writer introduces a quotation by the words, "John Dewey is right." The reader who desires to pursue the literature of modern positivism further will find another good presentation of that point of view in E. C. Hayes, *Sociology and Ethics*. (New York: D. Appleton & Company, 1921).

an intellectually reactionary character; for, like all positivism, it can survive in its present form only by refusing to think about its own presuppositions.

It is a very familiar argument that positivism is self-refuting if it both reduces knowable reality to sense data and also speaks of society, for society includes many persons, and the other persons are not my sense data: they are metaphysical so far as my consciousness is concerned. No sense experience can reveal to me the inside of another's mind. Behind his words, his smile, his acts, there are his thought, and feeling, and will. It will be a long time before the pan-behaviorists convince us that consciousness is bodily behavior. No, society is a realm of persons, whose conscious life is an entirely different fact from their bodies. If so, the very concept Society is a metaphysical one. But it is in assertions about personality and society that the essence of Dewey's thought consists. "When the consciousness of science is fully impregnated with the consciousness of human value," he tells us,[7] then the dualism of material and ideal will be broken down. That is, a metaphysical proposition about human personalities is the key even to the meaning of science. But if so much metaphysics be good, why not more? If we need to acknowledge our fellows and their value, does not religious experience make it justifiable to go further and to acknowledge the being of an eternal spiritual person to interpret the profoundest experiences of life?

To summarize: instrumentalism, according to its most recent expression, would appear to deny the truth and value of almost everything that has been precious to the characteristically religious experience of the human race, and to frustrate the spiritual desires of religion for

[7] *Op. cit.*, p. 173.

the eternal in the interest of the desire for change. This bald statement says nothing of the ethical and social values of instrumentalism, but is concerned only to point out its unsatisfactoriness as a philosophy of religion. Dewey's positivism has, however, contributed one idea that is of very great importance to religion, namely, the idea of the value of human consciousness, individual and social. It is probably this factor in his philosophy that makes it seem to many the gospel of a new age.

4. THE NEW REALISM AND RELIGIOUS VALUES

Alongside of instrumentalism as a vigorous recent movement in philosophy should be named the new realism which has shown great productivity and energy both in England and America. The neo-realistic movement is no one clearly unified body of doctrine, but it is marked by several outstanding traits. Its method is to analyze the given into terms and relations which cannot be analyzed further; that is, it proceeds like chemistry or mathematics.[8] It finds the aim of philosophy to be that of understanding experience; and it holds that one always understands by analyzing. The new realism thus differs sharply from instrumentalism. The latter desires action, life, motion; the former, knowledge, understanding, analysis. For instrumentalism the center of interest lies in the human person, his needs and desires; for the new realism the presence of the human person in a situation is an incident from which thought can and must abstract: nothing is added to an analysis by the remark that it is the work of a man.

The new realism has directed its polemic, however, not chiefly against pragmatism, but, rather, against idealism. Idealism has been characterized by interest

---

[8] See Chapter I of this book and E. S. Brightman, *An Introduction to Philosophy*, pp. 22–29 and 231–236.

in consciousness, mind, and organic wholes, such as personality and values. Neo-realistic method, carried out to the bitter end by its American exponents, analyzes these wholes into elements and regards them as relations among terms which in themselves are neither personal nor valuable. Mind and value[9] are like the rainbow—lovely and insubstantial, an evanescent radiance which science analyzes as consisting of certain relations among entities which in themselves bear no resemblance to rainbows. So the realist analyzes experience into its elements, which the American new realists call "neutral entities." This term, coined by Dr. H. M. Sheffer, indicates that the ultimate terms and relations at which analysis arrives are in themselves neither mental nor physical. Now, these terms and relations turn out to be of many irreducible kinds. This philosophy is therefore pluralistic. Such in broad outline are some of the phases of a type of thought that has developed very rapidly in the past ten or fifteen years.

How does such a philosophy deal with religious values? Instrumentalism, as we found, sought to undermine, or at least to explain, religion by tracing it to its origin of religion in desire, as distinct from matter-of-fact knowledge. Neo-realism also finds the origin of religion in desire, for religion is an outgrowth of the values of life, and the valued is the desired. Dewey, as we saw, used this fact to discredit religion; but some of the neo-realists are distinctly more friendly to religion than is instrumentalism. Since realistic method calls for a complete analysis of experience, no such major outstanding fact as religion could well be overlooked.

Let us cite a few instances of the school's interest in

[9]See E. S. Brightman, "Neo-Realistic Theories of Value," in E. C. Wilm, *Studies in Philosophy and Theology.* (New York: The Abingdon Press, 1922), pp. 22—92.

religion. Professor Perry's *Present Philosophical Tendencies*[10] reveals the author's interest in the second chapter, on "Scientific and Religious Motives in Philosophy"; and the concluding chapter, "A Realistic Philosophy of Life," sketches the author's philosophy of religion. His later book, *The Present Conflict of Ideals*,[11] deals with the moral problems of national ideals from a philosophical standpoint; and this involves frequent discussions of religious questions. The book closes with an appeal for religion, as James conceived it. Professor Spaulding's *The New Rationalism*[12] is, as he tells us in the Preface, "a Neo-realism of ideals that are discovered by reason, as well as of those reals that are disclosed to the senses and that form what we call nature." The world, he believes, needs a philosophy "that holds to the actuality of ideals . . . rather than one that justifies our living only in accordance with our biological nature." In harmony with this aim, the closing chapter of the book is on "Realism's Teleology and Theology." Mr. Alexander, the English realist, published two volumes of Gifford Lectures, entitled *Space, Time and Deity*,[13] which has aroused international attention as a work of the first magnitude. It is evident, then, that religion is an object of genuine concern to the neo-realists.

We shall now consider briefly how the philosophers just mentioned work out their philosophy of religion. Particular stress will be laid on Perry. In stating the views in question, the writer will necessarily condense, freely paraphrase, and interpret; if he fails to do full justice to the meaning of the authors discussed, he takes

[10]New York: Longmans, Green & Co., 1912 and later editions.
[11]New York: Longmans, Green & Co., 1918.
[12]New York: Henry Holt and Company, 1918.
[13]London: Macmillan & Co., 1920.

refuge in the plea of Perry, who writes, "I have assumed it to be more important to discover whether certain current views were true or false than to discuss with painstaking nicety the question of their attribution" (PPT, p. vii).[14]

For Perry, religion is an attitude toward the fortune of values in the career of the human race. He holds that the characteristic religious attitude combines faith and action. Faith is essentially the hope that values may prevail (PPT, p. 340), until they shall "enter into possession of the world at large, as they have already come to possess it in part" (ib., p. 343); the goal for action is thus set. Value, in his theory, relates to interest or desire; nothing is inherently valuable, but anything may acquire value in proportion as it fulfills interest; the more interests it fulfills, the more valuable it becomes. This is clearly a quantitative, subjective, and humanistic theory of value. Apart from man and man's interests, there is nothing good or valuable in the whole universe; the eternal order of terms and relations which is the ultimate being of everything is as valueless as a chest of bank notes in the depths of the Pacific. Only in so far as terms and relations and banknotes fulfill human interests are they of value. This view permits Perry to assert that "realism explicitly repudiates every spiritual or moral ontology" (PPT, p. 344); the universe is not already or eternally a moral order, and there is no spiritual reality at its heart. If the moral and the spiritual were already the true reality of things, what more (our author asks) would there be to do in such a world? "He who judges the world to be what he aspires to have it become is the last man in the world to act effectively for the world's betterment" (PCI, p. 370).

---

[14] In quoting from Perry, we shall refer to *Present Philosophical Tendencies* as PPT, and *The Present Conflict of Ideals* as PCI.

But religion, on Perry's view, is far from the belief
in the existence of a perfectly good reality; it is action
for the world's betterment, which presupposes that reality is not now perfect. "Religious belief is a confidence
that what is indifferent will acquire value, and that
what is bad will be made good through the operation of
moral agents on a preexisting environment" (PPT, p.
334). The faith in progress, in the forward movement
of life, in man's ultimate complete possession of his
world—this is religion. Perry finds support for such
religious faith in observed facts: things do happen on
account of the good which they will serve, men are in
some sense free to choose the good, "nature has yielded
life," "the forms of life which are most cherished—intellectual activity, the exercise of the sensibilities, and
friendly social intercourse—are the very forms of life
which are capable of maintaining and producing themselves" (PPT, p. 345). In short, evolution and human
history are, on the whole, a progress, in the indefinite
future continuance of which we are free to believe.

What shall we say of such a philosophy of religion?
One is struck, first of all, by its similarity in result with
instrumentalism, in spite of their differences in starting
point and in relative interest in the problem of
religion. The substantial identity of these two schools
in their practical religious outcome is significant, and
is a witness, if not to the truth of the position held, at
least to its influence in current thought. This agreement
is the more striking in view of the radical differences in
general outlook between the two schools. Instrumentalism is frankly positivistic and practical in its standpoint. Neo-realism appears to be metaphysical and
intellectualistic; yet its religion is as positivistic and
practical as Dewey could desire.

But even the reduced and impoverished religion which

remains when Perry reaches his conclusion has the air of being strangely out of place in his realistic world. The philosophy which began with strictest analytical method ends by allowing a place for faith and hope. That which began by swearing allegiance to science ends with an outlook for the future that goes far beyond what science warrants. Science expects that the time will come when all life on this planet will cease and when no conscious being will survive from the entire human race to carry on the torch of progress or to remember the history of civilization. Such expectations of science Perry regards as unproved. "To pretend to speak for the universe in terms of the narrow and abstract predictions of astronomy is to betray a bias of mind that is little less provincial and unimaginative than the most naïve anthropomorphism. What that residual cosmos which looms beyond the border of knowledge shall in time bring forth, no man that has yet been born can say. That it may overbalance and remake the little world of things known, and falsify every present philosophy, no man can doubt. It is as consistent with rigorous thought to greet it as a promise of salvation as to dread it as a portent of doom" (PPT, p. 347).

Perry thus explicitly admits that when it comes to living, religious faith must supplement—nay, replace—scientific knowledge. But if, in principle, he is willing to make this breach in the walls of his system, and if analysis is, in the end, not the only instrument with which the mind should envisage life, why is thought restricted to faith in the future of earthly civilization? If one is going to have faith, why not look to the eternal as well as to the future? Why not have a faith that corresponds to the facts of religious experience? In short, if faith be admitted, why not face its full implications? Such faith as Perry feels goes too far for the strict logic of scientific method; it does not go far enough to satisfy the logic of religious experience.

Religion, it is true, looks to the future with confidence, but not merely to the welfare of future generations on this earth. It looks also to a life beyond the grave. It bases its faith in both futures, here and hereafter, not merely (with Perry) on a cautious maybe, but on the conviction that the Eternal Real is the sort of being that can be depended on to increase the values of life forever. It lifts up its heart in prayer to God and communes with him; it regards life as a cooperation with God. These facts are disregarded by the philosophy in question; and any theory that leaves facts out of account is dubious.

For another reason it appears probable that neo-realism can have no satisfactory account of religion, namely, the conflicting attitudes toward religious values that have come to expression within the school. We have seen Perry's theory. It is in express contradiction to the view of the distinguished realist, Bertrand Russell, whose philosophy of religion has found an already classical expression in the essay, "A Free Man's Worship."[15] Mr. Russell refuses to comfort himself with any hopes or faiths. He pictures man for a brief period emerging in a universe of blind and unconscious force, conscious that he and his race with all their achievements must soon utterly perish, yet cherishing "ere the blow falls, the lofty thoughts that ennoble his little day, . . . proudly defiant of the irresistible forces that tolerate, for a moment, his knowledge and his condemnation, to sustain alone, a weary but unyielding Atlas, the world that his own ideals have fashioned despite the tramping march of unconscious power." Mr. Russell remarks, in the

---

[15]B. Russell, *Mysticism and Logic.* (New York: Longmans, Green and Co., 1921), pp. 46–57.

preface to the volume in which this essay is printed, that he now feels less convinced than when he first wrote the essay of the objectivity of good and evil; as if that were possible! We have seen that Perry is not satisfied with Russell's philosophy of life; yet, after all, is it not more consistent with the method and presuppositions of realism than is the faith that he proposes?

5. THE NEW REALISM OF SPAULDING AND ALEXANDER

A still different philosophy of religion is advanced by E. G. Spaulding, who believes that among the real entities revealed by an analysis of experience are values which "are real parts of the objective world, external to and independent of not only their being perceived, conceived, and appreciated, but also of the physiological organism."[16] Unlike Perry, who made value dependent on a relation to desire, Spaulding asserts the Platonic theory of the objectivity of values. "Justice and beauty and truth themselves do not change, but remain eternal, quite outside of time and space." He takes as seriously as Russell the scientific prospect that "the physical universe is 'running down'" and that "seemingly its end . . . is to become wholly 'run down,' and then, no more process." But there are factors in evolution of which physical science does not take account, namely, values. New values emerge in the process; hence, evolution is creative; hence, also, "there is an efficient agent or power to produce all values." That which produces values must itself be a value, he argues. The realm of objective values which produces values is God, "the totality of values." God is denied to be "a psychical being of the nature of will or of intellect, and absolute ego, etc., who is relator of all entities, and so

[16]*The New Rationalism.* (New York: Henry Holt and Company, 1918), p. 508.

the fundamental underlying reality of the universe."
And yet, apparently conscious of the vagueness of
his thought, Spaulding speaks of this God in the third
person masculine, remarks that "if God is personality,
he is also more than personality," and designates his
solution as theistic.

It is not our purpose to comment on the vagueness or
looseness of analysis in such theism. Much more significant than these obvious defects is the fact that the
objectivity and transcendence of religious values here
win recognition; that within the school that defines the
universe as indifferent to all value and builds a religion
on the denial of spiritual or moral ontology, a voice is
raised to proclaim that spiritual values are real, objective, eternal, and efficient. Thus the metaphysical asserts itself as against the positivistic.

No account of important realistic contributions to
religious thought would be complete without a reference
to Alexander's Gifford Lectures on *Space, Time, and
Deity*.[17] It is impossible here to do more than sketch
in barest outline the standpoint of these lectures, which
have exerted a wide influence. They are based on a
thorough analysis of the world from a realistic standpoint, which results in the view that the spatio-temporal
order, or Space-Time, as Alexander calls it, is "the
stuff or matrix out of which things or events are made,
the medium in which they are precipitated and crystal-
lized; that the finites are in some sense complexes of
space and time." This means a universe of motion, of
"continuous redistribution of instants of Time among
points of Space." Everything in our universe is made
of this Space-Time. But it is a characteristic of the
universe to be constantly differentiating itself into

---

[17]London: Macmillan & Co., 1920.

higher and higher complexes.   At present the highest
is mind.   But just as every stage below mind has striven
toward something higher, so mind looks above and beyond, strains and strives for something still higher.
This tendency toward ever higher forms Alexander calls
a *nisus* toward Deity; and for any given stage, the stage
above is Deity.   Deity, then, is the upward urge of evolution.   Alexander speculates, with a quaint sort of neo-
gnosticism rather than realism, that the next stage
beyond man will consist of beings which he calls angels
or finite gods, so that our deity is plural and our religion
is a twentieth-century polytheism.

Here, then, are the neo-realistic philosophies of religion: that the universe is blind and without value, but
that man, in his short span of life, with no prospect for
the future, must bravely and defiantly assert his ideals;
or, that in the same general sort of universe it is profit-
able to hope that the human race will indefinitely
progress; or, that the universe is of a quite different
sort, with real values eternal and supreme, causing and
controlling evolution without existing in a divine intelligence; or, that the world-process is eternally developing from the stages of subhuman existence through
the human to the superhuman, and that this fact is
Deity.   In the face of such conflicting judgments, must
we not agree that religion is a fact which realism is compelled to face, but which it does not know what to do
with?

6. ABSOLUTE IDEALISM AND RELIGIOUS VALUES

The classical tradition in English and American
philosophy since the middle of the nineteenth century
is that of absolute idealism, the philosophy (largely
under Hegelian influence) that regards the universe as
one absolute system, one coherent whole.   This whole is

sometimes considered as a self, sometimes as a supra-personal absolute, sometimes as an X of which you can only say that it is the complete solution of all problems and fulfillment of all meaning, the final synthesis of all theses and antitheses. On any interpretation of absolute idealism, nothing finite has any self-existence or value by itself, or short of its relation to the organic whole of reality.

In 1920 a little book appeared which interpreted the meaning of religion for a distinguished representative of this school. I refer to Bernard Bosanquet's *What Religion Is*.[18] This may be taken as a typical expression of the attitude of absolute idealism (or speculative philosophy, as Bosanquet prefers to call it) toward religious values.

Its less than one hundred pages contain a beautiful series of meditations on the meaning of religious experience. It might almost be regarded as a manual of devotion rather than of philosophy. It transports us at once to an atmosphere very different from that in which instrumentalism and neo-realism move. On the whole, they have room only for just so much of religion as is embodied in the faith in human progress. Bosanquet, too, writes on Hope and Progress for Humanity, it is true. But even this means something very different to Bosanquet from what it means to them. For Dewey and Perry, at least, religion means the emotional glow that accompanies perpetual growth, the hope that by his own striving man may eventually possess the whole world in the name of value, a world which, without him and his striving, would have no value. For Russell, it is the grim determination to grit your teeth and fight,

---

[18]London: Macmillan & Co., 1920. For an excellent critique of Bosanquet's views see R. A. Tsanoff, *The Problem of Immortality*. (New York: The Macmillan Company, 1924), Chap. X.

even though the universe is hostile and the future hopeless.

Bosanquet, however, finds ground for human hope not primarily in anything man can do or needs to do, but, rather, in the nature of the universe, which as an absolute whole is itself the source and criterion of value. Man's life derives its meaning from the perfect Whole to which it belongs. "The religious man," says Bosanquet, "trusts in no strength of his own, and to be perfect apart from that in which he trusts would be for him sin and self-contradiction." This trust means "that there is always more to be learned, a further power of the values, a spiritual progress at least." The similarity and difference between this and Dewey's final law of growth are both striking. Each believes in growth; but Dewey regards growth as the ultimate value and end-in-itself, whereas Bosanquet measures growth by its relation to absolute value. Bosanquet's hope for the human race rests not so much on belief in the perfectibility of man's nature as on confidence in the Eternal, the trust "that through all appearances, good is supreme."

It is at once evident that Bosanquet's view is metaphysical rather than positivistic. It is also evident that it is closer to the facts of religious experience; for religion does not merely hope that the future may be better than the past, but it also trusts in an eternal perfection. Bosanquet points this out when he says that "it only requires us to rise above the appearance and keep our unhesitating grasp on the reality which is wholly good." It is faith of this sort that expresses itself in genuine religion everywhere; a more-than-human giving meaning to human life. Such idealism offers man a metaphysical and eternal basis for hope rather than such comfort as can be extracted from the cheery confidence that things will perhaps turn out better than science predicts. Its hope, furthermore, is a rational one, grounded on the interpretation of experience as a whole.

Not alone does Bosanquet thus offer a very different interpretation of progress, which seems to do more justice by religious experience than the other philosophies that we have been considering, but he also envisages a wider range. We find him writing of the peace of God, salvation, justification by faith, freedom and power, unity with God, man and nature, the nature of sin, suffering, prayer, and worship. It appeared to be the aim of the other philosophers whom we have studied to whittle religion down to a minimum in order to fit the facts of experience to their theory, while it would seem to be Bosanquet's aim to be catholic and inclusive, to take up into his system as much as possible of religious life; that is, to fit his theory to experience. He, then, is more reasonable, in the sense in which reasonableness was defined in Chapter I.

Dominating his account of the various aspects of religious life is the idealistic faith in a more-than-human whole, a universe to which man belongs. Religion is, so to speak, recognizing one's membership in the universe. "You cannot be a whole unless you join a whole." This sense of not being our own, of belonging to the eternal and supreme good, which is the whole, is freedom and power, is religion, "the only thing that makes life worth living at all." Since we thus belong to the eternal, our life is itself eternal. This does not mean for Bosanquet that our personality is immortal; the meaning of our life, rather, its loyalty, its cause, is eternal. Whether human consciousness shall survive bodily death or not is unimportant. What matters is that the value of the whole survives and we are somehow one with the whole. How, we do not know or need to know. Likewise, prayer finds its interpretation from this same standpoint; it is "the very meditation which *is,* or at the very least which enables us to realize and enter into the unity which is religious faith." Only this unity (and our unity with the whole) is essential to religion. Religion leads man beyond himself to reality.

Thus in a single uplifting and almost ineffable idea Bosanquet finds the heart of religion. Everything else is superfluous. This idea is sufficiently flexible and rich to serve as a center around which to group much of the life of religion. It aims to interpret everyone's religious life; not to destroy but to fulfill. But, after all, does it not reflect one mood and aspect only and not the whole of religious life? Its language is rather that of the pantheistic and extreme mystical types of religion than of the active and ethical. It forthwith excludes the type which sees in personality, human and divine, the supreme value, and interprets the human relation to the divine in terms of ethical cooperation and social companionship as well as in terms of mystical union. What absolute idealism thus excludes is precisely that part of religion which is and has been its life for most believers.

7. A Review of the Preceding Interpretations of Religious Values

The philosophies thus far examined differ at many points, but they all agree that religion is an essential part of human experience. Philosophy must be tested (we have held all through this discussion) by the adequacy and inclusiveness with which it interprets experience.

In this investigation, it is true, we are not concerned with all values, but only with those that we call religious. From the standpoint of these values, at least, that philosophy will be most adequate which is able to find the fullest meaning in the religious experiences of humanity. It is obvious that no philosophy could regard as true all of the religious experience of the race; conflicting valuations and contradictory beliefs condemn such an enterprise at the start. A philosophy of religion must be primarily a principle of inclusion and interpretation; it must also be a principle of criticism and exclusion. It must take care that neither of these principles interferes with the legitimate work of the other.

Applying this point of view to the philosophies hitherto considered, we observe that in the positivistic systems the aspect of criticism and exclusion greatly overbalances that of interpretation and inclusion. To most of the religious experiences and values instrumentalism says, "No, there is no place for you; for mysticism, for prayer, for the very problem of evil, to say nothing of its solution, there is no room. There is no God other than humanity, hence no communion with God; and no future life except that of the future generations of humanity on this earth." Only to the religious hope for growth, that is, only to the optimistic or melioristic aspect of religion, does instrumentalism say, "Yes, enter thou into the kingdom prepared for pragmatically true ideas as long as they work."

The predominant result of neo-realism, as we have seen, is substantially the same as that of instrumentalistic positivism, in spite of its greater interest in religion and its more evident desire to interpret it.

Bosanquet's treatment of religion is, however, far more catholic and inclusive. But his treatment, like that of instrumentalist and neo-realist, excludes the belief in a personal God. Belief in growth, in progress, in the unity of a universe that is somehow supremely good—these items of religion are conserved; but faith in a Supreme Person who understands all, loves all, works in all—this is vetoed. Such a situation is one of the many serious cleavages in the spiritual life of the modern world. On the one side, the philosophers, with their positivistic programs and beautiful though vague visions of the world's unity; on the other, the vital religious life of Christianity, Judaism, Mohammedanism, and many movements in other religions, deriving their vigor from faith in a personal God. Greek and Barbarian, Jew and Gentile, theory and practice!

8. Personalism and Religious Values

At least one type of philosophy, however, refuses to regard this cleavage as hopeless. The theistic aspect of religious experience finds interpretation in that philosophic movement to which the name "personalism" has been attached (notably by Renouvier in France and Borden Parker Bowne in this country). This philosophy is an idealism which holds that persons only are real, that every item and fragment of our world exists only in and for persons, and that there is one Supreme Person who is source of the world-order and creator of the society of persons. Insofar as he is regarded as fulfiller of the ideals of highest value, he is God. Such a standpoint is no modern fad or erratic provincialism of a peculiar group of thinkers; but, with numerous variations in detail and in supporting argument, it is one of the classic traditions in the history of philosophy. The roots of it may be found in Plato, Aristotle, and Augustine; more specifically it has been held by Berkeley, Leibniz, Fichte, Hegel (according to many of his interpreters, if not all), T. H. Green, Maine de Biran, Renouvier, Bowne, Ladd, Royce, Howison, James Ward, Richardson, Carr, Pringle-Pattison, Sorley, Rufus M. Jones, Youtz, Flewelling, J. S. Moore, Mary W. Calkins, Hocking, Edgar Pierce, Knudson, Strickland, R. A. Tsanoff, and many others.

By way of illustration, let us look again at Sorley's Gifford Lectures on *Moral Values and the Idea of God,* which we have already discussed briefly in Chapter II. This book does not aim to be a complete philosophy, nor even a complete philosophy of religion. In a sense it is not a philosophy of religion at all. It is a novel argument for personalistic theism, based on the interpretation of moral experience. Following Rickert, Sorley holds that our mind takes two attitudes: one, that of interest in universals; the other, that of interest in individuals. The former is embodied in the natural sciences; the latter, in history and morals. The former is ultimately interested in causes; the latter, in values. Each realm in which the mind is interested has its laws. A study of the meaning of value shows that intrinsic value belongs to persons only—a statement in which Sorley is at one with Dewey and Perry. But—and here he parts company with them—the laws of value in the moral sphere are as objectively valid as the laws of causal connection in nature, although they are very different and differently apprehended.

It is this last point which is the center of Sorley's contribution and which does much to establish the claims of personalism to be a more adequate philosophy of man's total experience than any of the other philosophies which we have considered. For, he holds, the laws of moral value point to a real objective order of value in the universe, just as truly as the laws of nature point to an objective natural order, and for the same sort of reason, namely, the appeal to the logical ideal of reasonableness. In this he agrees with Spaulding's Platonic argument for the objectivity of value. Our valuations, our conceptions of justice and benevolence, love and veracity, point to and presuppose an ideal standard to which they ought to conform. If this ideal standard is actual, as Sorley and Spaulding agree it is, in what does its actuality consist? It is no simple task to answer this question. An inclusive answer (what Sorley would call a synoptic view) must give an account of the objectivity not alone of value, but also of the laws of nature, and of the observed incongruity between the order of nature and the order of value—all of this in the same universe! The universe seems to be divided against itself. It not only does not always embody, but seems often to oppose all that the order of value would demand.

Sorley offers as the only postulate that meets all the conditions the standpoint to which we have referred as personalism, which views the world as an expression of an Intelligence which is at once a will to goodness and a source of power, but which leaves to finite persons a certain measure of freedom or self-determination. This view accounts for the apparent hostility of nature to value by the hypothesis that it is a manifestation of divine purpose aiming at "the fashioning and training of moral beings." The objectivity of values would then mean their existence as purposes of the Divine Mind. This breaks with Spaulding's impersonalistic value-theory, for Sorley cannot understand what would be meant by a value that could operate apart from a person. Thus Sorley, applying the standard of coherent inclusiveness, which has been our logical guide, arrives at a theistic personalism that suggests a theory of progress as well as a theory of value.

Obviously, the same sort of logic which led to the objectivity of moral value in a Supreme Person would also interpret religious value as a clew to the Divine Person, more intimate and more revealing than moral

value, significant as that is. The remaining chapters
will study the central experiences of religious value
more in detail.

9. SUMMARY

We are now ready to summarize our results. Religion
experiences human life as related to a superhuman and
eternal reality. Positivism, we saw, omits this relation
and thus falls short of expressing what religion means.
We have examined several current philosophical tendencies with reference to their interpretation of religion,
assuming as a criterion the tests of inclusiveness and
coherence. Any theory we hold is true in proportion
to the range of facts which it explains. The more experience it makes intelligible, the truer it is.

Testing current philosophies by their capacity in-
clusively to interpret religious experience, we have
found that instrumentalism and the predominant
tendencies in the new realism include faith in progress
(which is in some sense part of every real religion), but
that their positivism excludes the more-than-human
values of religious experience. The speculative philosophy of Bosanquet is more capable of finding room for
those values. But since it regards the One to whom in
religion we are related as the organic whole of reality,
which is not a person, it excludes all those experiences
which imply relationship between divine and human
persons, with understanding, love, and response on the
part of the divine.

Personalism must also be judged by the same standard. Does it include faith in progress? Dewey objected to
any ideal of perfection except the law of growth. Perry
objected to any spiritual or moral ontology. Personalism
asserts that there is an ideal of perfection in eternal
reality. But is this assertion incompatible, as these

critics hold, with taking our human tasks seriously? By no means; for, although the ideal is real in God, it is not yet real in finite persons, and the discovery and realization of it sets them an infinite task. The objectivity of value in God doubtless means that it is not possible for God to be any better than he is; it certainly does not imply that man has no more to do. It may be that even God's perfection is a perfection of life and growth rather than a static completion.

If progress means advance in acquaintance with true values and their possibilities, personalism offers a more satisfactory goal for human striving than does positivism. It surely includes the values of growth and progress. Does it also include the sense of belonging to a whole? It does not agree with absolute idealism in regarding man as an organic part of God, it is true, and unlike absolute idealism in most of its recent forms, it holds to the belief in personal immortality.[19] It does not, therefore, favor the Nirvana-like absorption of the individual dewdrop into the shining sea. But whatever value there may be in whole-hearted devotion to a cause infinitely beyond and above oneself or in mystical membership in an eternal whole, is amply provided for in the relation between human and divine personality, which is at once a cooperation and (on the human side) a surrender. Theistic personalism would thus appear to be the most comprehensive philosophy of religious values, including all the aspects recognized by other views, but finding room for other aspects which they crowd out.

If a religion be one-sidedly mystical or one-sidedly intellectual or one-sidedly practical, it may build for itself a pantheistic or a positivistic creed; but if it be

---

[19]But see E. S. Brightman, *Immortality in Post-Kantian Idealism* (Harvard University Press, 1925).

an expression of the whole of life, it will utilize the principle of personality and thus tend to become theistic. Philosophy will in turn react on life and either render religious life more rich and fruitful or more barren and narrow. If the religion of the future is to be deeply rooted in the soil of human nature, it must be metaphysical and personalistic.

CHAPTER VII

THE EXPERIENCE OF WORSHIP

1. THE PROBLEM OF THE CHAPTER

THE progress of thought in this book may be briefly summarized. We have aimed to interpret religious values. As a preparation for that task we inquired into the meaning of interpretation, that is, of reasonableness, as applied to the beliefs of religion (Chapter I). We then found it desirable to define the relation between the values of religion and of moral experience, coming to the conclusion that moral values are as necessary a presupposition of any religious values as is reasonableness a presupposition of any interpretation of religious belief (Chapter II). We then noted that the experience of value is a datum in need of interpretation as truly as is sense experience; and so there was developed the distinction between apparent value and real value, between value-claims and true values (Chapter III). We went on to examine the value-claims of religious experience. At first, not yet facing the question of the truth of religion, we considered its value in terms of human experience (Chapter IV), and in terms of the more-than-human object of its devotion (Chapter V.).

In the process of this investigation it became more and more apparent that any estimate of the value-claims of religion would be merely superficial if it did not face and think through the distinction between a positivistic and a metaphysical interpretation of religion, and consider the relative adequacy of current philosophical systems as coherent and inclusive accounts of religious experience. Chapter VI, therefore, in which these sys-

173

tems were investigated from this point of view, is the watershed of the book. Using its results as our working hypothesis, we shall return in this chapter to the facts of experience, by which every philosophy stands or falls, and consider afresh the actual life of religion.

The heart of any religion is whatever it regards as of highest value. To this highest value it usually gives the name of God; and the religious attitude to God includes and finds its consummation in worship. In studying the experience of worship, therefore, we shall be at the very center of what religious men and societies have judged to be the supreme value of religion. The present chapter aims to define that experience as a preparation for its evaluation in later chapters.

2. THE NEED OF REFLECTION ON WORSHIP

Worship as it is spontaneously experienced is usually not reflective or critical. The object of worship and the methods of worship are for most people given in the religious traditions of the group to which they belong. Primitive man worshiped long before he asked why he should do so. It has not been reflective deliberation about the truth and value of religion that has led most men to serve their gods, no weighing of reasons; but from the beginning men have worshiped because impulse and need, tradition and custom have urged them to it. "In their blindness," uncritically, they have bowed down before whatever gods there were.

In the twentieth century there are still worshipers. But there are also men who do not worship. If one may judge about such matters, these are many more than those who worship. Among educated people the number of worshipers appears to be less, if anything, than in the preceding century. Should one inquire into the grounds for the diminution of worship, the impartial investigator would have to admit that they are on the whole fully as nonrational as the original social and instinctive causes of worship. Worship seems to have gone out of fashion. Other arts, as Hocking has shown, have crowded out religion, their mother; the mode of the day fulfills the command, "Thou shalt not worship nor bow down."

Yet all the while, whether in fashion or out of fashion, worship has been either truly hurtful or truly helpful to the best interests of mankind. Religion has always taken for granted its own value. Yet the most ardent worshiper cannot deny that from time to time great spirits have arisen among men who, for reasons given, challenged that value and refused to bow the knee either to Baal or to Jehovah. "If there were gods," cries Zarathustra, "how could I stand not being one?" An Auguste Comte regards belief in God as a stage of thought that must be superseded by positive scientific knowledge of matters of fact; yet he would save two legs or the piece of an ear of worship by making humanity its object. But this is a halfway measure. A twentieth-century critic comments: "Humanity is not an object to be worshiped. The very attitude and implications of worship must be relinquished. In their place must be put the spiritually founded virtue of loyalty to those efforts and values which elevate human beings and give a quality of nobility and significance to our human life here and now."[1] For such critics of worship, God is dead. Worship, they assume, self-evidently gives no quality of nobility or significance to life.

How, then, can a worshiper of sensitive mind avoid reflecting on his own experience in the face of such a challenge? "A just thinker," says Emerson, "will allow

---

[1] R. W. Sellars, *The Next Step in Religion* (New York: The Macmillan Company, 1918), p. 7.

full swing to his skepticism. I dip my pen in the blackest ink because I am not afraid of falling into my inkpot."[2] When we confront religious skepticism, no mere exercise in academic speculation is at stake; it is a question of whether the modern man wishes to achieve spiritual integrity. It is the duty of the religious man who wishes to preserve the values of religion, as well as of the philosopher who wishes to understand, not to take the experiences of religion thoughtlessly for granted but to reflect on them and evaluate them critically.

3. WHAT WORSHIP IS NOT

If we are to undertake the task of reflecting on the experience of worship, we must have some working notion of what worship is. It should be remembered that any definition that could be offered would be meaningless apart from the system of experience and thought of which it is the deposit. This is true of all definitions and especially of the definition of worship. To try to capture the life of it in a phrase is a bolder venture than it is wise.

Instead, then, of looking for a formal definition, it would perhaps be better for us to meditate for a while on some of the expressions of worship. This method may bring our study nearer to the spirit of Thomas à Kempis, who said, "*Opto magis sentire compunctionem quam scire eius definitionem.*"[3]

In doing so we shall limit our thought chiefly to the higher types of worship among civilized man rather than to inquire curiously into origins or averages. Genetic studies have an important place which is at

---

[2]"Worship," in *The Conduct of Life*, etc. (Everyman's Library), p. 248.

[3]*De imitatione Christi*, I, 1. "I desire rather to feel compunction than to know its definition."

present in no danger of being overlooked; on the contrary, there is need of reminding some students of religion that the Bushmen of Australia are no better authorities in the philosophy of worship than they are in the science of physics. The genetic method becomes an enemy of truth if it leads us to a prejudice in favor of origins and against mature development.[4] Likewise the statistical method, much in vogue at present, is, to say the least, not likely to yield any criterion of truth or value. The so-called questionnaire has its uses; it also has its limitations. The answers of ten thousand Sunday-school teachers, normal-school pupils, college freshmen, or professors, to questions about religion have about the same relation to the lofty heights of worship as the answers of the same number of limerick writers would have to the secret of poetic inspiration. In our study we shall not be looking for average levels, but for the secret place of the Most High.

The ground may be cleared in a preliminary way by some negative considerations. Worship is not, as sentimental religionists would often have it, the whole of life. Daily work and play, politics and business, science and art, are doubtless related to worship, but they are not themselves part of worship. Worship, then, is not the whole of life; and, it may be added, it is not even the whole of religion. Religion includes or causes much that is not worship. Brotherly service to our fellow men is believed by many to be a very important part of religion; but to call it worship would be an instance of the pathetic fallacy. Worship is an inner posture of the individual, his attitude toward God. "Souls," says Emerson,[5] "are not saved in bundles. The Spirit saith

---

[4] See G. A. Coe, *Psychology of Religion* (University of Chicago Press, 1916), p. 25.
[5] *Op. cit.*, p. 254.

to the man, 'How is it with thee? thee personally? is it
well? is it ill?'" Again, religion includes belief; but belief is not worship. Belief, it is true, is a necessary presupposition of worship. A worshiping unbeliever is impossible. Man cannot worship his own ignorance; nor
can utter mystery be a god, Herbert Spencer to the contrary notwithstanding. The element of belief in some
worship may, it is true, be very slight. It is probable,
as we have said, that primitive cults arise apart from
rational faith; but their ritual is not worship until the
soul is in it and a god is believed in. Civilized man, certainly, must believe in an object worthy of his worship
before he can kneel and adore. But true as all this is,
an act of belief is not an act of worship; it is the precondition but not the fruition of worship.

Our thought will therefore at its present stage presuppose belief in God. The history of religion among
civilized races points to monotheism as the highest type
of religious belief. Our study in Chapter VI vindicated
it as the most adequate philosophy. For monotheism
there is one God, a Supreme Person who is at the same
time the Supreme Power and the Supreme Value in the
universe. Our discussion will work with this idea of
God, without considering what worship would be if
some other idea of God were believed. This will narrow
our scope, but make the study more definite. Some idea,
at all events, is a prerequisite to true worship; yet, let us
repeat, no idea, however worthy, is itself worship. Sim-
mel's extraordinary definition of religion as "enthusias-
tic apprehension of any content"[6] will serve to remind
us how barren religion becomes when the idea of God
is omitted. But, important as it is, that idea is not
religion.

Nor should worship be confounded with its external

---

[6] Quoted by Max Scheler in *Das Ewige im Menschen*, p. 521.

manifestations. Ceremonies and rites as forms of behavior are suitable objects for scientific investigation
in this behavioristic age; but the behavior of a human
organism or community must always be interpreted in
the light of the conscious attitudes which the behavior
expresses. Worship is never identical with its objective
expression, but is always a conscious attitude of the
worshiper to his god. Without a conscious attitude to
God, no true worship is transacted. If the conscious
attitude to God be feeble and meager, the worship is
feeble and meager, whatever its external forms may be
or whatever other values than worship may be present
in the life. If the conscious attitude to God be vivid and
rich, the worship is vivid and rich. This does not mean
that rite without true worship is valueless, for it im-
plants in the hidden recesses of the soul a background
for the later fruition of worship; none the less, it remains true that cult is not worship. It is wholly instrumental to conscious experience of God; it is quite literally a "means of grace," not grace itself.

4. THE FOUR STAGES OF WORSHIP

What, then, is the nature of worship? Of what attitudes does it consist? Attitudes we say, not attitude;
for worship is no fixed or single point of consciousness.
It is a stream which becomes deeper and often stiller as
it flows, a life which begets life. From observation of
its historic and present forms we find it to consist of
reverent contemplation, revelation, communion, and
fruition. If we thus single out its stages, it is not intended to give the impression that they are all separate
and distinct from each other or that the order given represents the constant or usual order of psychological development. Sometimes the stages seem to occur almost
simultaneously. The point of importance is that each

higher stage includes and presupposes those that precede it on the list, and that all four attitudes are present in all fully developed worship. Contemplation, revelation, communion, and fruition are all essential.

Contemplation is the first stage of worship. It is worship in its lowest terms; yet it involves more than belief in God. By contemplation is meant the fullest possible concentration of reverent attention on him. Man meditates on the mystery of a Creator who is also a Redeemer. As Richard Baxter quaintly puts it in the *Saints' Everlasting Rest,* there is "the set and solemn acting of all the powers of thy soul in meditation upon thy everlasting rest." The soul may be silent before Jehovah in contemplation, or may break forth into praise and thanksgiving.

But, however contemplation expresses itself, this stage of worship is incomplete without a higher. He who patiently waits upon the Lord finds that the Lord inclines unto him. Contemplation is followed by revelation. In contemplation man is seeking; in revelation God is giving. In contemplation man's attitude is active; in revelation it is passive. Each is necessary for the normal fulfillment of the other. First, "I saw the Lord"; then, "flew one of the seraphims unto me." First, meditation under the bo tree; then, the illumination of Nirvana.

> "Who in heart not ever kneels
> Neither sinne nor Saviour feels."[7]

Reverent contemplation fits us to receive God's judgment of our character and of his.

Yet it would be an error to regard this revelation as the end of worship. The saint who aims only at illumination is not the perfected saint. The passive

---

[7] G. Herbert, in "Business," *Herbert and Heber's Poems,* p. 96.

recipient of revelation should become active again; yet now he does not return to mere contemplation, for he can enter into a mutual relation with the God who has revealed himself. This is most often expressed in prayer; but the practice of the presence of God may take many forms. Communion with God, then, differs from contemplation as fellowship with a present friend differs from thought about an absent one; for, although God is truly present to the mere contemplater, a God whose presence is not revealed is as good as absent. And a God revealed but unresponsive to our spirit's need is as though he were not. The literature of devotion is full of expressions of the intimacy of communion with God and warnings against its possible loss. To quote Richard Baxter again, "Frequency in heavenly contemplation is particularly important to prevent a shyness between God and thy soul."[8]

Sometimes this shyness is so successfully broken down as to destroy reverent contemplation and to produce an undue familiarity, akin to that which in the end breeds contempt. The extremes of so-called gospel songs may be matched in the Pietistic movement of the seventeenth and eighteenth centuries. Such "hymns" as the following were produced:

> "Call me, Oh call me, thy bride,
>   Call me, I pray thee, thy dove;
> Bring me to thy dear side,
>   Fill me with trusting love."

A production of twenty-three stanzas gave twenty-three attributes of Jesus in the following style:

> "Little Easter Lamb, how sweet,
>   How sweet thy taste to me.
> Honey flowing from thy wounds
>   Brings felicity.

---

[8] *Op. cit.*, p. 339.

> Of thy grace my soul has boasted.
> Life sprang up when thou wert roasted!"

Twenty-three stanzas of this would suffice to prevent shyness.

It was such excesses in the Pietistic movement that led Ritschl to denounce all mysticism.[9] Nevertheless, it was Ritschl who said that "the fellowship which sinners may have with God is as close as that between the head and the members of a family," and that "in the personal sanctuary of this peculiar knowledge of God, of the world, and of oneself, which consists more of states of feeling than of intellectual reflections, one is absolutely independent over against men; or, if not, one has not yet attained the enjoyment of reconciliation."[10] Communion with God thus gives man a sense of membership in an eternal spiritual whole that cannot fail; yet it is not the final stage of worship.

God is too overwhelming for man to endure long the intense feeling of direct communion with him. Conscious life is rhythmic, and attention must alternate, as Hocking has pointed out, between the whole and the part. This thought is allegorically expressed in a well-known passage in the *Theologia Germanica* (Chapter VII):

"Now the created soul of man hath also two eyes. The one is the power of seeing into eternity, the other of seeing into time and the creatures, of perceiving how they differ from each other as aforesaid, of giving life and needful things to the body, and ordering and governing it for the best. But these two eyes of the soul of man cannot both perform their work at once; but if the soul shall see with the right eye into eternity, then the left eye must close

---

[9]*Geschichte des Pietismus;* where the hymns given in the text are also quoted, Vol. II, pp. 489, 491. The translations are by the present author.

[10]*Rechtfertigung und Versöhnung*, Vol. III, pp. 94, 617.

itself and refrain from working, and be as though it were dead. For if the left eye be fulfilling its office toward outward things, that is, holding converse with time and the creatures, then must the right eye be hindered in its working; that is, in its contemplation. Therefore whosoever will have the one must let the other go, for 'no man can serve two masters.' "[11]

But the mystic writer has gone to extremes in the separation of the functions. God and his world are not two utterly distinct universes. When the worshiping mind turns from its moments of direct communion with "the center and soul of every sphere" to a concern with our fragmentary human experiences, it carries to them the power of the Whole which draws them to itself. God is the magnetic pole of our spiritual universe; and, contrary to the old mystic, he gives meaning to our life in the world.

Just as the mariner should not leave the lanes of navigation and flee to the pole, so the soul should not leave the world and flee to God. To be in the world yet not of it is the worshiper's portion. He steers toward port through tempest and sunshine, his compass held steady by a power beyond the clouds and the very sun. Then at last within his soul there dawns the final stage of worship, which is fruition. Not the ecstasy of mystic communion but the fruit of the Spirit—love, joy, peace, longsuffering, gentleness, faith, meekness, temperance— is the true goal of worship. These virtues when they grow out of a life of worship have a very different inner aspect than when they are cultivated for their own sakes. Fruits grow out of the life of the organism; so the fruit of the Spirit. As is the love of human person and human person, so is the love of human person and

[11]Tr. by Winkworth in the Golden Treasury Series (London: Macmillan & Co., 1893).

divine person: first, contemplation of the Loved One; then revelation of the mysteries of the true nature of the Loved One; then, a communion of life; and, finally, creation of new life, "birth in beauty," as Plato calls it. This should not be taken to mean that the worship of God is merely a means to an end, a mere instrument to personal character or social sentiments or conduct; it means, rather, that, unless the end sought is one of which worship is both root and integral part, the human personality will never find its maturest fruition.

5. TRANSITION TO THE NEXT CHAPTER

Worship as it has just been described is worship at its best. But the actual average falls short of this ideal composite of selected experiences. Only a rare spirit in a rare moment truly worships as we have defined the act. Perhaps the mass of men never worship. Perhaps, indeed, enlightened men would not desire to worship. Perhaps there is no room for worship in culture. Perhaps it is fantastic. There may be a God, but his existence may be a remote and barren fact.

No mere description of the experience of worship could tell us whether worship is truly valuable. The worshiper must think his way through to a reasonable view of experience as a whole if he is to maintain his right and obligation to worship against all critics. Not only must he construct a positive view, but he must also face ultimate doubts about the value of worship before it can be his secure possession. If this is to be done, the sooner the better; hence the next chapter will consider these doubts; and the following one will inquire into the creation of the fruit of the Spirit.

CHAPTER VIII

DOUBTS ABOUT THE VALUE OF WORSHIP

1. The Problem of the Chapter

WORSHIP, as we have seen, is contemplation of God, revelation, communion (or supposed revelation and communion), and fruition. In this process of worship the religious man believes that he finds life's highest value. For simplicity's sake we may for the present waive consideration of whether our conclusion in Chapter VI that God really exists is valid or not. Let us, rather, scrutinize doubts about the value of the experience of worship. Such doubts are fully as devastating as theoretical atheism; for, if philosophy and theology were to "prove" that there is a God, but experience were to find no true value in worship, this practical refutation of faith would outweigh all theoretical proof. The life of religion depends upon the worth of worship. The value of worship, it is true, would not by itself justify the beliefs that accompany or sustain it. But the valuelessness of worship would destroy those beliefs beyond repair; and its value would be evidence for religious belief that might acquire logical force when interpreted in the light of a synoptic view of our whole human experience. It is just as irrational to ignore real consequences as it is to fall into easy-going acceptance of results as a criterion of truth.

Can worship survive doubt? That acts of worship are still satisfying to devout souls cannot be questioned; but, if these souls paused a while to think, would they still be satisfied? Is worship reasonable? Some would say that one must not try to reason about such matters;

they are too high for our wit. Oswald Spengler is their spokesman when he says, "The desire for system is the desire to kill the living";[1] that is, we should take life pragmatically as it comes, without trying to reason about it. Reason, Spengler thinks, is a foe to life. But if this way of thinking be applied to religion, the outcome is disastrous. Such a defense of worship is, in the end, a pessimistic and skeptical betrayal of what is most precious; for if there be ultimate warfare between life and logic, between worship and truth, God is not reasonable; in short, there is no God. The defense of religion by appeal to skepticism is treason within the camp. When a friend of religion can write, as one has written, that "the heart-hunger of the world to-day is not for a reasonable religion, as some would have us believe, but for a satisfying God,"[2] it seems like a frank admission that there probably is in reality no God, and so we may as well make one that suits us. It is not, then, altogether surprising that a Reinach can ironically define religion as "a collection of scruples that hinder the free exercise of our faculties."[3]

If worship is to deserve survival it must justify itself before reason. Can the modern man worship? Can he confront the whole wherein he lives and find there a God to adore? Or is man to-day so occupied with fractional living, with fragments of business, or art, or science, that he is impotent to worship? Must he always fail to see the forest for the trees? Was Mehlis right when he judged that culture is dying of its own beauty? Is there no beauty that is both truly adorable and permanent? Must the busy present veil the object of wor-

---

[1] *Der Untergang des Abendlandes*, (1st–15th ed., Munich: Beck, 1922), Vol. II, p. 16.

[2] E. L. Pell in *The Christian Advocate*, 99 (1924), p. 1553.

[3] Reinach, *Orpheus*, p. 4. Cited *Ere*, Vol. XXII, p. 756b.

ship, the God in whose hand are past and future, present and eternity?

Our problem in its most general form is well stated by Willa Cather. "Life," she says, "was so short that it meant nothing at all unless it were continually reinforced by something that endured; unless the shadows of individual existence came and went against a background that held together."[4] Is it possible, we ask, in the experience of worship truly to find such a background, or does worship fail us? This is the doubt that we must face.

2. THE DIALECTIC OF DOUBT

Doubts are many. There are doubts of blank ignorance and doubts of dull incompetency, doubts of perversity and doubts of temperament and mood. All of these doubts are below the level of reason and are both unworthy and incapable of a rational refutation. Not reason but enlarged experience or the gift of a new intellect is their sole refutation. We shall pass by these unreflective stages of doubt in order to grapple with the deeper questions raised by a reflective doubt.

When thought once begins to criticize, doubts spring up like weeds on every side. There is a wild luxuriance, a seemingly planless productivity of doubt. Yet, just as there are laws of biology to be found in the growth of the rankest weeds, so laws of reason are discoverable at work in doubt. Rational doubt about any object always reveals some truth both about that object and about reason itself. Hence, out of the apparently meaningless profusion of doubts about worship in the modern mind it is probable that some rational meaning can be constructed. Perhaps the ungainly fragments may be fitted to each other as in a puzzle-picture, so that, when all our

---

[4] *One of Ours* (New York: Alfred A. Knopf, 1922), p. 406.

doubts are put together, they will be seen both to refute their own character as doubts and also to contribute something to the picture of the whole life of true worship. If this be true, the real danger to worship lies far less in systematic and thorough doubt than in random doubting, which is merely analytic or partial. When all our doubts are seen together, synoptically, they will experience a change and become a rational vision of faith. If you doubt thoroughly, your doubts will answer each other. Emerson expressed this conviction most vigorously in his essay on Worship. "If the Divine Providence," he says, "has hid from men neither disease, nor deformity, nor corrupt society, but has stated itself out in passions, in war, in trade, in the love of power and pleasure, in hunger and need, in tyrannies, literatures, and arts—let us not be so nice that we cannot write these facts down coarsely as they stand, or doubt but there is a counter-statement as ponderous, which we can arrive at, and which, being put, will make all square."[5]

Doubt, then, has a dialectic structure that keeps our reason restless until it finds both reason and rest in God. Each doubt leads to a contradictory doubt that cancels it and thus rises to a higher faith. Only by facing our doubts fully may we see beyond them and attain faith that is really "the substance of things hoped for." Perhaps Bacon was right when he said, "In contemplation, if a man begin with certainties, he shall end in doubts; but if he be content to begin with doubts, he shall end in certainties." To the words of Bacon should be added the profound advice of Boehme: "Now it behooves the wise seeker to consider the whole process."[6] Each thesis of doubt, as Hegel might say, generates its

[5] *The Conduct of Life, etc.*, p. 248.
[6] *Signature of All Things*, etc. (Everyman's Library), p. 64.

antithesis; and out of their opposition arises a synthesis, which in turn generates new oppositions until a view of the whole is reached in which there is an inclusive vision of experience that is completely coherent.

3. First Thesis: Doubt About Contemplation: "All Is Within"

How shall we go about our task of doubting thoroughly? There is no royal road to the discovery of truth. In any problem the prescription is to start where we are and think from chaos toward order. For our present purpose it may be useful to try to discover the progress of the dialectic of doubt through an examination of the four stages which have been described, namely, reverent contemplation, revelation, communion, and fruition.

Our starting point, then, will be doubt about contemplation. Worship begins with solemn thought about God, meditation on his supreme excellence. But thought, says the doubter, is mere human reasoning and opinion which easily becomes overcertain of itself and eventuates in dubious creeds. Contemplation of God is thus at best no more than reliance on our reasoned opinions; at worst it descends to the deification of our dogmas. "Orthodoxy," as Herrmann used to say, "is too rationalistic." Hinduism illustrates the danger of a sterile contemplation that ends in itself. To quote a modern Hindu writing: "If a man be skilled in words and learned, let him compose histories of the Holy One. . . . Often hath it been said to such an one, 'Cleanse thy voice and thy heart by telling of the glory of the Holy One,' and this one will give answer, 'Sir, I am busy describing the doctrine of the identity of the universe with the deity.' "[7] Some Christians might judge

---

[7] N. Macnicol, *Indian Theism* (London: Milford, 1915), p. 218. From the *Bhakta-kalpadruma* (1866).

that the peril from such intellectualism is not confined to Hindus.

The doubter who complains of the rationalism and dogmatism of religion is right in so far as he sees that religious worship rests on rational belief; but he is wrong in his inference from that fact. He supposes that, because the truth and value of worship depend on believing certain human ideas, therefore worship is only a play of human fancy or—to borrow a term from psychology—mere rationalization. Because worship is contemplation he argues that it is all within. This doubt arises from isolating the moment of contemplation, cutting off its meaning from experience as a whole, and staring at the artificial abstraction thus created. Idea, any idea, apart from its meaning is all within; believing as a psychological process is merely subjective. But if worship is to be condemned on this ground, then all beliefs about everything, from the objects that I see before me to mathematical truths, from tar-water to God, must fall in one and the same ruin. If worship is worthless because it requires ideas in our minds, then all experience is worthless and life is vain. Such doubt forgets that ideas are to be condemned as false not merely because they are in our minds but solely because they are unreasonable. Contemplation cannot justly be rejected merely because it is contemplation. It must, rather, be tested by its power to interpret the objects that we experience; the within stands or falls by its power to mediate what is beyond.

4. First Antithesis: Doubt About Revelation: "All Is Beyond"

Worship asserts its virtue when thus tested, for contemplation yields revelation. He who meditates on God finds that there is revealed to him more than his own

reasonings could ever produce. The "numinous" majesty of the Almighty, his exalted righteousness, his pity-
ing and healing love, the beauty of his holiness are in
due season revealed to the worshiper who seeks him. In
the presence of these transcendent revelations he ex-
claims: "What am I but what I have received? . . .
I believe because it is absurd!" He is conscious of having found something that is quite beyond his native
powers to produce. For many souls this phase of worship is overwhelming; and it has produced extremes of
experience and doctrine. Implicit, blind faith; unques-
tioning belief in authoritative creeds as containing the
essence of revelation; acceptance of tradition or Scripture as final standard, fear and distrust of science and
philosophy—these are some of the bitter fruits of the
overvaluing of the experience of revelation. For good
or ill, the experience is a power in life.

Such fruit comforts and sustains the soul of many a
worshiper. To the average man it is the bread of life
delivered at the front door. But, like the little book of
the Apocalypse, though sweet as honey in the mouth, it
is bitter in the belly. When worship tarries passively
at the moment of revelation, and the reason prays, "Oh
to be nothing, nothing!" the doubter is always on hand
gleefully commenting on answered prayer. He has,
moreover, won no mere victory of satire. If worship be
nothing but a passive recipience of revelation apart from
any rational belief in a moral and personal God, our God
is, as Rudolph Otto recently remarked, a mere idol.
The worshiper who lingers too long at this stage of
worship says in effect, "All is beyond," and thus cuts off
God as effectively as the mere contemplator who says,
"All is within." The errors of ultraconservative theology arise mostly from persisting in this antithesis.
Revelation is not the whole of worship.

5. FIRST SYNTHESIS: COMMUNION: "THE BEYOND THAT IS WITHIN"

There is, we must admit, a thoroughly justified doubt about any worship that is either mere subjective contemplation of one's own ideas, or mere passive acceptance of a supposed revelation, no matter what that revelation may be. The position of the mere rationalist and that of the mere authoritarian are equally false both to reason and to worship. On the other hand, each makes an essential contribution. Without reverent and rational contemplation within the mind worship is mere mummery. Without revelation from beyond the mind worship is a groping that does not find, a looking that does not see. What is needed, therefore, is the deepening of worship that arises in conscious communion between the contemplating worshiper and the revealing God. We seek not alone the within of contemplation nor the beyond of revelation but, rather, in the beautiful phrase of Rufus M. Jones, "the beyond that is within," a God whom we can find through our own inner life, yet who is infinitely more than our experience of him.

6. SECOND THESIS: DOUBT ABOUT COMMUNION: "ALL IS FEELING"

versus

SECOND ANTITHESIS: DOUBT ABOUT FRUITION: "ALL IS BEHAVIOR"

Although communion is a solution of the doubts provoked by the defects of contemplation and revelation, it is itself not final. It leads to the consummation of worship in fruition. Neither can be fully appreciated without the other nor without the inferior stages of contemplation and revelation. Communion is a deepened and personalized contemplation; fruition is the interpretation in life of the divine revelation, the cooperative product of God and man.

But at each of the stages of worship doubt arises. Against contemplation the reproach was brought, All is within and hence worship is subjective. Against revelation it was said, All is beyond and hence worship is irrational and therefore unattainable for the thinking man. Likewise the higher stages of worship are doubted. Of communion it may be said, All is feeling, and hence worship, although attainable, yet is irrational. Against fruition the accusation runs, All is behavior, and hence God is superfluous; the Golden Rule suffices without the golden streets; supernatural sanctions are unnecessary.

The doubts that grow out of the belief that communion is mere feeling and fruition mere behavior are as complicated as are human nature and civilization. We must be content therefore with a bird's-eye view of these doubts.

When the doubter hears it said that worship is communion with God, his comment is ready to hand. Communion? What is this but mere emotional mysticism? Is it not a mere surrender of rational self-control in the interests of lawless feeling? Is it not pure subjectivism on a far lower plane than that of rational contemplation? On the other hand, when this same doubter looks for the fruition of mystical experience in behavior, he may say that worship reduces to a few forms and ceremonies. Worship is socially expressed as ritual; and ritualism is mere externalism. Thus, worship as communion is too inner; as fruition, too external. Its value is therefore doubly doubtful.

Two tendencies in the intellectual world will serve to illuminate the twin doubts that have just been mentioned, namely, psychoanalysis and the social interpretation of religion. An instructive popular exposition of the psychoanalytic view of worship has recently appeared in Mr. E. D. Martin's book, *The Mystery of Religion*.[8] For this type of thinking, the essence of religion lies in the reconciliation of man with the heavenly Father. Who, then, is this heavenly Father who reveals himself to us as the forgiver of sins? Well, he and all of religion are but the "symbolic expression of our wish that the universe were run in our interest." God is simply a "Father-complex" of the general type familiar to the psychoanalyst. The Father-complex is a defense mechanism that enables man "to forgive his own sins by conceiving of them as having been forgiven by the Father." Animal sacrifice provides the emotional shock necessary to break the emotional fixation upon the actual parent. This is, of course, thoroughgoing subjectivism. Religion is "the solution of conflicts which lie wholly within the psyche." "We must," says Mr. Martin, in Vaihinger's spirit yet on very different grounds, "find the meaning and value of our lives in fiction and illusion."[9] We have here a point of view which, so far as the object of worship is concerned, may well be called psychoanalytic solipsism. For it, religion is a purely subjective transaction.

Over against this view of worship as communion with our own Father-complex may be set what has been called the Uncle Sam theory of God. Instead of looking within and below consciousness, as do the psychoanalysts, a numerous school of writers look out toward the social fruits of religion. These men—Durkheim, Ames, King, Haydon, and many others more or less influenced by

---

[8] New York: Harper & Brothers, 1924.
[9] *Op. cit.*, pp. 99, 192, 217, 334, 337.

Auguste Comte—all define religion as group consciousness or social mind of some sort.   What religion expresses, these men believe, is the solidarity of some human group; humanity is the Supreme Being; God is the
social mind, "the idealizing Social Will, or Spirit of the
Group," as E. S. Ames phrases it.[10]   A representative of
this view is said to have remarked that organized cheer-
ing on the football field is a religious experience, because social.   It is, then, not a captious caricature to
call this the Uncle Sam theory or to describe it as social
solipsism.

It would be no lover of truth who would damn psychoanalysis and positivism with a label and cast them thus
to one side.   There is a real truth in each.   Psychoanalysis reveals some of the individual and subjective
roots of worship, and shows the need and value of symbolism.   It recognizes the great truth that, as Mr. Martin remarks, "there is a sense in which each man, if
left alone, would be religious in his own way."[11]   It
explores the hidden depths of the soul.   Likewise, social
positivism contributes to truth.   It teaches the fragmentary character of worship that centers about God
and me instead of about God and us; the absurdity of
a God who is God of the individual and not of society.
It has only scorn for the idea of God as a guardian
angel for the individual; a guardian angel is verily no
God.

As a corrective to gross externalism and superficiality,
psychoanalysis is valuable; as a corrective to excessive
individualism in worship, the social view has a function;
but as the whole truth each refutes the other.   Worship
is neither wholly inner psychic struggles nor is it wholly
external social relations.

[10]*Jour. Rel.*, 1 (1921), p. 468.
[11]*Op. cit.*, p. 342.

7. Third Thesis of Doubts: "Communion is Beyond Good and Evil"

versus

Third Antithesis: "Fruition is a Fanatical Assertion of Morality"

We have found that the second thesis and antithesis refute each other, but we have not yet found the synthesis which solves their contradiction. While we are waiting for this synthesis to appear another conflict may engage our attention. No thoughtful reader of this book (and especially of Chapter II) could overlook the problem of the relations of worship to the moral life. This problem is also suggested by our consideration of the social aspects of religion. It is of pressing theoretical and practical importance. Here, too, doubts and apparent contradictions multiply. The experience of the communion of the worshiper with his God does not bear on its face the majesty of the moral law; it seems to be experience of a different order. In the average religious group some will be found who seem to have mystical communion of a sort, but whose moral character is dubious. The one does not necessarily involve the other. In moral experience will is the central fact; in communion, feeling. The moral man is active; the communing worshiper receives from God infinitely more than he gives. The worshiper's conviction is expressed by Sadhu Sundar Singh, "The wonderful peace which the man of prayer feels while praying is not the result of his own imagination or thought, but is the outcome of the presence of God in the soul."[12] Communion with God seems to carry the worshiper beyond himself, even, perchance, into realms beyond good and evil. Good and

[12]*Reality and Religion* (New York: The Macmillan Company, 1924), p. 8.

evil are human categories, it is sometimes felt; when God speaks, human judgment is stilled.

Here the voice of the doubter is raised. If communion carries the mystic to a point where moral categories fail, the doubter asks, what becomes of the moral life while worship is going on, and what effect does such worship have on morality? If the mystic is a stage superior to the moral, as many mystics have held, may not the ardent worshiper not only feel a *contemptus mundi* but even come to acquire a contempt for morality itself as mere works without that blessed mystery called faith? Has he not described morality as of no avail for salvation—yes, as filthy rags? Does not pursuit of the infinite rainbow lead men to contemn goodness, the rarest jewel of our finite lives? If the doubter be persistent, he will point out that many a worshiper has seemed to glory in the surrender of self-respect, describing himself as a very worm of the dust. Communion with God, he will conclude, discourages morality and humiliates the soul. The net result of this aspect of religion is (so Karl Marx thinks) that it becomes the "opiate of the people."

The same idea is often expressed by calling religion other-worldly. The theme of religion has often been, "I am a stranger here, heaven is my home." The history of asceticism is largely a history of withdrawal from active life here for the sake of supposed benefits hereafter. God and eternity may become the sole object of real interest. *"Et ipsa_ist beata vita, gaudere de te, ad te, propter te; ipsa est et non est altera"*[13]—"This is the blessed life—to rejoice about thee, unto thee, because of thee; this is the blessed life indeed and there is no other." But if there be literally no other interest in

---

[13]Augustine, *Conf.*, X, 32.

life than God, the outcome is an empty and barren worship as well as the destruction of normal life. Communion with a God who is wholly of another world cuts the nerve of life in this world.

These doubts would perhaps prove annihilating were it not for a set of opposing doubts that arise when we face the fruition of worship in life. Is the worshiper, as some think, beyond good and evil? Then why is it that a Jesus, a Paul, a Calvin, a Gandhi are so loyal to their moral perceptions as to occasion the charge that religion is hyperconscientious? Does communion with the Eternal humiliate man? Why then does he who has met the Lord go forth exalted, with convictions so intense that he seems to identify his own will with that of the Almighty, and elicits from those less religious than himself the judgment that he is extremely self-assertive? Is Karl Marx right in saying that religion is an opiate of the people? Then why have so many prophets of past and present been social revolutionaries, striving for the true brotherhood of mankind? No more disturbing foe to social injustice has ever entered human history than the worshiper's faith that God, the all-Father, is love. Or, is it true that worship is other-worldly? If so, why Oliver Cromwell, John Calvin, John Wesley, the Salvation Army, and the Pope of Rome? Why is there so much force in the counterdoubt which criticizes the worshiper on account of his undue concern for temporal power and his zeal to set right all that now is in the conduct of social life, becoming Puritanic censor of

> "all that I think,
> Yea, even of wretched meat and drink"?

Those, then, who doubt worship because communion is deficient in morality are met by those who doubt it because its fruition suffers from an excess of morality, a surplus of activity. Far from disregarding morality, it is almost fanatically moral. These doubts, taken together, are a tribute to the balance and comprehensiveness of true worship. They show that the worshiper is a citizen of two worlds, and that his experience unites and perfects the essence of each.

8. FINAL SYNTHESIS: WORSHIP AS CONSCIOUS RELATION OF THE WHOLE PERSONALITY TO GOD

Communion is doubted, we said, because it holds, or is believed to hold, that all is feeling. The fruition of worship in conduct occasions doubt because it appears to assert that all is behavior. But if anything stands out clearly in the actual commerce of the soul with God, it is that neither a mere feeling of communion nor any form of behavior (however socialized or democratized it may be) is the goal of religion. The nature of the true fruit of worship is foreshadowed in the defects of its partial forms. Complete worship will engage the complete personality of man, not his feelings alone, nor his conduct. The doubts that have been raised about the fruition of worship were permissible and necessary just because that fruition was regarded as mere behavior. The true fruition of worship is found in the development of the whole personality, which finds itself and realizes itself through a consciousness of its relations to God. Keats and Bosanquet are right; this world is "a vale of soul-making."

Can the value of personality as the worthy fruit of worship be doubted? This is the ultimate question about the value of religion. Personality, it may be replied, when fully itself, conscious of its ideals and relations, living in harmony with God, is self-justifying. It is what we mean by value. The doubter who questions the value of personality does more than he intends to do; for he not only denies the worth of worship, but he denies all value whatever, even the value of doubt and so of his own question. Thus, at last, worship is self-justifying because it brings life to a coherent whole; doubt, self-destroying because in contradicting worship it contradicts all else, including itself.

Doubt, then, moves on toward truth, as all life, when sound, seeks higher levels. The thought of this movement of life is fittingly expressed in the lines of Father John Bannister Tabb:

> "Out of the dust a shadow,
>   Then, a spark;
> Out of the cloud a silence,
>   Then, a lark;
> Out of the heart a rapture,
>   Then, a pain;
> Out of the dead, cold ashes,
>   Life again."[14]

9. Survey of the Chapter

When the self-refuting character of these doubts is seen, they seem almost too absurd to be real. Why, one may ask, do men not see it so? This is equivalent to asking why everyone does not live a complete life in the clear light of reason. Why, indeed? But there can be no question of the fact. Such doubts are entertained. Men stop short not alone of the unattainable Absolute but even of the whole truth that is within their grasp. It is no marvel that this is true, since worshipers themselves give occasion to the doubter. The worshiper who tarries in contemplation and does not press on to receive revelation, or who accepts revelation but does not seek communion, or who enjoys communion without looking for fruition, or who is satisfied with fruition in conduct

---

[14]From Norman Ault, *The Poets' Life of Christ* (London: Milford, 1922), p. 113.

without nourishing the total personality which is both root and fruit of good conduct, such a worshiper gives rise to the doubter who sees maimed and imperfect worship going on before his very eyes. This, he says, is what worship is; and it is not good. Fractional worship begets fractional doubting. Total worship challenges total doubt; but total doubt, while we doubt, refutes itself and turns again into faith.

The worshiper, however, is not to be too severely censured for these his defects. Many of them are due, it is true, to unspiritual causes, some of which might be removed were he willing to seek the Lord with a whole heart. But many of those excesses are due to the very value of worship. Every element and phase of the pilgrim's progress toward the Celestial City of the Spirit is so precious that, like the lover who is overcome with joy in the presence of a single lock of his lady's hair, the worshiper lingers lovingly in contemplation or revelation, communion or conduct, and gives to the part the value that rightly belongs only to the whole. Worship, as we have seen, is a process that leads from moment to moment until the whole is attained. Every moment is indeed precious; but woe to the worshiper who forgets that only to him that believeth is the preciousness, believeth, that is, in a whole God to whom the whole worship of the whole personality is due! Woe to him whose partisanship for one element makes him an enemy of the whole! Woe to dogmatist and moralist, intellectualist and æsthetic, woe to solipsists, whether psychoanalytic or social!

We return, then, to the thought of God. If there is to be a revival of worship in the modern world, it will come in large part through a revival of thought about God. This means no return to a barren intellectualism. Among worshipers not uniformity but unanimity is the need; not one form of cult or of dogma, but one spirit. Yet the one spirit is itself an empty form unless it mean devotion to a common cause, the cause of God among men. Without the idea of God the spirit of worship perishes. And it must be added that not every idea of God is worship-inspiring. God as Father-complex needs not worship but psychotherapy; God as social mind needs the United Charities; God as occasional doer of this or that, miracle-worker and inhabiter of sacred buildings, demands the incantations of the medicine man; but God as immanent Spirit of the whole universe, Creator and Redeemer, inexhaustible Person—this God invites the rich adventure of the soul that we call worship. Such a God as this I believe to be real; far more real than any human idea about him. The worshiper who has found fruition will recall that there are many stages of worship, many roads to God, and he will not fear lest God and his world may become estranged if God does not chance to be in the center of to-day's fashion of thinking. God lets himself be found afresh in many ways; but he always lets himself be found.

CHAPTER IX

WORSHIP AS CREATIVITY

1. THE PROBLEM OF THE CHAPTER

WORSHIP we have found to be a process that includes reverent contemplation of God, the receiving of some revelation from him, the experience of communion with him, and a consequent fruition of personality—the fruit of the Spirit, a new birth.

It is this new life that is the true goal of worship and the essential value of religion. If worship be truly consummatory (to borrow a term of John Dewey's), it is an experience worthy the loyalty of a man or a God. It is perhaps as near to the secret of the purpose of man's existence as we are likely to come. The claims of religion, then, are transcendent.

Precisely because so much is at stake it is imperative to scrutinize those claims most narrowly. The boasted prerogative of religion is its power to save. What does the saved life come to? Does worship truly yield its fruit in its season—the human being redeemed and transformed? On the title page of the English translation of the *Theologia Germanica* that book is described as one which "setteth forth many fair lineaments of divine truth and saith very lofty and lovely things touching a perfect life." "Lofty and lovely things"—are they the genuine experience of the worshiper? "Glorious things of Thee are spoken"—but what is the reality in experience to which these glowing words refer?

Worship is the inner shrine of religion. Religion cannot be assured of its right to a perpetual place in human experience unless worship have an intrinsic value of its own. The *Theologia Germanica* puts the case forcefully:

That which is best should be the dearest of all things to us; and in our love of it, neither helpfulness nor unhelpfulness, advantage nor injury, gain nor loss, honor nor dishonor, praise nor blame, nor anything of the kind should be regarded; but what is the noblest and best of all things should also be the dearest of all things, and that for no other cause than that it is the noblest and best.[1]

Here is a Christian idealism willing to count all things loss for Christ, an idealism beside which our cautious utilitarian pragmatisms stand revealed as tawdry tinsel.

Religion will always lead a precarious existence if it be regarded merely as a means to other ends, social, æsthetic, hygienic, or what you please. Those ends might be attained in some other way; in which case the services of religion would be no longer required. It would be superfluous. " 'Tis certain," says Emerson,[2] "that worship stands in some commanding relation to the health of man, and to his highest powers, so as to be, in some manner, the source of intellect." It is doubtless true, as Emerson believes, that worship stimulates intellect; but even though worship were hitherto the sole source of intellectual health, this fact would not guarantee the place of worship for the future. Intellect might at any time issue a declaration of independence.

If religion is to be worth having, it must produce some value of its own; within its own domain it must exercise creative power. He who faces God must say with the prophet, "Woe is me," and with the apostle, "Wretched man that I am," when he measures himself with the measuring-rod of God. If there be no cleansing

---

[1]Chap. VI, p. 17.
[2]*The Conduct of Life* (Everyman's Library), p. 255.

fire, no redeeming Lord, that is, no unique work of grace, worship can only be a source of deeper despair or (at best) of self-deception. But he who observes the facts of religious life, wherever the religious experiment has been made in good faith, cannot doubt that something has been created in the human soul that is felt to be of infinite value. "When the true Love and True Light are in a man, the Perfect Good is known and loved for itself and as itself."[3] The author of *Theologia Germanica* had no doubt about the creativity of worship. What, then, is the spiritual treasure that is created by the worship of God? To a consideration of this problem we shall address ourselves in the present chapter.

2. A CREATIVE UNIVERSE

The problem of creation has always been of interest to religion. God is usually regarded as the Creator. But theology has tended to stifle the very life of divine creativity by making creation a prerogative of the Almighty exercised once and for all long ago, and quite beyond the range of present human experience or understanding.

Yet if we are to say anything whatever about creation, it must be as an interpretation of human experience as we know it. All that we can say of God or man or nature is inevitably such an interpretation. If creation be something utterly remote, utterly unlike anything that we have experienced or known, all that may be said on the subject is mere elaboration of ignorance. If, however, creation be revealed as a fact of our conscious experience and of the world in which we live, then we have some clew to the creative Spirit of God who brooded on the face of the waters.

A creative God is the only sort of God worthy of wor-

[3] *Theologia Germanica*, Chap. XLIII, p. 167, Eng. tr.

ship. A God who has already done all that he proposes
to do and has left the universe in its present state may
be an object of compassion or of upbraiding; certainly
not of worship. A God who can change nothing, bring
nothing into being, create no new life, is a pitiable thing
—scarcely a God at all. Yet such a God has been the
residual Deity deposited by the mechanistic philosophy
which has been the official doctrine in many quarters
since the waning of idealistic influences in the middle
of the nineteenth century. Such a God is not worth
worshiping. So long as we believe that we live in a universe from which genuine novelty is excluded, the whole
enterprise of worship must, if we are conscious of the
implications of our own thinking, appear as futile self-
deception.

Modern thought, long in the bondage of this mechanism which denies all novelty, has been awakening to the
central importance of such facts as change, variation,
growth, and freedom. The theory of evolution, once
held to eliminate the Creator, is now seen to be patent
evidence of a creative force at work. When L. P. Jacks
calls this a *Living Universe,* or H. A. Youtz writes of
"creative personality" in a cosmos in which the spiritual
is supreme, or William Temple speaks of *Mens Creatrix,*
"Mind the Creator," these men are epitomizing the
newer insight that is coming to supersede mechanistic
interpretations of experience.

If the universe be truly creative, it is, insofar forth,
congenial to worship. It is the sort of universe that
worship takes it to be. We must, therefore, if we desire
secure intellectual foundations for our thought about
worship, consider some of the currents of thought that
are friendly to the idea of creativity.

Bergson's *Creative Evolution* (1907) comes to mind
at once as the modern classic of this point of view. The

world, he holds, is not a finished product but is in the making, being created constantly. Pragmatism, too, sounder in some of its metaphysical insights than in its doctrine of truth, has been a steady foe to any sort of block universe, and a friend of hope and novelty and freedom. Mr. Schiller expressed this aspect of pragmatism rather vividly in his presidential address before the Aristotelian Society (1921) on "Novelty." John Dewey and his collaborators wrote a volume called *Creative Intelligence* (1917), in which, it is true, "intelligence" has a special and restricted meaning, but which, none the less, dwells on its creative function.

It would, however, be a provincial error to suppose that interest in creativity is confined to Bergsonians and pragmatists. In many forms and sometimes in unexpected quarters the principle finds repeated expression. Wundt's doctrine of the creative resultant and his belief that spiritual energy tends to increase both imply creativity. One of the most original and influential of recent books on metaphysics (already discussed briefly in Chapter VI) is S. Alexander's *Space, Time, and Deity* (1920). For Alexander, Space and Time are the ultimate stuff of reality; but his real interest is in the movement of reality to higher levels rather than in this Space-Time stuff. This movement is creative; it is a cosmic process which strives toward the production of higher and higher qualities, new and better levels of existence. To this creative aspect of the cosmos he gives the name deity. Lloyd Morgan in his *Emergent Evolution* (1923) has continued and synthesized the work of Bergson and Alexander, setting forth at large the evidence for the emergence of new qualities, that is, for real creation, in the world of our experience.

The renewal of confidence in human freedom is another fact to be taken in this connection. The advocacy of freedom by Bergson, James, Royce, and Bowne has long been familiar. In the past few years writers so diverse as Müller-Freienfels, the German irrationalist, and Spaulding, author of *The New Rationalism* (1918), have alike defended freedom. Charles Peirce's writings on the subject have lately been made more available and influential by the publication of *Chance, Love, and Logic* (1923). Louis Arnaud Reid has shown the relations of reason and freedom in the *Monist*, 34 (1924), p. 528.

For our purpose the position of William McDougall is particularly instructive, since he rests the defense of freedom on the fact that mind creates. "That the human mind, in its highest flights, creates new things," says McDougall,[4] "thinks in ways that have never been thought before, seems undeniable in face of any of the great works of genius. . . . Why should we doubt that organic evolution is a creative process and that Mind is the creative agency?" Sorley has written that "the self is the cause of its own actions; and each action, although connected with the past, is yet a true choice determined by itself, a true creation."[5] The relations of purpose, freedom, and creativity are also brought out in the book by Edgar Pierce called *The Philosophy of Character* (1924). Jung, the psychoanalyst, brings support to belief in freedom from his very different approach. Driesch's *Metaphysik* (1924), a concise exposition of his present view, makes the doctrine of freedom a cornerstone of his system. It is true that Driesch interprets it as mere "Jasagen" or "Neinsagen" to a content which is determined, a mere "saying yes"

---

[4]*Outline of Psychology* (New York: Charles Scribner's Sons, 1923), pp. 447f.

[5]*Moral Values and the Idea of God* (2nd ed., Cambridge: University Press, 1921), p. 442.

or "saying no"; but this narrowing of the scope of freedom does not preclude its relation to a genuinely creative process.

Outside of the field of technical philosophy and psychology there has been a similar development of thought. Edward Carpenter's *The Art of Creation* (1894), one of the earlier products of this stream, was referred to with approval by James. Of late the idea has been popularized and applied in many fields. We may speak of a whole literature of creativity. Slosson's *Creative Chemistry* is a familiar illustration in the field of natural science, and Miss Follett's *Creative Experience* is an important application to the social sciences of the principle under discussion. It was doubtless inevitable that the idea should be put to such further use as is made of it in E. S. Holmes' *Creative Mind and Success.*

For our present purpose the application of the principle of creativity to religion is of primary interest. There is an abundant literature here. Cross has written of *Creative Christianity,* Drown of *The Creative Christ,* and Mrs. Herman of *Creative Prayer* (a book of high devotional value). In the philosophical interpretation of worship as creativity we undoubtedly owe most to Hocking's *Meaning of God in Human Experience;* Bennett's *Philosophical Study of Mysticism* makes further fruitful suggestions. The significant concept of creative personality is made central to the interpretation of religious experience both in Youtz's *The Supremacy of the Spiritual* and in Flewelling's *The Reason in Faith.*

This literature of creativity and freedom is not recording any utterly new discovery of modern times. There are few wholly new ideas in the world and the concept of creativity is not one of those few. What is happening is that a new emphasis is being given to a neglected aspect of experience. A hundred years ago Hegel saw, perhaps more clearly than any other thinker, the dramatic movement of creation both in our conscious experience and in the world of nature. The Hegelian *Idee* was a process, not a "block," as James wrongly thought. Hegel saw that life is a conflict of contradictory forces which lead to ever higher syntheses, and that every true synthesis, whether in the objective or the subjective order, is genuinely creative.

Poets and artists have always known the secret of creation. In the familiar and profound words of Browning, the musician's creativity is described:

"But here is the finger of God, a flash of the will that can,
    Existent behind all laws, that made them, and lo, they
        are!
And I know not if, save in this, such gift be allowed to man,
    That out of three sounds he frame, not a fourth sound,
        but a star.
Consider it well: each tone of our scale in itself is naught:
    It is everywhere in the world—loud, soft, and all is
        said:
Give it to me to use! I mix it with two in my thought:
    And there! Ye have heard and seen: consider and bow the
        head."

Historic religion has always known of God as creative power.

"Father Bel, faithful prince, mighty prince, thou createst the strength of life!"

"Since the gods created man, Death they ordained for man, Life in their hands they hold."[6]

The higher religions hold before their devotees a shining goal, the achieving of a new life in God, his gift.

"Then is the mortal no more mortal,
    But here and now attaineth Brahma."[7]

---

[6] G. A. Barton, *Archæology and the Bible* (American Sunday School Union, 1916), pp. 401, 412.

[7] G. F. Moore, *History of Religions* (New York: Charles Scribner's Sons, 1913), vol. I, p. 276.

Christianity fairly teems with the creative spirit. Its sacred book is the New Testament. It commands a new birth, promises a new heart. It is new wine, new cloth, a new commandment; to its followers is promised a new name; they shall sing a new song. They long for the New Jerusalem, a new heavens and a new earth, yes, a new creation. "Behold, I make all things new." Christian worship in early times, at least, was a novelty-creating force in the experience of men. The Christian God was a Creator who was a Redeemer. When a sect arose, the Gnostics, who sought to separate the two functions by declaring that the God who redeems is not the God who creates, it aroused great popular interest, but soon became a powerless intellectualism.

Now by roundabout ways, as we have seen, current thought is returning to the ancient insight of philosophy and art and religion, that reality is creative. Nevertheless, considering the intellectual temper of the age, it is somewhat surprising that the rediscovery of creativity has occurred so soon. This is an industrial, realistic, mechanistic age. Necessity has been in the saddle. Nature and society, life and mind, have all been conceived as subject to iron laws. Perhaps just because of the reign of determinism, it was time for freedom and creation again to emerge. Whatever the reason may be, on every side we see the insurgence of free life. The world is in a ferment. New forms of life are coming to birth in the realms of intellect and art, politics and industry; the revolt of youth is as symptomatic of the times as it is of youth.

It is easy to ridicule many of the forms that are assumed by the contemporary thirst for freedom. The search for new beauty in poetry and art seems often to be distracted and aimless. Yet behind it all there is a spiritual fact. Freedom is again emerging in the human

spirit; and the hunger for freedom is essentially a hunger for new powers and new values; that is, a hunger
for God, the Supreme Power and the Supreme Value.

It is an auspicious moment for religion to speak its
revealing word about the worship of God. It must be
admitted, however, that the authentic accent of spiritual
creativity has none too often been heard from the interpreters of religion. In too much of what has been
said and written under the name of creative Christianity the emphasis has been on changing forms of doctrine and belief, new views of the Scriptures, new husks!
If true religion is to be understood, there is less need of
fervid reiteration of commonplaces about intellectual
honesty and evolution than of more insight into the values that emerge when worship is evolved. Thought, we
are told, must seek higher levels in each generation;
the mind must make new forms and new adjustments.
Obviously, obviously! But why not take up the order
of the day: How does man, at any level, find God? In
the deeper literature of creativity and mystical experience there are signs that religious thought is turning
from the barren truisms of a shallow intellectualism to
a search for reality, for God himself.

3. What Worship Creates: Perspective

If religion be right in its faith that the true worship
of God is one of the highest points of the universal
creative process, there arises the problem, What is it
that worship creates? What qualities of life are produced? What sort of persons are made?

A complete account of the fruition of worship would
be impossible within the limits of a single chapter.
From the many fruits of the Spirit four will be selected
for special consideration, namely, perspective, a spiritual
ideal, power, and a community of love. These are a few

of the many "very lofty and lovely things touching a perfect life," which are the peculiar property of worship.

First, as has just been said, worship gives man perspective. The natural man starts with his body and its needs, what his senses experience and his desires demand, and with the conventions of his group. A certain perspective is given in the very conditions of existence; but it is not the ultimate perspective that man needs. The accidents of life soon force him to acknowledge that he and his are not all that exists. There are powers beyond his domain. He tries to explore their ways of acting, and to understand and control them for his own ends. But in worship he comes to his most intimate relations with those powers, relations of a quite different order from those of his natural life. Worship enables him to look at his life not alone from his own point of view, or from any human standpoint, but, in some measure, from the point of view of his God. If creative prayer be, as Mrs. Herman calls it, "the soul's pilgrimage from self to God,"[8] when one finds God, one finds a new perspective, which is not only new but unique.

This perspective is not identical with the emotional glow of a conversion experience or a mystical ecstasy. It is, rather, the insight that comes to man when his life and the whole world are set into relation to his God and when he thus recognizes himself as member of the whole in which God is supreme. For many mystical souls this experience of perspective and its attendant emotions are the whole of religion. For all who truly worship it is most precious. He who said, "Unless a man say in his heart, I and God are alone in the world, he will never find peace"[9] was expressing the common faith of most deeply religious natures. The vitality of pantheism

[8]*Creative Prayer*, p. 8.
[9]Abbott Alois, quoted by Herman, *Creative Prayer*, p. 65.

among mystics is probably due largely to its interpretation of this perspective. We are the branches; he is the vine. We are thus one with God. The intellectual defects of pantheism are, in the eyes of the mystic, atoned for by its religious genius. In recent times Bernard Bosanquet, as we saw in Chapter VI, has made the religious perspective beautiful and persuasive in his booklet, *What Religion Is*. "You cannot be a whole," he there told us, "unless you join a whole." John Dewey, a very different sort of thinker from Bosanquet, also speaks of religion in one of his books as "the freedom and peace of the individual as a member of an infinite whole."[10] Thus it is evident that religious worship connects man's inmost life with a realm that is more-than-human, more-than-social—the realm of what is eternally real.

Such a perspective is no mere barren theory, if, indeed, theories are barren; it is a force in life. It gives man what he most needs, namely, the combination of a sense of his personal worth with a sense of personal subordination. Either of these alone is easily achieved. A sense of personal worth is the native element of the natural man. A sense of personal subordination is the ready attitude of the fawning politician, the self-seeker, or any man who is in a mood of depression. But how easily each of these changes into something less valuable than itself! It takes but little to transform the sense of personal worth into intolerable self-conceit and the sense of subordination into false humility. But every true value creates the union of the two to some extent. Loyalty to the true or the good or the beautiful nourishes the worth of the individual and yet subjects him to the law of the ideal which he is seeking to attain. Yet no experience in life deepens and intensifies both of these

[10]*Human Nature and Conduct*, p. 331.

aspects in such perfect balance as does the worship of God. "The practice of the presence of God," says Jeremy Taylor, "is the cause of great modesty and decency in our actions . . . when we see ourselves placed in the eye of God."[11]

To be truly and inseparably a member of the whole of which God is the Supreme Power creates the sense of personal worth. Man communes with God! The Infinite God condescends to man, and seeks him as a shepherd seeks his lost sheep! Yet the sense of the value of one's own soul, while preserved, is set at once into violent contrast with an idea that serves as its check and balance. To be truly a member of the whole exalts my self-esteem; but to be member of such a whole! A whole of which God is center and source! Overwhelming power, blinding beauty, ineffable wisdom, stainless goodness, all reveal to me my dependence and my subordination. The transcendent God is infinitely beyond and above me. Positivism cannot at all understand this secret of worship. The language of worship never stops short with the consideration of the worth of the human soul or of human society; it speaks in utter humility and adoration the sacred name of God.

Personal worth and personal subordination thus fuse in the worshiper's experience. Out of this tension of opposites is born religious personality with its peculiar qualities—a poise that, while worship lives, can never become apathy, a peace that cannot become mere passivity, a joy that cannot become frivolity, a confidence that cannot become overconfidence. True religious worship, therefore, will feed the springs of inner life with a secret calm that supplants the fears which paralyze humanity. A popular writer has well said that "if hope and courage go out of the lives of common men, it is all

[11]*Holy Living*, p. 29.

up with social and political civilization."[12]   The rebirth
of worship is an urgent need of civilization.

No lesser and no other good than God gives to man
the perspective of which we have been speaking.   Out
of this perspective emerges the trust that leads the author of the *Theologia Germanica* to say, "I would fain
be to the Eternal Goodness what his own hand is to a
man," or the more tragic writer of Job to cry, "Though
he slay me, yet will I trust in him."   Without God-con-
sciousness culture may be a magnificent human achievement, but at its soul it will lack the absolute center of
peace which only the worshiper knows.

> "There is a point of rest
> At the great center of the cyclone's force,
>   A silence at its secret source;—
> A little child might slumber undistressed,
> Without the ruffle of one fairy curl,
> In that strange central calm amid the mighty whirl.
> So in the center of these thoughts of God. . ."[13]

Your programs of social reform, your ancient and op-
pressively solemn rites, your modern intellectualisms
are, if the truth were spoken, no worship, no religion,
unless they interpret God to men.

4. What Worship Creates: A Spiritual Ideal

Wherever true worship has created perspective the
current of spiritual life begins to flow deeper.   Worship,
we found, has a fashion of intensifying and enriching
itself as it proceeds from contemplation to revelation,
from revelation to communion, and from communion to
fruition.   These stages, as was remarked in the previous

[12]A. E. Wiggam, *The New Decalogue of Science* (Indianapolis:
Bobbs-Merrill Company, 1922), p. 262.

[13]Frances Ridley Havergal, in *Oxford Book of English Mystical
Verse* (Oxford: Clarendon Press, 1916), pp. 285f.   By permission of
Nisbet and Company, London, owner of the copyright.

chapter, do not necessarily follow any one order of development in time, but stand in most complicated interrelations. The perspective of which we have been speaking is that fruition of worship which is the outgrowth of reverent contemplation. The revelation which comes to the contemplating worshiper also creates its fruit, which we shall call the spiritual ideal.

The fact that man is an ideal-forming being is one of the most significant facts about him. How he comes to form ideals is a subject for psychological investigation. But let psychology describe that process in any way it please, for the worshiper two things will be true: he will see the law of that process as his God's way of working in the mind of man, and he will know that his ideal assumes its actual form precisely because he worships. When true worship creates perspective, it brings in its train an ideal of what spiritual life ought to be. The infinite perspective generates an infinite ideal of perfection. As Eucken has pointed out, the *Geistesleben,* the experience of ideal and eternal values, reveals a power at work in man beyond the merely human. Worship creates a vision of perfect life and an intense desire for its attainment. The most repellent forms of asceticism and fanaticism are at their heart but a perversion of the soul's longing to attain perfection.

God is perfect goodness, perfect value. The worshiper of such a God has had revealed to him an ideal of his own personality as completely devoted to the perfect values of his God. In the nature of this spiritual ideal lies its peculiar creativity. It is an unattainable, an inexhaustible ideal; one the pursuit of which is self-justifying and utterly satisfying, yet one which requires eternity for its realization. No infinitely repeated cycle of world history, of which the ancients dreamed, could express or exhaust this ideal. Nietzsche's doctrine of eternal recurrence is too meager a vehicle for it. "The spiritual ideal is," as Radoslav Tsanoff has recently pointed out,[14] "not eternal recurrence but eternal aspiration. God work is always being done, and never done with." The pragmatic notion of adjustment to the natural environment is but a mutilated fragment of what this ideal demands.

The nature of the spiritual ideal gives rise to problems, one of which we may now examine. Just how is the worshiper to think of the realization of this ideal? He believes that it has been revealed to him by God; in God, then, is its home, its guarantee, its eternal realization. Yet there is a peril in dwelling too exclusively on the realization of the ideal in God. If the universe be already perfected, there is ground for faith, but there is also ground for inaction, as was shown in the chapter on "The Moral Basis of Religious Values." The Divine Sovereign, divinely perfect, has made his universe the home of value. What has the religious soul to do but to accept and contemplate the divine perfection? Quietism is the natural conclusion from this premise. The logic of certain forms of absolutism, of pantheism, and of Calvinism all points in the same direction. Worship, then, is in peril of causing a barren and passive inaction. To "fold the hands and calmly wait" is the highest achievement of which this phase is capable. Calm faith is assuredly a blessing when it engenders loyalty, a curse when it creates indifference to the duties of life.

In order to avoid this peril of indifferentism some fly to the opposite extreme of holding that the ideal is to be made real, if at all, by man's own efforts. This is the typical attitude of the entirely nonreligious person; within the religious camp it develops the purely human-

[14]*The Problem of Immortality* (New York: The Macmillan Company, 1924), pp. 177f.

istic religion (if it may properly be called religion) which identifies the whole of religion with the Golden Rule, makes service its motto, and regards worship and inner spirituality as superfluities, or at best luxuries. Bertrand Russell, John Dewey, Ralph Barton Perry, and many other writers agree in this humanistic religion.

If these opposed perils are both to be avoided, the spiritual ideal of religion should constantly be viewed in the perspective of which we spoke earlier. When thus regarded, the realization of the ideal is seen to be an infinite cooperative process in the whole to which man belongs; yet man's part in that process, however small, is seen to be essential to the whole. The ideal that is born into the worshiping soul cannot then lead to mere blessed contemplation of a perfect universe when it is fully grasped in its total meaning; nor can it lead to mere feverish, despairing activity. What religion offers is the high adventure of cooperation with God.

5. WHAT WORSHIP CREATES: POWER

If religion created no more than the perspective and the ideal of which we have been speaking, it would have justified itself. Yet perspectives and ideals seem to the average man feeble and futile. He craves something that makes it possible for him to live in accordance with the ideal. That something is the creation of communion, the third stage of worship. The fruit of communion at its highest levels is power. From its most primitive forms to its most developed, religion has been a search for power, a faith that there were untapped reservoirs of spiritual energy in the unseen. He who in worship becomes conscious of communing with the Eternal God is able to report that he is endued with power from on high. "I am God's, who knows that I am. . . . And thus," says the shoemaker mystic, Jacob Boehme, "thus is the cure of my soul's sickness; he that will adventure it with me shall find by experience what God will make of him." "What is hereby intimated to the magus?" he asks in another quaint passage. "A mystery is hinted to him: If he will do wonders with Christ, and tincture the corrupt body to the new birth, he must first be baptized, and then he gets an hunger after God's bread, and this hunger has in it the verbum fiat, viz., the archeus to the new generation. . . . But I do not speak here of a priest's baptism; the artist must understand it magically; God and man must first come together ere thou baptizest, as it came to pass in Christ."[15] Boehme experienced power—the *verbum fiat*, the new generation.

Religious power has certain striking traits. In common with all power, it makes a new future possible for the person. That new future may not be a control of environment or of bodily disease, but perhaps something more valuable—the control of inner attitude. But religious power has an additional aspect that is more characteristic. Not only can it, within limits, control the future; it can also transform the past. The common idea that the past is a record that has been written once for all and can never be altered in the slightest iota is true enough so far as the content of the past is concerned; but it is not true of the meaning of the past. One never knows what a picture means until one has seen the whole picture. One cannot understand a poem from the first few lines; one must read the entire poem. Likewise one cannot read off the meaning of one's past experiences without considering their relation to the present and future. This fact is of great moment to

---

[15] *Signature of All Things*, etc. (Everyman's Library), pp. 104f., 67.

religion. The worshiper, believing that present and future may be given new power by his communion with God, has faith that his whole life, including his past, is also transformed by that same power. He who worships will always know that his past has been what it was, with all its weaknesses, sins, and shames. But before he communed with God that past was sin; after meeting God his past is still the same sin, but that sin forgiven, the sinner redeemed. The same facts are there; but religion has power to give them a different meaning. As the final stroke of the artist's brush changes the whole effect of a painting, so the experience of the forgiving mercy of God changes the whole effect of a soul.

Since the power that religion imparts is not mechanical but personal, not coercive but cooperative, it is an original experience, a liberation of the soul. Institutionalized religion has been and is to a regrettable extent the enemy of freedom; but the experience of worship is the soul's charter of liberty. Communion with God means freedom from bondage to the past, to the environing world, to the future; a freedom that comes from commerce with reality itself. The church has been a force in society partly because it has this charter of freedom. Religious power, then, is freedom; and its freedom is power.

6. What Worship Creates: A Community of Love

No account of the fruit of worship in personality would be complete if it omitted what is the supreme consummation of worship, and, if the experiences of religion foreshadow truth, the very goal and purpose of the universe: I mean, the Community of Love, or, as Royce called it, the Beloved Community. So far we have been considering the creative power of worship in the experience of the individual worshiper. But, however true it may be that in the act of worship there is always a "flight of the alone to the alone," and that the moment of worship is a temporary forgetting of one's fellow-men, the experience of finding God is also a rediscovery of every other human soul. Worship needs and finds a God who is God of all. National and tribal deities, gods of a special race or class, are not the God of the perspective and spiritual ideal of worship. From the point of view of worship every man is seen in his rela-tion to a God of inexhaustible resources whose name is Love; and hence humanity is given the task of real-izing the Community of Love.

This social fruitage, we maintain, is a necessary out-come even of the most individual acts of worship, when they are truly understood. A genuine relation of one soul to God must generate a relation of that soul to all of God's children in all their interests.

But this is not the whole story. Individual worship in the secret places of the heart is indeed essential to all true religion; but experience shows that when individ-uals come together and become a worshiping commu-nity, new spiritual levels are reached, new values created, new powers released. No function of conscious-ness remains precisely the same when others are present as when the individual is alone. Social worship adds new depth and meaning to the experience of God. It is not a substitute for private devotion, any more than opinions of one's social group are a substitute for one's conscience or intelligence. But through social worship love is made more sacred, the feeling of unity with our fellow creatures (for which John Stuart Mill yearned) becomes more vivid and binding, and the fact that God is God of all is more adequately expressed than through any private worship. Hence, he who seeks to be reli-gious apart from the worshiping congregation of the

church is surrendering more than he can well afford
to lose.

Worship, then, is necessarily social at its highest
point. It has been said, for example by Coe, that certain
forms of mystical experience are anti-social; that they
"involve turning away from the neighbor whom one has
seen, away from the whole sphere in which love can
act."[16] It must be granted that excesses may often be
found in the history of religious mysticism. But no
type of experience should be judged by its abnormal
forms; as well condemn sense-perception on the ground
that there are hallucinations of sense! The wellspring
of social unity and spiritual love in the mystical worship of the God of love should never be forgotten. Religious worship, alone of all the forces known to man,
is able to perform that miracle of pity and of hope which
enables him who has seen God to see not his fellow worshipers only, but all mankind, as a potential Community
of Love. That miracle, I say; for the natural man lacks
this vision; and the presence of traces of such a feeling
toward the human race is almost universally regarded
as a token of the presence and work of God in the life
of man.

7. The Preparation of the Soul for Creation

These are the creation of worship: perspective, the
spiritual ideal, power, and the community of love. Yet
with the description of these or other products of worship the question has not been answered which we human beings most need to have answered if worship be
all that faith takes it to be. That problem is, How may
the miracle be wrought in me? What forces are at my
disposal to produce the fair fruit of the Spirit?

[16]*Psychology of Religion* (University of Chicago Press, 1916),
p. 285.

The first answer that one might give is that there is no human answer; it is the gift of God. "The Spirit bloweth where it listeth; thou canst not tell." Not by measure and rule does God give himself to man, but as he will. Yet this answer is singularly unsatisfying. A God of arbitrary whim is not the object of worship. The worshiper's God is a God who may be trusted. His ways are not our ways; but his way is perfect and so it is reasonable and good. Thus the worshiper may ground his hope of discovering some of the ways that lead to God's creative working in the soul.

It would not be unreasonable to expect that there might be some analogy between creativity in the spiritual life and that on lower levels of existence. Observation shows that what Wundt calls the creative resultant occurs whenever the proper elements are brought together. Give Shakespeare's mind the vocabulary of the English speech plus his imagination, and a new creation occurs. Paint and the artist's utensils and the artist's soul produce a beauty which it would be fatuous to explain in terms of the crude material stuff which he employed. The creative resultant is a new whole which contains more than the elements which seemed to make it up.

Creation, then, as a general rule, happens when elements which are not usually united are brought together under proper conditions to produce a new whole. Many elements in our world lie side by side, mutually inert. On a study table are articles of metal and paper, wood and leather, ink and glass and rubber. Each is indifferent to the other. They might lie there for decades and nothing might happen to them save the accumulation of dust. But if fire should come into contact with them, they would all be changed. Something new would be created—in this case, something pitiably worthless. But if an organizing mind should use these same materials, adding to them what serves its purpose, then the new creation may be a thing of power and beauty, a drama or a poem. The elements thus combined obey an ideal will and assume a new form. In worship the elements that need to be brought together are the soul and God. When they are consciously and truly together the miracle happens which no words can fully describe.

In the present consideration of the forces that make for creativity the "negative path" of the mystic will be omitted from consideration in order that our thought may dwell more exclusively on the positively creative forces.

Of these forces the first is what may be called the preparation of the soul. No human being can create anything new unless something in his life has prepared the soil of his spirit for the germination and growth of the seed of the new life. In the language that we have been employing, contemplation of God, revelation from him, and communion with him are the necessary preconditions of creative worship. Lack of intense preparation of the soul accounts for the emptiness and feverishness of much that is regarded as religious, or at least as social, service. To expect the fruit of the Spirit without spiritual preparation for the same is to expect the impossible; it is to substitute mechanism for spirit. Religious faith cannot doubt that God is equally near to the souls of all men, to the grossest and dullest as well as to the most sensitive and obedient. Yet, though God be there, the miracle cannot happen to the unprepared soul. That is why so much of the talk about being religious without going to church is largely cant, and not pious cant either. New life is not created by magic, nor by wishing well toward Deity, nor even by enjoying nature in spiritual emptiness. Germs of life must be planted in the invisible regions of our spirit ere the mystery of creation can be enacted. God's creation of new life in us is not *ex nihilo;* the human attitude furnishes the necessary material. The process of fruition comes only after a process of fertilization.

8. Conflict as Creative

After the preparation, what then? What is the way that nature shows us? Is it not the way of growth through conflict? "Strife is the father of all things." Conflict is indeed a force that makes for creativity. Out of the tension of opposites, new levels of experience arise.

It is all too easy to make irresponsible use of this principle. Is conflict a creative force? Then, say some, any conflict is good. Let him who would climb the heights of artistic creation descend to the depths of dissolute living. Let him who would achieve power begin by seeking to destroy the power of others. Yet human history teaches on every page how self-defeating are many forms of conflict. Not all conflict leads to God. Not every war is the Holy War.

The spiritual conflict that generates power is a special kind of conflict. It is first of all the struggle of the soul toward God; then, the effort of the rational will to discover and maintain the tension of opposing forces in such manner as to preserve the value in each, yet also to lift the spirit to a higher level. Jacob Boehme understood

the opposition and combat in the essence of all essences. . . . Seeing, [he says] there are so many and divers forms, that the one always produces and affords out of its property a will different in one from another, we herein understand the contrariety and combat in the Being of all beings. . . .

And then we understand herein the cure, how the one heals another, and brings it to health; and if this were not, there were no nature, but an eternal stillness, and no will; for the contrary will makes the motion, and the original of the seeking, that the opposite sound seeks the rest, and yet in the seeking it only elevates and more enkindles itself.[17]

That is, spiritual conflict is essentially a dialectic movement that does not destroy but uses the energy in the cross-currents of the soul. Worship is not merely negative. Asceticism, therefore, is not true worship; true worship is growth and creation through conflict, that is, through seeing the relation of conflict to God, "the essence of all essences."

This conflict is partly within the individual; partly between the individual and society. For religious faith, all of these conflicts are aspects of the divine conflict initiated by God himself for the making of souls. It is safe to add that the worship of God is the only human experience large enough in its scope to be able to speak the word of creative control to all the impulses in man's breast; worship alone is the experience in which every conflict becomes creative power.

Not only do the conflicts within the natural man and his world serve as occasions for the development of power, but worship itself also generates new conflicts. He who contemplates dwells on the God he knows, yet he finds that God to be a mystery. The recipient of revelation is passive yet impelled to activity. He who communes with God attains a blessed intimacy, yet is overwhelmed with awe in the presence of the Holy One. Knowledge-mystery, activity-passivity, intimacy-awe— these conflicts and tensions in worship are ever creative of new levels of life. New impulses, new standards, new virtues, pour into the worshiping mind. This aspect of

---

[17] *Op. cit.*, p. 13.

worship is perhaps a reason for the religious uses of parable and allegory that conceal and yet reveal the thought and thus challenge the inner life.

9. SILENT SELF-POSSESSION AS CREATIVE

To the preparation of the soul and the conflict of which we have been speaking an additional element must always be present if the value of worship is to be realized. The spiritual life is the single mind, unified by concentration on one supreme purpose. Hence, self-possession is one of the most significant sources of creative power. Concentration always leads to new vision or new life. If we

> "See all sights from pole to pole
> And glance, and nod, and bustle by;
> And never once possess our soul
> Before we die,"[18]

we may be sure that no great creative moment will occur in our lives. But he who focuses the rays of the sun of being in the burning glass of his mind will see the tiny bright spot turn dark and darker until it bursts into flame. The Chinese sage Mencius knew something of the meaning of the power of self-possession when he said, "He who brings all his intellect to bear on the subject will come to understand his own nature; he who understands his own nature will understand God."[19] The sophisticated modern may smile at the naïve faith of the Oriental philosopher, but let him who has truly concentrated on the soul and God, if he will, cast the first stone.

The power of self-possession is too abundantly illustrated in the history of mysticism to require detailed

---

[18]Arnold's *Poetical Works*, p. 404.
[19]Tr. Giles, in *Confucianism and Its Rivals*.

exposition. Yet an age that has forgotten how to be silent and fears to be alone needs to be reminded that new life springs up in moments of solitary, concentrated meditation. The pious Boehme expresses this truth in dialogue form. The disciple asks, "But wherewith shall I hear and see God, forasmuch as he is above nature and creature?" The master replies, "Son, when thou art quiet and silent, then art thou as God was before nature and creature; thou art that which God then was; thou art that whereof he made thy nature and creature; Then thou hearest and seest even with that wherewith God saw and heard in thee before ever thine own willing or thine own seeing began."[20] Even when we meet with our fellows, spiritual natures do not need constantly to talk and act. Friends who can be silent together are friends indeed. There is a wise pastor, seeking to develop this source of power among his people, who conducts services of meditation which lead up to a final period of utter quiet; and, to quote his words, "in the last creative silence, things begin to happen."

10. THE VISION OF GOD AS CREATIVE

The forces that create spiritual values in the human personality may be analyzed and described as fully as we please, yet in the end they all come to one force, one experience, which is the beginning and end of worship and all religion. This one supreme force, which is the root of all creation in human worship, is the experience of seeing God. Contemplation is looking for God; seeing him is the experience that is reported by every soul that has made to the full the experiment of worship. Made, I say, to the full; for there are not many to-day who have the patience to "look at anything," as Mr.

---

[20] *The Signature of All Things*, etc. (Everyman's Library), p. 228.

Squire puts it, "long enough to feel its conscious calm assault."[21]

There are substantial reasons why the idea of God is a creative power in human life, and therefore the truest religion is always theocentric. Some few of these we may consider briefly.

Seeing God is a creative experience, first of all, because to see God is to confront reality. An evil and adulterous generation seeketh a sign; that is, it seeks something foreign to reality. A neurasthenic generation seeketh alcohol or any form of stimulation that will conceal reality from eyes too weak to stand its light. Hope for new and wholesome human life dawns the moment men are willing to confront the facts. Now some have thought that religion was one more mechanism for escape from the stern realities of this life into a compensatory world of the imagination, where all is bright and fair. For this view of the nature of religion there is considerable historical evidence in the beliefs that have actually been held. But if one take a broad view of the purpose that has inspired the great religious personalities, one cannot believe that religion has been experienced by them as a mechanism of escape. They have sought the real, the living God; their prayer has been, "Thy will, not mine, be done." If genius be objectivity, then the religious genius must be one of the highest types; for religion, in its highest aim, is objectivity regarding those matters of value, destiny, and eternity regarding which objectivity is most difficult to attain.

Again in a still different way the worshiper's vision of God is creative. While it inspires him to confront the real, it leads him beyond the partial glimpse of reality

[21] J. C. Squire, in the poem, "Paradise Lost," *Poems, First Series* (New York: Alfred A. Knopf, 1919), p. 97.

that is his immediate experience to a broad view of the whole meaning of his life and his world.   Religious worship, then, fosters creativity by its breadth of view.   Miss Follett has recently remarked that a fact out of relation is not a fact; and quotes Mr. Justice Holmes as saying that it is not "the acquisition of facts (which is important) but learning how to make the facts live, . . . leap into an organic order, live and bear fruit."[22]   This is, in essence, the familiar Hegelian doctrine which Royce had in mind when he used to say that a hand apart from the body is no longer a hand.   If religion taught us only to confront reality as a collection of brute facts, it would be barren.   It bears fruit abundantly because it sets all the facts in relation to the plan of the whole, which it calls the will of God.   Thus it broadens the field of vision and gives an indescribable exaltation to the life that deeply experiences it.   "Whosoever obtaineth [the love of God]," says Boehme,[23] "is richer than any monarch on earth; and he who getteth it is nobler than any emperor can be, and more potent and absolute than all power and authority."   This extraordinary enlargement of self-consciousness arises from the infinity of the God who is seen.

Further, to see God is to catch a glimpse of universal purpose, of total meaning in life.   Even one glimpse of that universal meaning and universal love is enough to impart a new quality to a human life.   No worshiper believes that to see God is to understand him fully; but no worshiper believes that God remains wholly unseen to the spiritual eye.   If only for a moment we see God, we are like the scientific investigator to whom has occurred suddenly the clew that will explain the mass of

[22]M. P. Follett, *Creative Experience* (New York: Longmans, Green & Co., 1924), p. 12.

[23]*Op. cit.*, p. 258.

facts which he has accumulated, or like the poet who has been given the inspiration for a poem, or like the preacher in whose soul the plan of a stirring sermon has emerged—save that in the case of the worshiper the plan that is revealed is the total plan of the cosmos, veiled in mystery, it is true, but a mystery of wisdom and love. Saint Augustine reports a simple psychological experience which may serve as an illustration here. When he is about to repeat a psalm which he knows, he says, "Before I begin my expectation extends over the whole," *"in totum expectatio mea tenditur."*[24] This experience of memory is also typical of creation, *"in totum expectatio mea tenditur."* The whole over which the expectation of the worshiper extends is the very plan of God; and hence in worship some of the noblest fruits of human life are born. It is perhaps one function of the constant repetition of ritual forms to symbolize the ever-present oneness of the creative God.

One final aspect of the vision of God will be mentioned. He who worships is conscious of seeing a God who hides himself. The great philosophies and religions agree in this: that God does not reveal himself to sense, and that no revelation of him to man is complete; but that this God, partly revealed, partly hidden, is drawing the world to himself by love.

From sense God is wholly hidden; at best the objects of our sense experience serve as signs and symbols of the beyond. Of all that we can see we must say, God is not this, not this! Yet while God is wholly hidden from sense the discerning mind of the worshiper sees that sense is a veil which conceals hidden meaning; nay, more, it is, as Berkeley says, a divine language. It is not merely maya and illusion. But one must go beyond

---

[24]*Conf.*, XI, 27 (Loeb, II, 276).

the language to him who utters it if one is to find the God who hides himself.

Likewise from feeling God is hidden. It is true that the experience of worship is an experience of deep feeling. Worship without feeling is a barren thing, if it be worship at all. The mystic's experience is chiefly feeling; a feeling of which the author of the *Theologia Germanica* can write, "A single one of these excellent glances is better, worthier, higher and more pleasing to God than all that the creature can perform as a creature."[25] Yet assurance that the God experienced by feeling is indeed the God of reality is never given by any feeling, no matter how ecstatic or satisfying. Further, feeling at best gives us a single focusing of the life of God in the soul; its content may be intense and ineffable, but feeling is a meager interpretation of the rich life of the Supreme Person, God. God, then, remains hidden from feeling.

He is also to some extent hidden from thought. Thought, it is true, is necessary to worship. Without some idea of God a religious feeling could not be distinguished from the feeling of intoxication or anæsthesia, nor could fanaticism be distinguished from reasonable faith. The popular prejudice against doctrine is intelligible as a blind reaction against arid overemphasis on it; but it is not intelligible as an interpretation of the truth about religion. The intellectual interpretation of God is a necessary phase or adjunct of worship. The complete divorce between religion and philosophy means, in the end, the barbarization of religion, a thing even more to be dreaded than the Hellenization of Christianity, which troubles Harnack. Yet it must also be freely confessed that God remains hidden from the

---

[25] Chap. IX, p. 26, Eng. tr.

truest and loftiest philosophical thought. As Royce said, "The divine truth is essentially coy. You woo her, you toil for her, you reflect upon her by night and by day . . .; in fine, you prepare your own ripest thought and lay it before your heavenly mistress when you have done your best. Will she be pleased? . . . Will she say, 'Thou hast well spoken concerning me'? Who can tell? Her eyes have their own beautiful fashion of looking far off when you want them to be turned upon you; and, after all, perhaps she prefers other suitors for her favor."[26]

Some conception of the Divine Person may, I believe, be attained by thought and must be understood as well as possible if the worshiper is to maintain his self-respect. But thought must always hold its results humbly and open to correction, with the awareness that there is infinitely more beyond the best thought of the present. No theology, no philosophy, is absolute. Only the Absolute is absolute. God does not wear his heart upon his sleeve. His face is not an open book. Thought about him is an *unendliche Aufgabe,* an infinite task— a creative life-career for an immortal soul, indeed, but a career in which the hidden God will forever be sought, revealing much, yet ever luring on by hints of a mystery that lies beyond.

11. THE CENTRAL PLACE OF THE WILL

All that God is can never be revealed to man. The vision of God will never be perfect. Yet the experiment of worship reveals the fact that the adoration of this God who is known yet unknown, present yet absent, found in our feeling and thought yet transcending all

---

[26]*The Spirit of Modern Philosophy* (Boston: Houghton Mifflin Company, 1892), p. 73.

that we shall ever find, is the secret source of what is perhaps the mightiest creative power on which our human life can rely. The God who is hidden from sense and feeling and thought is most completely revealed as the creator of the fruits of worship. Yet this statement is misleading unless it be at once added that God creates the fruits of worship only in the life of the worshiper. To use the language of James Bissett Pratt, the benefits of subjective worship come only to him who engages in objective worship. Worship is the complete personality of man directed toward and responding to the presence of God. Hence, the vision of God that is truly creative will use the facts of sense and of feeling and of thought, but will not rest content with any one of those phases. It will learn that the hidden God is found adequately for our human needs only by the whole personality in action, that is, controlled by what we call will. In the end, the will of our total personality to cooperate with God is the key to the vision of God and to the ingress of the creative Spirit of God into human life. It is this will that disciplines the preparation of the soul, holds it steady in conflict, that is necessary to self-possession, and that seeks a vision of the God beyond ourselves. A will steadily directed to God is the chief essential to creative worship. That this standpoint is not a mere moralistic perversion of worship, a shallow salvation-by-character, is evidenced by the testimony of the mystic whom we have frequently cited, Jacob Boehme. "Therefore," he says, "let the true Christendom know, and deeply lay to heart, what is now told and spoken to her, viz., that she depart from the false conjecture (or opinion) of comforting without conversion of the will."[27]

---

[27] *Op. cit.*, p. 203.

12. Conclusion of the Chapter

This brings us to the end of our study of creative worship as the essence of religious value. We have only to summarize our results and hint briefly at one inference from them.

We have shown that contemporary thought, in many of its currents, is recognizing the principle of creativity and freedom as a real factor both in man's psychological experiences and in the objective world. This tendency of thought is a revolt against mechanism and sets the stage for the conception of a creative God. When we seek signs of the creative work of God in the experience of worship, we find at least the four traits that we mentioned, namely, a unique perspective, a spiritual ideal, power, and the creation of a Community of Love. When we ask how these values are created in man's life or on what forces he may rely for their attainment, we find several powerful factors—the preparation of the soul, conflict, self-possession, the vision of God, and the will of the worshiper.

A few words about the God revealed in worship will bring the chapter to a close. Theology and philosophy alike have, on the whole, thought of God not only as eternal, absolute, and infinite, but also as changelessly perfect. He has usually been viewed as one to whom and in whom nothing can really happen, for all possible happenings are present to him in one eternal Now. The experience of worship, like the experience of obligation, suggests that God's life may be richer and more plastic than this traditional absolutism has believed. God is not found as a static being; he is found as one who works and creates, a God whose favorite method is evolution, process, novelty-producing. Worship, then, is an experience which opens new vistas in human life and gives us a God whose acts of creation are as eternally new as the laws of his being are constant. The miracle of religion is the ever-creative God and his symbol is "the tree of life which bare twelve manner of fruits and yielded her fruit every month."

CHAPTER X

PHILOSOPHY AND RELIGIOUS EDUCATION

1. The Problem of the Chapter: Topsy and an Elephant

THE preceding chapters of this book have developed a theory of religious values based on what is believed to be a reasonable interpretation of experience and its implications. According to our view, religious values, in order to be truly valuable and worthy of devotion, must be both coherent and moral; and yet in them is revealed more than mere reasoning or moral effort could produce if there were not a more-than-human Person, the eternal God, who reveals himself to man and creates in him values that elevate his life above the plane of natural instinct and desire.

If this be true, religion is essentially a matter of man's conscious relation to God. It is not a set of useful habits or of socially adjusted behavior-patterns; nor is it mere loyalty to any abstract ideals, however true or useful those ideals may be. Religion bears habits, behavior, ideal loyalties, as its fruit; but these things are not its root. Its root, if we are right, is in man's inner consciousness, where he seeks and finds a God to worship—or loses God and seeks some substitute for him.

This conception of religious value, as we have seen in our discussions, is not held by all. Many find in "service," in devotion to "science and democracy," or in some other social ideal what they believe is an equivalent for worship; and some call this supposed equivalent by the holy name of religion. It is as though the apple were

238

called an apple tree. The apple contains seeds of potential apple trees; and service, likewise, contains the seeds of potential religion. But until those seeds are planted and watered, until they send their roots deep down into the earth and their sprouts up into the air and sunshine, the apple remains an apple, and its seeds may die; and service is merely service and not vital religious life.

The problem, then, that confronts the thoughtful observer of modern tendencies is both theoretical and practical. He must not only ask, as we have done in this volume, whether the popular humanistic positivism of current thought and practice is true; he must also consider the possible consequences of his reflective thought for the actual religious life of humanity.

The philosopher should not assume an airy indifference to the effect of his teachings on life. Although pragmatism has greatly overemphasized the value of consequences as a test of truth, it must be granted that the whole truth about any idea can never be known until all of its consequences are taken into account.

Now, if the personalistic theory of religious values at which we have arrived is true, a radical criticism and reform of many current programs of religious education is called for. It may be said without exaggeration that religious education is in as serious peril from the dogmatic and uncritical provincialism of those who take the behavioristic pragmatism of the moment for the whole truth as it is from the dogmatic and uncritical provincialism of the so-called "fundamentalist." Uncritical affirmation and uncritical negation are equally unsound. There has been too much of both. The dogmatist refuses to think critically because he is too sure that he has a revealed metaphysics which needs no further thought; and the positivistic pragmatist is too sure that society can take the place of God, and socialized

behavior the place of worship. To both, the deeper problems of life are a strange tongue.

Both extremes, furthermore, are alike in that for them
the problem of religious education is essentially a problem of means rather than of ends. For the extreme
dogmatist the ends of religion are given in uncritical
conceptions about the Scriptures and revelation; for the
extreme humanist those ends are restricted to "science
and democracy," or the adjustment of human animals
to their natural environment. Neither extreme is willing to subject its preconceived ends to critical examination in the light of the total meanings and values of experience as a whole. Both, then, are, in their fundamental spirit, anti-philosophical. To any questioning
of their presuppositions they interpose a stringent
verboten—it is not done!

If our theory were merely one more dogma to be added
to the collection of dogmas, it would be in an equally
unreasonable position. But, while we have arrived at
a specific interpretation of religious values, the present
chapter is not written to persuade dogmatist and positivist to exchange old dogmas for new. The practical aim
of this chapter is, rather, to show that no theory of religious education is worth while unless it is based on a
genuinely philosophical interpretation of religious
values and therefore of the aims of religious education.
Religious life is molded by religious thought.

The view to which we are opposed may be called the
Topsy theory of the aims of religious education. Topsy
was not born; she "just growed." Holders of the Topsy
theory believe that the aims of religious education
should not be inquired into any more precisely than
Topsy wished to inquire into her nativity. These aims
may be found full-grown, on the one hand, in revelation,
or, on the other hand, in the spontaneous whims, fancies,

and desires of unenlightened, uncriticized human nature. Topsy is willing to think about how to get what she wants, but she is not willing to think about whether she wants what she ought to want. Whether Topsy swears by the Council of Trent or Calvin, or by Rousseau or Dewey, she remains Topsy until she is willing to face and think through the problems of a coherent interpretation of experience as a whole. She "growed"; let her also interpret as best she may to what end she was born. The "critical" or "creative intelligence" for which instrumentalism rightly pleads is needed not alone for understanding the instruments which shall make effective the ends that are given in revelation or in biological instinct, but it should also be set to work on the task of reinterpreting the meaning of what Rufus M. Jones calls "the fundamental ends of life."[1]

As this book began with an interpretation of the theory of reasonableness as coherence, so let it end with an interpretation of the practical task of religious education as rooted in a coherent view of religious values. Religious education is in great need of a genuine philosophical background against which it shall "see life steadily and see it whole."

John G. Saxe was not a great poet, but his whimsical stanzas on "The Blind Men and the Elephant" contain much wisdom. Both philosophers and religious educators might well lay its teaching to heart. The six blind men gave six different descriptions of the elephant. He seemed very like a wall, a spear, a tree, a fan, or a rope according to the part of his body that the blind men laid hold of. The poem ends with the following stanzas :[2]

---

[1] R. M. Jones, *The Fundamental Ends of Life* (New York: The Macmillan Company, 1924).

[2] *The Poems of John Godfrey Saxe* (Diamond ed., Boston: Houghton, Osgood and Company, 1880), p. 136.

"And so these men of Indostan
  Disputed loud and long,
Each in his own opinion
  Exceeding stiff and strong,
Though each was partly in the right,
  And all were in the wrong!

"So oft in theologic wars,
  The disputants, I ween,
Rail on in utter ignorance
  Of what each other mean,
And prate about an Elephant
  Not one of them has seen!"

It may be remarked if any one of the blind men had continued his investigations as far as he could, even though blind, he would have been able to give a reasonably correct account of the elephant. If the group had been willing to pool results the outcome would have been very near the truth. But as long as each man sticks to his dogma without seeking a completely coherent view, only confusion will result. Philosophy suggests that Topsy consider the entire elephant; at least that we omit no observation which we can make with the equipment which nature has given to us.

Philosophy is the habit of considering the whole. Let us now proceed to inquire what contribution philosophy can make to the theory of religious education.

2. THE AIM OF RELIGIOUS EDUCATION

The aim of religious education may be very simply put; it is to teach the human race to live religiously. It is the thesis of the present chapter that anyone who wishes to succeed with such an aim needs a comprehensive philosophical outlook. This thesis receives immediate support from a comparison of the aim of religious education with the aim of philosophy. The aim of philosophy is to interpret human experience as a whole. Philosophy tries to consider all the facts there are, and all approaches and points of view, and then to unify and interpret them by a world view. It includes the results of science, the values of life, all that is "practical" as well as all that is "theoretical," and aims to understand experience as a whole in the light of all the facts and meanings that we can find. Philosophy is the habit of taking everything into account and of thinking coherently about everything; a rare attainment, but an alluring and necessary ideal!

It is evident, as has been said, that the two problems are related. To define what it means "to live religiously," and whether religion be true and worth attaining, clearly requires philosophical perspective. It is true, as we have seen, that there are many men of many minds at work on philosophy, and that their results are not in agreement, nor are all friendly to religion; yet it is clear that if religious education is to commend itself to men of intelligence, religion itself must appeal to their intelligence. This appeal can be made only by setting religion in relation to all human thinking and living; that is, by a philosophical study of its truth and value.

We may go so far as to say that if ideas and beliefs play any part in religion or in education, philosophical criticism is imperative to save fundamental ideas from dogmas and from fads, from prejudices and from provincialism. The words of the great Bishop Berkeley may well be applied to the religious educator: "Whatever the world thinks, he who hath not much meditated upon God, the human mind, and the *summum bonum,* may possibly make a thriving earth-worm, but will most indubitably make a sorry patriot and a sorry statesman," and, we may add, a sorry teacher of religion.

3. Objections to Recognizing the Place of Philosophy in Religious Education

The case for the need of philosophy is so clear that, if logic were the only force in human life, objections could be ignored. Unfortunately, however, we are not all logical, and we kick against the pricks of reason.

The "plain man" (and especially the plain child) is evidently no philosopher. He is not trained in the universities; and even if he is, that does not prove that he can think. Now, religion is for the plain man, for his every-day consumption. Philosophy is quite above his head, and confuses and distresses rather than helps and enlightens him. Hence, it is argued, philosophy is religiously useless.

There is no doubt that many people have been and are good and religious without knowledge of or regard for technical philosophy. Indeed, many good and religious people abhor the word "philosophy" as they should abhor sin. Nevertheless, it may be safely asserted that no person has ever been either good or religious without doing some thinking, however meager it may be. The good man, even though wholly untrained in theories, must be able to grasp a moral principle, to distinguish right from wrong, and to apply his principles to his conduct; the religious man must also have thought somewhat about God and God's relation to him. No religion is possible without some conception of the values that religion is after, and it is a religious need, as well as an intellectual demand, to give a reason for the faith that is in us. All such thinking—about obligation, about God, about ideals—is in principle philosophical. It may not be skillful, or technical, or learned; it may not use the language or come to the conclusions of the schools; but it is philosophy, good or bad, adequate or inadequate. Whatever is wholly below the thought-level, without idea or belief or ideal, is neither morality nor religion. The dumb devotion of the dog is either more or less than it appears to be; either the dog has some ideas or he does not know what he is doing at all. Utterly dumb devotion, whatever else it may be, is not religion.

From these facts it follows, not that a man must study philosophy before he has a right to worship the Almighty, but that he has a right to expect and demand help from those who have studied philosophy. Even though the plain man may never grasp technical philosophy, his religious educators should do so, if they regard their task seriously. The physician must know anatomy, physiology, pathology, and much more that his patients need never know; but the patients must take some thought for their bodies and must have some respect for the knowledge of their physicians if they are to be treated. Likewise the religious educator should have an expert knowledge that will command respect, and that will be available for application to the needs of the humblest.

The objection in behalf of the humble believer is, therefore, without force. The more humble believers there are, the more need there is for intelligent leadership. The plea for blind guides to guide the blind is so often made that its intrinsic folly is sometimes overlooked. But from a different quarter there arises another sort of objection to philosophy in religious education. The dogmatic traditionalist objects to philosophical criticism because he has observed that philosophical thinking often leads to readjustment, and readjustment is fatal to the comfortable finality of his dogmatism. But the position of the anti-philosophical dogmatist is most precarious. His own system of doctrine is a highly rationalistic conceptual structure and makes an intellectual appeal. He must either say that his system is so final that it is futile and even wicked to question it, or he must make his appeal to the forum of reasonable thinking—that is, to philosophy. The recent book by E. Y. Mullins, *Christianity at the Crossroads,* is an able, but unsuccessful, attempt to get along with and without philosophy at the same time. The greatest defenders of religion, Protestant and Catholic and Jewish and Mohammedan and Hindu and Buddhist, have usually agreed in holding that religion is based on reasonable considerations and is in harmony with reason, however far beyond reason the Infinite may lie. If this belief be true, philosophy is necessary. If it be not true (as some extreme dogmatists hold), then, lo! philosophy has crept in unawares—namely, the philosophy of skepticism. Free philosophical investigation cannot destroy truth and must in the end help it; such investigation is truly disturbing as well as arduous, but it is necessary if religion is to avoid skepticism, and if religious thinking and secular thinking are to be correlated. The truth-lover must constantly readjust practice and belief to truth.

Not all dogmatism is in the camp of traditionalism. Topsy is two-sided. There are also dogmatic devotees of what Perry has called "the cult of science." Such dogmatists join hands with religious traditionalists in wishing to exclude philosophy. They base their results (so they say) on what can be tested by the senses and experimentally verified. Philosophy, they declare, not only deals with what we can never perceive by sense, but also with what is essentially unverifiable. Philosophers squabble forever, world without end, and come to no conclusion, while men of science are agreed in their main results. Without seeking to defend philosophy from these strictures we must remark that the devotee of science who rejects philosophy on these grounds has also logically included religion in what he rejects. He who will believe only what may be verified by the senses cannot believe in duty, or in ideals, or in God; he can recognize no values and can believe in no human consciousness, his own or that of another. If only what can be observed by sense-perception is true, then literally nothing is true but sense objects and reason itself must be abandoned. The cause of reason and the cause of religion stand together.

Fortunately, no men of science carry the logic of the cult of science to this extreme. The great scientists are the first to recognize the limitations of scientific method, and the fact that the values of life have a validity that does not rest on laboratory results. This was significantly shown in the well-known joint statement issued by representative scientists, religious leaders, and men of affairs and published in the press of May 26, 1923. This statement contained the following:

The purpose of science is to develop, without prejudice or preconception of any kind, a knowledge of the facts, the laws, and the processes of nature. The even more important task of religion, on the other hand, is to develop the consciences, the ideals, and the aspirations of mankind. Each of these two activities represents a deep and vital function of the soul of man, and both are necessary for the life, the progress, and the happiness of the human race.

Such an utterance, signed by scientists like R. A. Millikan, Charles D. Walcott, H. F. Osborn, E. G. Conklin, J. R. Angell, J. M. Coulter, W. J. Mayo, and numerous others, ought to silence the narrow idea that science precludes consideration of the higher values of life. On the contrary, the very form of the statement challenges thought to a philosophical investigation of the relations of the point of view of science and the point of view of value.

One further comment should be added. The results of science are, of course, of the utmost importance in religious education. They reveal effective mechanisms for the control of experience. But he who studies these mechanisms without studying the extra-scientific assumptions made by all moral and religious beliefs and experiences will be out of contact with religious realities; he may be efficient, but he will be ineffective; he may be practical, but his work will be shallow and empty. He will be like a contractor who has the materials for building, but no architect's plans.

Again, it is said by some social theorists that philosophy is, on social grounds, incompatible with the calling of the religious educator. These persons regard philosophy as essentially anti-social. They are not wholly without a basis for their strictures. It must be admitted that philosophy is in a sense a luxury; one has no time to philosophize unless the body has been clothed and fed. Now, the social thinkers of whom mention was made regard it as sheer self-indulgence and intellectual snobbishness to engage in reflections about the nature of matter and of mind when the social needs of the world are so great; thought should be devoted to bringing war to an end, to solving the problems of labor and capital, to international understanding and cooperation rather than to metaphysical niceties.

A reference to the true function and task of philosophy refutes the charge brought by these objectors. What is philosophy? It is a patient, thorough, persistent attempt to inquire what human experience means, what is truly valuable and worthy of our belief and our allegiance. If ever there was a time when such an inquiry was a pressing social necessity, it is to-day.

To a large extent the ills of the world are due to the beliefs and the valuations of the human mind. The social worker must either aim to give people what they want or what they ought to have. To continue to aim at giving them what they want is to continue the low standards that now exist. To aim at giving them what they ought to have means that someone must do the work of the philosopher and reflect on what that may be, and then put it in a form so intelligible and so persuasive as to convince the minds of unprejudiced men. The task of interpreting the highest values of life needs to be undertaken afresh by or for every human being. To suppose that this task has been completed, so that we need trouble no more about philosophy, or to suppose that it ever will be completed, is to suppose that the human mind can stand still, and find no new problems. A social philosophy, founded in our general world view, is an imperative need of the distracted present.

In spite of the foregoing considerations, it must be admitted that some philosophers have held that there was no relation between philosophy and life. Philosophy, they have held, is a mere play of the intellect, a purely theoretical activity, while practical life goes on in a "water-tight compartment" by itself. Historically, David Hume represented this point of view. He admitted that his philosophy gave him no light on the problems of life, but, rather, obscured them. He says:

The intense view of these manifold contradictions and imperfections in human reason has so wrought upon me, and heated my brain, that I am ready to reject all belief and reasoning, and can look upon no opinion even as more probable or likely than another. Where am I, or what? From what causes do I derive my existence, and to what condition shall I return? Whose favor shall I court, and whose anger must I dread? What beings surround me? and on whom have I any influence, or who have any influence on me? I

am confounded with all these questions, and begin to fancy
myself in the most deplorable condition imaginable, envi-
roned with the deepest darkness, and utterly deprived of
the use of every member and faculty.

Most fortunately it happens, that since reason is incapable of dispelling these clouds, Nature herself suffices to that
purpose, and cures me of this philosophical melancholy and
delirium, either by relaxing this bent of mind, or by some
avocation, and lively impression of my senses, which obliter-
ate all these chimeras. I dine, I play a game of back-
gammon, I converse, and am merry with my friends; and
when, after three or four hours' amusement, I would return
to these speculations, they appear so cold, and strained, and
ridiculous, that I cannot find in my heart to enter into
them any further.[3]

Among present-day thinkers Durant Drake is an
earnest advocate of the position that our epistemological
and metaphysical conclusions can have no useful effect
on life. It must be said, however, that this represents
a failure to take note of the full function of philosophy.
If philosophy does not interpret life, and show the relations between our living and our thinking, it fails in its
task. If the world of thought and the world of action
are to be severed, then we have on the one hand life
without meaning, and on the other meaning without life.
Each is inadequate, incoherent, self-defeating. We have
not thought our way through to a true philosophy until
we have interpreted the relations between the two.

Others take the opposite position, namely, that philosophy should be debarred from the training of the religious leader because there is danger in too intimate a
relation between philosophy and life. Two instances of
such possible danger will be mentioned.

As a first instance let us consider the psychological
effect of philosophizing. Too much philosophy, we are

---

[3] *Treatise of Human Nature* (Everyman ed.), pp. 253-254.

told, is bad for a man. Those who take this position mean, in the bottom of their hearts, by "too much," "any at all." Philosophy, these people say, overdevelops the intellect, starves the emotional and active nature, stimulates criticism, and chokes appreciation and creativity. That this is a real danger no one with a wide acquaintance among young doctors of philosophy can doubt. Leonard Bacon's satires on *Ph.D.'s* (New York: Harper & Brothers, 1925) are joy to these critics. But that the danger is so serious as is supposed by those who urge it is very doubtful. The great philosophers have been men of rich and many-sided interests, of creative genius, appreciative of art, morality, religion, in close contact with life. While it is true that narrow devotion to certain types of philosophical problems leads to a shriveled soul and a barren intellectualism, such devotion is no full expression of the philosophical spirit. Indeed, it may safely be asserted that, of all the subjects that a religious educator could study, no subject is so broadening, so challenging to every side of life and thought, as is philosophy. It unifies and stimulates activity in all fields of any value at all. Every other study is confined to some special field, however broad that field may be; philosophy alone includes all fields. It is the most human, the most inclusive, the most spiritual of disciplines. The objection under discussion, then, is not an objection to philosophy, but to certain would-be philosophers, who find it difficult to assume a genuinely philosophical point of view.

A second instance is of very different nature. A prominent religious educator has expressed himself to the writer substantially as follows: "If you are going to lay so much stress on philosophical background, is there not a danger lest only such men as have the 'right' philosophical background should be able to find employment?" In short, is there not a danger of a new orthodoxy, a new dogmatism, based on economic pressure? This would appear to the writer to be a highly academic objection. It would seem that the tendency of philosophers to think fairly independently would take care of this possibility. Nevertheless, it must be granted that, theoretically at least, there is something in it. The danger may be lessened in two ways: first, by training a philosophical and a religious spirit that will guard intellectual and spiritual integrity over against economic and social pressure; and, secondly, by recognizing the right of society to demand certain standards of its teachers. Regarding the first suggestion, it must be granted that in every field the economic imperative makes itself felt; more and more is it necessary that the philosopher shall raise the standard of the ideal imperatives of reason and value. This cannot be done by insisting on conformity to any one system; but it does demand devotion to the truly philosophical spirit.[4] As to the second suggestion, it will surely be admitted that no one has the right to be a secular teacher if he denies the value of secular education; and no one has the right to be a religious teacher if he denies the value of religious education. That is to say, society has the right to demand that her teachers, if not her kings, shall be in some sense philosophers—shall have thought through the meaning and value of what they are doing.

The theoretical arguments having been exhausted, many will at this point in the discussion fall back on practical objections. Such persons would admit that philosophy ought to be included in the background of religious education, but hold that it is practically impossible to require it. On the one hand, the practical

[4]See E. S. Brightman, *An Introduction to Philosophy*, Chaps. I and XI.

demands on the religious worker are too great; he must act constantly, he has no time to think, that is, no time to think about philosophy. On the other hand, philosophy is said to be too arduous for the average religious educator to master; it requires a special talent, a special type of mind; why impose it on those that lack this talent? Nothing could be truer than that it is impractical to expect all religious educators to be scholarly experts in philosophy, or, for that matter, in psychology, or pedagogy, or knowledge of the Bible, or in any subject. But it is one thing to be scholarly and expert in a subject; it is another to be thoughtful and intelligent in that field. The latter is the least that should be required of trusted leaders.

If it is impractical for a person to "meditate much upon God, the human mind, and the *summum bonum*," it is impractical in the highest degree for such a person to undertake the tasks of leadership in religious education; or, should he undertake such tasks, to expect to be more than a hewer of wood and a drawer of water.

4. Reasons for Recognizing Relations Between Philosophy and Theory of Religious Education

In the course of the previous discussion, which was concerned with objections to recognizing the place of philosophy in religious education, there have emerged implicitly and explicitly numerous positive reasons for such recognition. We shall now undertake to formulate those reasons more systematically.

The fundamental ground for giving philosophy a place in the theory and curriculum of religious education is that philosophy interprets the values of religion and the objects of religious faith in the light of our knowledge and experience as a whole, as we have undertaken to do in the earlier chapters of this book. Philosophy correlates and interprets the facts gathered by the history and psychology of religion; in short, it evaluates religious experience. Our choice does not lie between philosophy and no philosophy; if we have any interest in the value or the truth of religion, our choice can only lie between a carefully thought-out philosophy and a slipshod and uncritical one. If religion is worthy of the best we can give it, then it is worthy of our thoughtful attention, our best philosophical reflection.

Further, philosophy, better than any other study, is a safeguard against the twin perils of religion, namely, dogmatism and skepticism. As was pointed out above, both traditionalism and modernism are in danger of dogmatism, if they lack the truth-loving, open-minded, objective philosophical spirit. And dogmatism, with its appeal to assertion instead of to reason, is the twin sister of skepticism. It may indeed be said, with a show of truth, that philosophy itself sometimes has produced skepticism. Yet, in a deeper sense, philosophy is the only refutation of skepticism. There are various ways of banishing doubt. There is the grim will to believe, accompanied by the refusal to think; there is the crowding out of doubts by action or intense emotion; but there is no permanently satisfactory way of dealing with doubt save by facing the problem and thinking it through. Underlying the opposition to philosophy on the part of some is a latent skepticism—the fear that thought is necessarily skeptical and that philosophy must lead to rejection of religion. More philosophy is needed to uncover and refute skepticism of this and every type.

Philosophy is needed in religious education also because it gives the religious leader a perspective that enables him to diagnose movements of thought and see their larger bearings. The philosophically trained mind is not easily taken in by religious, theological, or psychological fads; and the woods are full of fads. Philosophical perspective is worth more than many rifles in hunting such game. To mention only one instance, current tendencies in psychology of education are marked by overemphasis on conduct and behavior. He who knows the history of philosophy, and is aware of the philosophical problems of consciousness and of value is not going to be swept away by the latest eddy in the current of thought. He will realize that conduct is only part of life and not all, that there is an inner life of consciousness, where the mystic spirit communes with God, where conscience and duty dwell, where ideals and thought have their home; and he will know that conduct alone, behavior alone, is as futile and empty as is thought without conduct. The present over-emphasis on the external and physiological will be understood as a justified reaction against faculty psychology and excessive inwardness in religion; but it will be seen to be a situation which, in the end, is more destructive of religious development than was the inwardness against which it is a revolt. The truth is that many religious educators have been taught these modern exaggerations, and have founded their thinking and religious life on them, without knowing what they were losing or what they were accepting. Philosophical training would make the attitudes assumed toward current tendencies more sane and intelligent.

Finally, it is noteworthy that the need for philosophy is being recognized by observers of the practical work in religious education. The position of Dean Athearn, of Boston University School of Religious Education and Social Service, is most significant; he has led his faculty to require substantial amounts of philosophy of all students receiving any degree from his institution.

He found that many students came to Boston University with a philosophy, such as it was, of half-understood materialism, and proposed to rear a religious training on such a foundation. He saw the blunders in programs and ideals that resulted from a lack of broad philosophical perspective; and he has carried through his radical proposal with success.[5] A. C. Knudson, of Boston University, who travels widely through the country meeting preachers, reports a new interest in philosophy among the clergy. F. W. Hannan, of Drew Theological Seminary, has remarked that while some time ago the great demand of preachers was for methods and programs, the great demand now is for a fundamental philosophy of life that will enable them to carry the burdens of the modern religious leader with understanding. President Scott, of Northwestern, says:

Progress in the nineteenth century was largely dependent upon the study of nature. Progress in the twentieth century will probably depend largely upon the study of man. It is important to support chemistry, physics, astronomy, geology, botany, and zoology. It is imperative in this twentieth century to encourage the discovery of truth in psychology, philosophy, education, economics, sociology, history, literature and religion.

In this connection it may not be amiss to call attention to the fact that "The Conversion of a Sinner"[6] took place while Mr. Cabot was reading "the Bible, *The Meaning of Prayer, The Varieties of Religious Experience,* and other books on philosophy."

By way of contrast with the appreciation of philosophy by religious educators, mention should be made of Mr. George Babbitt's adventure in the church school.

---

[5]See W. S. Athearn, *Character Building in a Democracy* (New York: The Macmillan Company, 1925), pp. 119-124.

[6]By Philip Cabot in the *Atlantic Monthly* (1923) and since become famous and republished in book form.

It is true that Mr. Sinclair Lewis's *Babbitt* is already antiquated as a best seller, and may always have been antiquated as literary art; but if anyone is tempted to believe that religious education should be practical, without any philosophical frills, let him read those pages of *Babbitt* that describe Mr. Babbitt's career as an unphilosophical religious educator in a church with an unphilosophical pastor. *Babbitt* might well be made required reading for all students of religious education.

5. The Fundamental Issue in the Philosophy of Religious Education

Very briefly, now, let us state the fundamental issue that confronts religious education, from the point of view of its philosophical background. It is this: Are we going to abandon ideas and ideals, and give ourselves (like the traditional revivalist) to the mere cultivation of emotions, or (like too many educational psychologists) to the attempt to develop certain habits of conduct, without due regard to the ideal motives and the devotional experiences which are the heart of religion? We have swung from extreme rationalism to extreme irrationalism. Rigid orthodoxy is rationalistic, ultra-intellectual, and doctrinal, while extreme behaviorism eliminates the reality of intellect entirely and, by its exaltation of conduct and of reaction as opposed to thought, is becoming a kind of irrationalism. An inclusive philosophy is needed that finds room both for the rational and the extra-rational in an ideal of the whole personality meeting and interpreting its whole experience.

6. Specific Contributions of Philosophy to Theory of Religious Education

a. *Preliminary.*—Philosophy, we have seen, is essential for the theory and hence for the practice of religious education, if that practice is to be intelligent. In order to make clear just what this fact implies the remainder of the chapter will be devoted to a survey of the typical philosophical problems toward which every attempt at religious education must take some attitude. Regarding each of the problems discussed the author has had his own convictions, which he will present. It is, however, to be hoped that no one will draw the unwarranted inference that one type of philosophical opinion is all that the religious educator needs. On the contrary, every possible solution is of moment, and whatever solution may be reached will have its inevitable effect in practice. All important solutions should be understood by him who hopes to lead the life of his generation to better things. To attempt no solution is to grope blindly—however loyally and enthusiastically —in the dark.

b. *The Problem of the Criterion of Truth.*[7]—Religious faith asserts propositions about God and man, the world here and hereafter. It believes that these propositions are true. Unbelief contradicts these propositions, holding that they are not true; different propositions are believed by different religions, and by different advocates of the same religion.

How are we going to distinguish between what is true and what is not true in this strife of claims and counterclaims? When the skeptic tells us that no one can know absolute truth, or read the mind of God—if there be a God—every thoughtful person is willing to grant that we see through a glass darkly, and that no man can know what the Omniscient knows. But most thoughtful persons will agree that there is a difference between

[7]See Chap. I for a more technical discussion of the subject.

the unrestricted reign of error and the striving for truth; and that actual progress has been made in human history in the direction of truth. The question, therefore, about the criterion or test by which we may know what is true is fundamental to religion and to all sound social progress; for whatever is not based on truth will sooner or later have to be undone. Logic is the branch of philosophy that undertakes to answer this question and to sift proposed criteria.

At the present time it is doubtless true that the majority of the human race bases its religious beliefs on authority. Some holy tradition or authoritative interpretation thereof is accepted without question as the standard of doctrine. Much may be said for the social need and value of authority, wisely used. Yet, whatever the value of authority, nothing can be more evident than that mere authority is not the criterion of truth; the authorities conflict among themselves, and when authority comes to a decision for itself it has to judge by some standard other than authority. True authority inheres only in truth.

Many who doubt religion base their doubt on an appeal to sense experience as final criterion of truth. God and conscience, prayer and immortality are not objects that can be inspected by the senses, and hence are rejected by those that use this criterion. But it does not require much reflection to show that sensation is logically defective as a test of truth. Does any man live who has believed as true only what his senses tell him? If so, he has not believed that he or anyone else was a conscious being, or that geometry or algebra or trigonometry was true, or that there was a world before he was born and will be after he dies; nor has he any means of telling whether any given experience he has is a genuine sensation or an illusion or hallucination. It is thus easy to show that sensation is not the final test of truth, but that every mind recognizes truths that are super-sensuous and that sensation itself must be interpreted by a higher function of the mind.

There is scarcely a philosopher in the world who would base his criterion of truth on mere sensation. The two theories that are most widely held are known as pragmatism and the coherence theory. In this country it is probable that the former has more conspicuous advocates than the latter, and will be discussed first.

Pragmatism is the belief that an idea or belief is true if it works, has satisfactory practical consequences, is capable of verifying itself by leading up to the particulars that it predicts. This seems to be at once the method of laboratory science and of religious experience; it brings the plain man and the philosopher together; and it bears the label, *practical*. Anything trade-marked *practical* will sell in this fair land like hot-cakes or *The Saturday Evening Post*. Pragmatism has thus made a wide appeal to a very diversified following.

There is doubtless much merit in the pragmatic point of view. Every practical consequence, every working of an idea, is indeed part of the data that truth must acknowledge and interpret. Yet, important and popular as is pragmatism, its criterion is defective because it is ambiguous. What is meant by the word "practical"? Attempts to answer this question on the basis of the utterances of the pragmatists have led to the discovery of at least thirteen different meanings. To the capitalist it may have one meaning; to the laborer another and to the burglar yet another. The scientist means one thing by it; the religious devotee another. Within the realm of philosophy the differences are fully as great. At present the dominant tendency is to interpret it in terms of biology. The practical means what expresses itself in activity of the organism. The body and its behavior become the final test of truth. If this is what is meant, it is surely an inadequate criterion. Either it reduces to sensation, and is then subject to all the criticism to which that criterion is open, or else it seeks to expand and include in biology all ideals and values, which means the surrender of the pragmatic principle.

The coherence criterion, on the other hand, asserts that in the end there is only one road to truth-finding, and that is the road of taking everything into account and seeing everything in relation to everything else, as far as a human being can. When we have done that, we discover that many of our beliefs contradict each other, and that many are consistent with each other; the task of truth-finding, then, is to organize our total experience, eliminate contradictions, and establish as many relations as possible in the self-consistent material. Truth is what coheres, that is, sticks together. While this criterion has obvious practical difficulties in its application, and has often enough been abused, nevertheless it commends itself as the best way we have of building up truth and of detecting error. It obviously includes the facts of authority and sensation, and all practical consequences of every kind, and also has room for facts that these criteria rejected. It combines the ideal of a growing human apprehension of truth with the ideal of an absolutely coherent truth.

It is evident that each of the criteria discussed above has consequences for theory of religious education. If sensation be the test of truth, let man live the life of sense; there is no truth in religion or in moral values. If authority be the criterion, there is room for religion just as long as the flock can be induced to attend

only to the "proper" authority and no longer; the problem of religious education is, then, that of indoctrination
and the cultivation of the attitude of the closed mind.
If pragmatism be true, the religious educator must ask
cautiously, Which kind of pragmatism? If he follow
the fashion and adopt the biological brand, he must then
pare his conception of religious life and religious aspirations down to the biological model. He will have little
room for what has been the essence of religion, the inner
life of communion with God, of spiritual aspiration and
achievement; immortality will vanish and God become
scarcely more than a name for certain relations of biological organisms to each other. If coherence be the
criterion, there is no magic solution of all our woes
which can be turned out by the million and sold on all
news stands, but there is an available instrument which
recognizes the rights of inner life as well as of outer
relations, of principles and of ideals as well as of particulars and real things, and which may lead the
thoughtful and the honest mind to God. Such an instrument we have used in the present volume and found
it to be suited to the interpretation of religious values.

At any rate, if religious education should base its conception of religious truth on the reasonable and coherent
interpretation of experience as a whole, it would have
a foundation that would challenge every fair-minded
person. It would also have a principle that would protect it against the narrow and doctrinaire fads of the
moment, which usually overemphasize some group of
facts, while ignoring their relations to life as a whole.
The soul of religious educators may well be sick of men
who know their field, but do not know what their field
means for life.

c. *The Problem of the Nature of Consciousness.*—
Another fundamental problem of philosophy is the prob-

lem of what consciousness is. The contact of philosophy with religious thought is here too evident to be questioned. Religion has much to say about the soul. So has psychology—by implication, if not explicitly. The psychological study of consciousness as a science may be purely empirical and may disavow all "metaphysics"; but the results of psychology require and receive a philosophical interpretation, even from those that abjure philosophy.

In answer to the question, What is consciousness? tradition has a theory that has unfortunately been regarded by many as the only view compatible with religious faith. I refer to the traditional soul theory. This theory arises somewhat as follows: Our consciousness is gifted with many powers and possibilities that are not present before the mind at any one time; further, it is active in sleep, and possibly ceases in deep sleep or in other moments of "unconsciousness." Nevertheless, experience testifies that we are the same person all the time, and have all our powers or "faculties" at our command in our normal waking life. In order to explain both the fact of personal identity and the real existence of our faculties, the soul theory asserted that the soul is not our conscious life, but is a something that expresses itself in consciousness, although itself not conscious. It is what persists when we sleep, or are otherwise unconscious; and it is what is immortal. Yet when one asks an adherent of this theory what the soul is if it is not a conscious being, or what the soul is when we are unconscious, one receives strong assurance that the soul is something, but no clear statement about what it is. On account of the vagueness, bordering on agnosticism, that marks this theory, and on account of perplexities in understanding the relation between the "soul" and consciousness, this traditional account of the soul is almost universally rejected by psychologists and philosophers. The rejection of this theory is not, however, as will later be seen, tantamount to a rejection of all belief in the soul.

Psychology, having abandoned the "soul," experienced a reaction to the left. There arose the doctrine of associationism, of which David Hume was the most famous exponent. This doctrine would have nothing to do with mysterious essences, such as the traditional soul, but held that knowledge was confined to what could be actually experienced. Actual experience, Hume held, was wholly made up of sensations (or impressions, as he called them) and ideas (pale copies of sensations); and his theory saw in mind nothing but sensations combining and separating in accordance with the law of association. Associationism has the merit of trying to explain consciousness in terms of itself; but it fails because it does not take all of consciousness into account. Hume himself admitted that he was not satisfied with his account of personal identity.

The failure of both the transcendent soul and the associated sensations to give a reasonable account of mind left psychology for a long time gasping for breath. It has seemed to be without fundamental principles, and to be spending its energies in detailed experiments and tests, without any satisfactory view of the nature of consciousness as a whole. Indeed, as the naturalistic science and philosophy of the nineteenth century developed, it dawned on the minds of psychologists that consciousness, with its peculiar nonspatial and time-transcending properties, was out of place in a naturalistic universe. Instead, then, of adjusting theory to experience, the persistent attempt has been made to adjust experience to theory. Behaviorism is the logical outcome of this attempt.

By behaviorism is meant the theory which defines mind in terms of the behavior of the physiological organism; all that has been called conscious experience is for this view only certain movements of the bodily mechanism. What we have just defined is metaphysical behaviorism in its extreme form; there are milder forms which acknowledge the fact of consciousness, but hold that it is to be explained wholly in terms of behavior (as in Allport's *Social Psychology*). Metaphysical behaviorism is to be distinguished from methodological behaviorism, which means only the familiar fact that the consciousness of others must be studied by observing the behavior of their bodies. Everyone who does not rely on telepathy would agree with the truth and value of this type of behaviorism. But metaphysical behaviorism goes much further and says that the whole meaning of consciousness is to be found in behavior. To be conscious means for the organism to move in a certain way. To be angry is no "conscious" feeling or emotion; it is to grit the teeth and clench the fists. To think is not to reason "consciously"; it is to mutter certain words, either audibly, or, as Watson puts it, "sub-vocally."

Behaviorism has the advantage, such as it is, of explaining "consciousness" in physiological, that is, materialistic terms. It is a very neat system. It solves the riddles of the mind-body problem by the simple expedient of saying that the mind is the body in action, so that the relation of mind and body is no problem at all. The way, as they say, is not through, but around the problem. Thus it simplifies many ancient puzzles. But it fails because it omits so many facts. Consciousness is experienced as self-identical, as aware of the past, the absent, the future; it is not merely or chiefly response to present stimuli. Further, conscious response to stimuli is never identical with any part of the "reflex arc" as a material fact. Conscious feeling and purpose, knowledge of universals and abstractions like the square root of minus one, sympathy with other persons, communication with them and with the unseen, are all facts with which behaviorism is impotent to cope.

Yet it should be emphasized that behaviorism is superior to the antiquated theory of the transcendent soul, in that it remains within the field of the intelligible and the actually experienced; and to associationism, in that it views consciousness as living movement, action, and reaction, instead of as a collection of separate sensation atoms loosely held together. These advantages are not to be despised; but no account that leaves out the wide range of conscious experiences mentioned above can be a final or a broadly fruitful view of mind. It can be only a passing phase of psychology.

There remains one other theory, namely, self-psychology, or psychological personalism. This theory starts from the experienced unity of consciousness. It holds that all experience is self-experience. There are no "floating adjectives," no states of consciousness existing by themselves apart from others. Consciousness is always a complex that belongs together as some one identical person or self. It experiences itself as belonging to a whole which is a self. The true "soul" is no transcendent entity which no one can define, but is this fact of self-experience. There never were any separate sensations out of which to construct a self, for all sensations already belonged to a self. The self expresses itself through behavior, but it is not that behavior any more than the pianist is the piano. Self-psychology finds that one of the most characteristic traits of selves is their purposiveness, their striving for ends; indeed, conscious striving for ends has meaning only relative to the purpose of some conscious self.

Personalism thus has the merits both of association-ism and of behaviorism—the banishing of a meaningless soul and the active, functional view of consciousness—without the defects of either. It has the further advantage of being loyal to the experienced facts as other theories are not.

One occasionally finds surprisingly naïve attitudes toward self-psychology. By some psychologists it is wholly ignored, as by Bode in his otherwise incisive little book, *The Fundamentals of Education,* which purports to give an account of the theories of consciousness, mentions the soul-theory, associationism, and behaviorism—and stops there, evidently (if the matter was considered at all) confusing soul and self! By others, the self-psychology is avoided on the amusing ground that it is a product of theological prejudice. One must indeed be a victim of theophobia if one refuses to face the empirical facts of consciousness in terror lest one might then be seduced to believe in God!

On the other hand, recent psychology shows hopeful signs. Movements such as the purposive psychology of McDougall and the *Gestalt*-theory of Koffka and other Germans are precisely in the direction of self-psychology. It is becoming increasingly clear that the real issue in psychology is, as Cunningham points out, between personalism and behaviorism.[8]

The significance of these different psychologies for religious education is almost self-evident. The older soul-theory is the basis of a mystical and magical view; it is the psychology of traditionalism. Religious education based on it would aim at some mysterious subconscious relation to God or some mechanical work of grace in the soul. The conscious life would be neglected in

[8] G. W. Cunningham, *Problems of Philosophy* (New York: Henry and Company, 1924), Chap. XVI.

the interest of the status of the soul and its salvation in
a future heaven. Associationism, on the other hand,
would explain away all spiritual life and all moral
responsibility; the higher values and ideals are for it
wholly derived from sense; and a personal God and personal immortality are alike highly improbable if personality be what this theory takes it for.   Religious
education would have scant basis here.

Behaviorism obviously emphasizes conduct, individual and social reactions, the development of life. So
far as it goes, it has points of contact with religion.
Since it deals with what is capable of common observation and control, it seems to be well adapted to serve as
the psychology of religious education.   It is well
adapted so far as it goes (we repeat), but it does not
go far. For behaviorism, a personal God and personal
immortality are even more improbable than for associationism; they are literally impossible. Not only does it
exclude these vital truths as mere excrescences, but also
it externalizes and mechanizes the life of religion. True
religion, as our investigation of religious values has
shown, has at its heart an inner spiritual experience, a
mystical relation to God, a devotion of the soul to ideal
values. Now a behaviorist may have these experiences
and devotions, but his theory precludes his recognizing
them. The religious education programs that he pre-
pares are consistently directed toward the development
of conduct and social relations. The inner life, prayer,
the sources of spiritual power and energy, are ignored.
In their stead is a scheme based on chain-reflexes. The
moral and religious experiences which behaviorism thus
excludes are no mere fantastic superstitions, but are
real experiences to which the universal religious consciousness bears witness.

Personalism is, therefore, at once the most truly empirical and realistic theory of consciousness and also the one that recognizes and utilizes to the fullest the experiences that are central to religion. As Miss Calkins puts it, self-psychology is the only "truly psychological behaviorism." A program of religious education that ignores the self, its ideal aims, its identity and responsibility, will move only on the surface of moral and religious life. When religious education takes the self fully into account, it will see, as of late it has not always seen, that man is not a machine but a person, and that only behavior generated and tested by inner ideals can truly be called religious.

d. *The Problem of Moral Values.*—As Chapter II has already shown, religious values rest on a moral basis.

Ethics, like psychology, is usually regarded as a special science. It is, however, in a special sense philosophical, for it is impossible to decide what one ought to do without taking all the possibilities that reality offers into account. When I say, "I ought to do thus and so," I mean that, having considered all that there is as far as I can, I believe that there is nothing better that I could do. The simplest obligation thus has a cosmic outlook. Ethics is philosophical.

In moral theory, as in all fundamental thinking, there are differences of opinion. Ignoring minor variations, one may say that there are three main views of the nature of the value for which the good man ought to strive, namely, the hedonistic, the formalistic, and the perfectionistic.

Hedonism is the view that the only value of life is pleasurable consciousness, and that the good life is the life which attains a maximum of pleasure. If the pleasure of the individual is made the standard, we have egoistic hedonism; if the pleasure of society, universal hedonism. Egoistic hedonism is plainly hostile to man's nature as a social and aspiring being; and universal hedonism has to appeal to other motives than the love of pleasure to arouse and maintain the altruistic spirit. Hedonism, therefore, is not generally regarded as a satisfactory theory of morality.

Formalism is the theory that received its classic form in the philosophy of Immanuel Kant. It holds that the only moral good is a good will; not the pleasure or any other end attained, but solely the intention of the act, the principles from which it flows, can decide its moral quality. The good will is the rational will, the will that rules itself by a universal principle. Moral autonomy obeys the categorical imperative of duty. In this ideal there is something austere and noble; and also something humane, for it judges man, not by his abilities and attainments, but by his inner purpose. Yet if formalism is to be taken seriously, it asserts that goodness is entirely independent, not merely of all consequences of our action, but even of all regard for consequences. This surely does not do justice by our full moral experience.

Perfectionism holds that moral value consists, not in pleasurable feelings only or in rational will only, but in the development of personality as a harmonious whole, in accordance with the most complete and highest ideal of personality that our mind can form. The good life, then, is the whole life—the life that aims at the richest and fullest development of its capacities. The basis of moral obligation is self-respect. Altruism is a duty because no self can develop alone, and no self can respect itself without respecting others.

It is all but incredible that any theory of religious education should ever be worked out without taking cognizance of the philosophy of moral values. It is evident that ethical theory profoundly affects one's conceptions of the aims of religious education. The hedonist will seek to develop pleasures, recreations, optimistic attitudes, cheerfulness; the formalist will strive to discipline his will and to inculcate a high-minded and even fanatical disregard of consequences; the perfectionist will make well-rounded personalities his aim and will therefore have a more difficult, but a more rewarding task than hedonist or formalist. Perfectionist theory alone commands unambiguously the realization of religious values as part of the moral task.

e. *The Problem of the Nature of Reality.*—When one thinks of philosophy one naturally thinks of metaphysics—the attempt to give a completely coherent description and interpretation of the nature of reality as a whole. Metaphysics is the acid test of fundamental thinking. He who evades the problem entirely can hardly be said to have the intellectual right to pose as an interpreter of religion, particularly if his whole position includes metaphysical assertions which have not been criticized or thought through. Metaphysics demands that we define what we mean by reality, by man's place in the cosmos, and by God. Any attitude toward God, and so any religious attitude, involves metaphysical assertions which need critical examination.

In a survey of the present kind only a brief account of some of the chief problems of metaphysics can be given. Perhaps the most crucial problem is that of mechanism *versus* teleology.[9] Physics explains the world in mechanical terms, that is, in terms of necessary laws of matter and motion. As a philosophy, mechanism is the view that explains everything which happens as a necessary consequence of past conditions. Teleology, on the contrary, holds that explanation in terms of previous conditions is never the last word, but that

---

[9]See E. S. Brightman, *An Introduction to Philosophy*, Chaps. VIII and IX.

ultimately all mechanisms and all reality are to be interpreted as the expression of purpose. The facts of biological adaptation, the direction of evolution, the function of consciousness, the values revealed in experience are among the data that point to a teleological explanation. There is, then, evidence both for mechanism and for teleology. It is one of the tasks of metaphysics to think through the mechanistic and the teleological aspects of experience.

It is obvious that if mechanism be the whole truth, and if the teleological facts are to be explained wholly in mechanistic terms, then, both purpose and freedom are mere illusions in the universe. It is little short of pathetic when men undertake the responsibilities of the religious educator not merely without having thought through the problem but without even being aware that there is a problem.

Religious education based on a purely mechanistic philosophy, or on a psychology and biology that presuppose mechanism as a sufficient account of reality, is a contradiction in terms. It is a religious education founded on a denial of the possibility of religion. It is equally true that religious education founded on a mere assertion of purpose and freedom, but leaving known mechanisms out of account and not facing the problems, is a trivial emotion, a zeal without knowledge. It injures religion both by its ineffectiveness and also by its tendency to inspire contempt for religion in the minds of men of science. The imperative need for a metaphysics of mechanism and teleology for religious education needs no further proof.

Metaphysics is, however, complicated business. Like all things excellent, it is as difficult as it is rare. Hence, there are those who rebel against metaphysics. These men (of whom we have spoken in earlier chapters of this book) urge that it is impossible to solve the metaphysical riddles and declare that we must abandon the attempt to interpret the nature of reality. We must, they teach, confine our attention to human experience and to discovering its possibilities. Nothing can be known save what is experienced; all "metaphysical" entities, like matter or energy or a personal God, are empty speculations that at best are mere symbols for facts of experience. This philosophy calls our thought away from the invisible God to the visible facts. Positivism, whether in its classical formulation by Comte or in the more recent garb of the "Chicago School" of pragmatism, substitutes for the God of metaphysics the God of social experience. Positivists may retain the term "God" for humanity or the social mind, but they belong to the school of logomachy founded by Humpty-Dumpty, who said, "When I use a word it means just what I choose it to mean—neither more nor less." For Christians, God has always been the heavenly Father, the Supreme Person who is both Creator and Redeemer, the "determiner of destiny," the one who hears and answers prayer. If this concept is untenable, it would be more ingenuous to abandon the use of the term "God," and substitute for it "social mind" or whatever may be the proper equivalent.

The essential issue here is, as we have shown in earlier chapters, no mere quarrel about words. It is the question about whether man lives in a friendly universe and can trust its powers to be good, or whether man must rely wholly on himself. In this chapter no attempt will be made to argue this question; but it may surely be said that the religious educator who does not know whether he believes in a Rock of Ages or an Uncle Sam as the object of his worship is a helpless director of the religious life of others. Religious education must be founded on an intelligent attitude toward metaphysics. What ought to be depends on what is.

The human mind, one may safely predict, will not rest satisfied with the positivistic veto against metaphysics. Difficult and dangerous as it is to think, it is even more difficult and dangerous in the long run not to think. The intellectual and religious aspirations of humanity will not surrender because their task is hard. It may be questioned whether anyone has ever completely avoided metaphysics. In proportion as one succeeds in being nonmetaphysical, one shuts oneself up into the prison of one's private consciousness and becomes a solipsist. No one, however, has ever seriously meant to be a solipsist. Positivism rests on a species of self-deception and is an artificial construction that men cannot wholeheartedly believe when they see its implications.

It is, then, one of the essential tasks of religious education to make these implications explicit. Religious education must become aware of its own presuppositions; must decide not only whether positivism closes the way to God, but also whether the metaphysical way leads to God or to an unspiritual universe; and if to a God, to what kind of one. Is the pantheistic, the deistic, or the theistic conception more tenable?

If pantheism be true, religious education should aim at developing the mystical consciousness of man's oneness with God. If deism, the aim should be to teach God's utter transcendence and to emphasize miraculous interventions in the natural order as the best evidence of God's existence. If theism, it should inculcate in the mind the thought of God's immanence in nature and in human persons, and should seek to develop mutual, conscious cooperation of man with God in developing personal life. Metaphysical differences breed far-reaching differences in theological tenets and in educational aims. These differences cannot and should not be smoothed over or evaded; they should be thought out. Problems remain to plague humanity if they are not faced and solved as well as men can solve them.

f. *The Problem of the Nature and Validity of Religion.*—The branch of philosophy most obviously necessary to the theory of religious education is philosophy of religion. It is only in modern times that this branch of philosophy has come to separate development. There are numerous reasons for this fact. Some have felt that metaphysics already covered the ground, others that theology was self-sufficient. Still others resented the application of logical methods to the study of religion, on the ground that religion is too sacred to be pried into by analytic curiosity. In spite of objections, it has come to be seen that if religion and logic are to dwell in the same mind, they must dwell together; and thus there has developed a philosophy of religion. This discipline seeks to discover, in the light of what religion has been, what religion ought to be. It tries to put religion in its proper setting in the real world revealed to us by experience and interpreted by science and philosophy.[10]

Some of the special problems of philosophy are: the nature of religious values, which we have been discussing in this volume; the relations of science and religion; the interpretation of prayer and mystical experience; immortality; the problem of evil. To mention these topics is to mention what belongs inevitably to the content of all religious instruction, either in foreground or background. Religious education faces the

---

[10]W. K. Wright, *A Student's Philosophy of Religion* (New York: The Macmillan Company, 1922), and D. M. Edwards, *The Philosophy of Religion* (New York: George H. Doran Company, 1924) are excellent surveys of the field.

question whether these and other very fundamental problems are to be ignored, treated dogmatically and superficially, or studied thoroughly and competently. If thorough and competent study be the choice, there is no way of avoiding the inclusion of philosophy of religion in the training of the religious educator.

7. RELIGIOUS EDUCATION AND RELIGIOUS VALUES

Herewith we have reached the end of our study of religious values. We have sought to interpret the meaning and worth of religion and particularly of the central religious experience of worship. We have felt that our task would have been left unfinished had we not also considered the bearing of the results of philosophical reflection on the task of religious education.

Religious education has to do both with technique and with content, that is, both with means and with ends. This chapter has been concerned solely with the problem of content. Kant was right when he said that form without content is empty. It is, of course, equally true that content without form is dead; and nothing that has been said in this chapter can rightly be interpreted as denying or minimizing the value of technique in religious education. In the past there was an overemphasis on content without technique; to-day there is too much technique without content. There is grave danger that religious education may learn how to teach but on the way will forget that there is anything to teach. A project method that projects nothing is futile.

Religion is a life-experience which relates man and God, transforming the inner life and the social relations of him who experiences it fully. Religious values do not dwell apart from life in an ivory tower; their roots are in the soil of our common life.

If religion be true to itself, it must express itself in

affirmations that imply philosophical beliefs about the nature of reality. Likewise, if philosophy be true to itself, it must include all religious values in its survey of experience as a whole. Reasonable philosophy does not pretend to be omniscient nor does it fall prey to the fallacy that it can prove everything, or can spin the universe out of its own interior. Philosophy is only the attempt of thought to do the best it can with the universal problems of experience. If religious education should try to get along without philosophy, it would be in the position of refusing to think about its own foundations.

The account of religious values which we have given will serve its purpose if it leads the reader to face frankly the ideal possibilities of religious experience and to think his way through, as well as man may, to a coherent interpretation that will do justice, in theory and practice, to those values.

INDEX